The War Over *Perpetual Peace*

The Palgrave Macmillan History of International Thought Series seeks to publish the best work in this growing and increasingly important field of academic inquiry. Its scholarly monographs cover three types of work: (i) exploration of the intellectual impact of individual thinkers, from key disciplinary figures to neglected ones; (ii) examination of the origin, evolution, and contemporary relevance of specific schools or traditions of international thought; and (iii) analysis of the evolution of particular ideas and concepts in the field. Both classical (pre 1919) and modern (post 1919) thought are covered. Its books are written to be accessible to audiences in International Relations, International History, Political Theory, and Sociology.

Series Editor:
Peter Wilson, London School of Economics and Political Science

Advisory Board:
Jack Donnelly, University of Denver
Fred Halliday, London School of Economics and Political Science
David Long, Carleton University
Hidemi Suganami, University of Keele

Also in the Series:
Internationalism and Nationalism in European Political Thought
    by Carsten Holbraad

The International Theory of Leonard Woolf: A Study in Twentieth-Century Idealism
    by Peter Wilson

Tocqueville, Lieber, and Bagehot: Liberalism Confronts the World
    by David Clinton

Harold Laski: Problems of Democracy, the Sovereign State, and International Society
    by Peter Lamb

Liberal Internationalism and the Decline of the State: The Thought of Richard Cobden, David Mitrany, and Kenichi Ohmae
    by Per Hammarlund

The War Over Perpetual Peace: An Exploration into the History of a Foundational International Relations Text
    by Eric S. Easley

The War Over *Perpetual Peace*

An Exploration into the History of a Foundational International Relations Text

Eric S. Easley

palgrave
macmillan

JC
181
K4
E2

First published in 2004 by
PALGRAVE MACMILLAN™
175 Fifth Avenue, New York, N.Y. 10010 and
Houndmills, Basingstoke, Hampshire, England RG21 6XS
Companies and representatives throughout the world.

PALGRAVE MACMILLAN is the global academic imprint of the Palgrave Macmillan division of St. Martin's Press, LLC and of Palgrave Macmillan Ltd. Macmillan® is a registered trademark in the United States, United Kingdom and other countries. Palgrave is a registered trademark in the European Union and other countries.

ISBN 1–4039–6652–4

Library of Congress Cataloging-in-Publication Data

Easley, Eric S.
    The war over perpetual peace : an exploration into the history of a foundational international relations text / Eric S. Easley.
        p. cm. — (Palgrave Macmillan series on the history of international thought)
    Includes bibliographical references and index.
    ISBN 1–4039–6652–4
        1. Kant, Immanuel, 1724–1804—Views on sovereignty. 2. Kant, Immanuel, 1724–1804—Criticism and interpretation. 3. Kant, Immanuel, 1724–1804. Zum ewigen Frieden. 4. Kant, Immanuel, 1724–1804—Views on peace. 5. Sovereignty. 6. Peace—Philosophy. 7. International relations—Philosophy. I. Title. II. Series.

JZ4034.E37 2004
327.1'01—dc22   2004044799

A catalogue record for this book is available from the British Library.

Design by Newgen Imaging Systems (P) Ltd., Chennai, India.

First edition: December 2004

10 9 8 7 6 5 4 3 2 1

Printed in the United States of America.

To my Grandfather, Johnson Easley, and my Grandmother, Jane Henry, for their intellectual inspiration and zest for life. What the former passed on to me, the latter continues to in ways she will never understand.

Contents

Acknowledgments

This book was fulfilling to write because the following people and places made it so: Dr. Peter Wilson, for his plentiful thoughts, immense generosity and patience in supervision, and during our many productive chats in his office, for making me laugh when I should have been thinking; Howard Williams, who examined my work as a doctorate and encouraged my work as a book; all of those at the British Library, the Library of Congress, and the British Library of Political and Economic Sciences, for their generous help and patience; my parents, Sid and Melissa Easley, who through their selfless devotion to family and community have helped me to understand the kindness of God's grace; my brother Don and sister-in-law Jacqueline, and my Aunt Janet and Uncle Vernon, for their unconditional love and support coupled with constant prodding to finish what I'm sure, at times, they thought would never be; Kamini Karlekar, who I cherish for her challenging intellect, her giving spirit, and her friendship; Greg Asikainen, one of the greatest constants in my life, for being the most amazing friend a guy could have; Charlie Weigle, Tom Call, and Chris Woolsley, for their loyalty, public service, and deep companionship; Meera Ballal, for setting me free, for teaching me valuable lessons about life, and for her friendship; the Gentlemen of Brown's Mountain; the London Goodenough College, an international community like no other, for providing me with countless friends for life; the Brewing Society, for being a most perfect diversion from my research; my favorite Local, the Postmen's Pub, for the fellowship and camaraderie only a good English public house can offer; and finally, all the simple chapels and glorious cathedrals of London, for taking me in and uplifting me when times were good and times were tough. To all of the above, I say thank you. Because of you, the book took longer to write than it should. Without you, it would never have been completed.

The views and opinions expressed in this book are solely those of the author and do not reflect the positions/views of the U.S. Department of State.

Introduction: The Perpetual Peace

A Dutch innkeeper once put this satirical inscription on his signboard, along with the picture of a graveyard. We shall not trouble to ask whether it applies to men in general, or particularly to heads of state (who can never have enough of war), or only to the philosophers who blissfully dream of perpetual peace. The author of the present essay does, however, make one reservation in advance. The practical politician tends to look down with great complacency upon the political theorist as a mere academic. The theorist's abstract ideas, the practitioner believes, cannot endanger the state, since the state must be founded upon principles of experience; it thus seems safe to let him fire off his whole broadside, and the worldly-wise statesman need not turn a hair. It thus follows that if the practical politician is to be consistent, he must not claim, in the event of a dispute with the theorist, to scent any danger to the state in the opinions which the theorist has randomly uttered in public. By this saving clause, the author of this essay will consider himself expressly safeguarded, in correct and proper style, against all *malicious interpretation*.[1]

T he prelude to Immanuel Kant's *Perpetual Peace*, first published in Konigsberg in 1795, is a prophecy. Kant predicted that suspicious political leaders would consider the essay a "malicious" tract. He had visions of practical politicians, then or at some later time, holding his new treatise responsible for endangering the state. By including these clever opening lines, he believed he was successfully guarding against this possibility.[2] Little was his concern that the very theorists he was trying to protect might argue endlessly over what he proposed in *Perpetual Peace* through the nineteenth and twentieth centuries. This, in fact, is exactly what they have done. Their commentary on Kant's text is the source of this book.

As a doctoral student at the London School of Economics and Political Science researching Kant's contribution to international political theory, I became intrigued with the number of competing interpretations of *Perpetual Peace* I found over the years. Observing that similar interpretations of the work were situated in relatively well-defined periods of history, it occurred to me that further research might reveal distinct patterns of interpretation of Kant's celebrated treatise. This book sets out to explore this possibility. Additionally, once the existence of the patterns is successfully established, the book asks: why have they formed? It puts forward two historical explanations, one principal, one subsidiary, for pattern formation, and in the process, reflects on the relationship between the historico-political context of the interpreter and his or her interpretation of a classic text of International Relations. More broadly, this book provides for the first time a thorough account of the way *Perpetual Peace* has been interpreted in the English language. It is hoped that an interpretive history of this treatise will be a meaningful and valuable contribution to an academic discipline in which it is viewed as a foundational text.

Outlining the Arguments

I argue that two clear patterns of interpretation of *Perpetual Peace* have arisen. These patterns emerge from interpretations of the text completed in the English language between the years 1845 and 2003. Chapter 1 offers an introduction to the text of *Perpetual Peace*. It discusses which portions of the text are of most consequence to interpretations that ultimately reveal each pattern. This chapter provides the reader with a general grasp of the diverse ideas and proposals within the full text of *Perpetual Peace*. In addition, highlighting the broad range of its subject matter facilitates understanding of the more detailed discussions of interpretations that must occur when arguments for the existence of patterns are made in the chapters to follow.

According to my analysis in chapters 2 and 3, interpretations from the mid-nineteenth to the mid-twentieth century maintain that the text of *Perpetual Peace* endorses peace proposals above the state level. This collection of interpretations constitutes Pattern One, the development of which occurred in two phases. Pattern One, Phase One emerges from interpretations completed between the mid-nineteenth century and the end of World War I. These interpretations are discussed in chapter 2. Interpretations during this period assert that the text calls for a significant restraint on state sovereignty through establishment of a centralized authority, in the form of an international state or strong federation, above the collectivity of states. Pattern One, Phase Two arises from interpretations completed between the end of World War I and the mid-twentieth century. These interpretations are considered in chapter 3. Interpretations during this period suggest the text requires the sovereignty of each state to be curbed through establishment of a less formidable federation—one that still exists, however, as an institutionalized authority above the level of states.

According to my analysis in chapters 4 through 7, interpretations from the mid-twentieth century to its end maintain that the text supports peace proposals at the state level. This collection of interpretations constitutes Pattern Two, and as with Pattern One, two phases of development can be identified. Pattern Two, Phase One emerges from interpretations completed between the 1950s and the early 1980s. These interpretations are examined in chapter 4. After a century of understanding *Perpetual Peace* as requiring the limitation of state sovereignty, interpreters during this period defend a state-centric reading of Kant's work, which sees the prevention of war occurring through peace proposals at the state level. Pattern Two, Phase Two arises from interpretations completed from the early 1980s through the post–Cold War era. These interpretations are explored in Chapters 5–7. According to my analysis, interpretations during this period similarly view the sovereign state as paramount in Kant's text and see it as the primary vehicle to peace. Yet these interpretations are better understood as a second phase of Pattern Two because of the special emphasis they give to the First Definitive Article, which proclaims that the civil constitution of every state shall be republican.[3]

Finally, the book puts forward broad historical explanations for the various patterns and phases of interpretation of Kant's treatise. Chapter 8 sets forth the principal explanation, which argues that pattern formation is a function of the rise and fall of hopes for peace through international organization. A subsidiary explanation developed in chapter 9 reflects on the steady increase in the number of liberal states in the western hemisphere over the past century and one-half and the affect of this evolving historico-political phenomenon on the minds of interpreters commenting on *Perpetual Peace* during this time period and living generally within this geographical space.

The Sociology of Knowledge

The final two chapters move the book in the direction of the "sociology of knowledge." The sociology of knowledge is associated with the thought of Karl Mannheim, specifically, his book *Ideology and Utopia*. Broadly stated, the sociology of knowledge considers "the significance of the non-theoretical conditioning factors in knowledge" and makes the following key observation: "mental structures are inevitably differently formed in different social and historical settings."[4] According to Mannheim, "the older method of intellectual history, which was oriented towards the *a priori* conception that changes in ideas were to be understood on the level of ideas (immanent intellectual history), blocked recognition of the penetration of the social process into the intellectual sphere."[5] Another way he states this is that "the emergence and crystallization of actual thought" does not "develop historically in accordance with immanent laws" or "follow from the 'nature of things'" or "from 'pure logical possibilities.'"[6] Neither is it "driven by an 'inner dialectic.'"[7] Instead, it "is influenced in many decisive points by extra-theoretical factors of the most diverse sort."[8] Mannheim's central concern is with the "perspective" of the thinking subject or, as he describes the term, "the subject's whole mode of conceiving things as determined by his historical and social setting."[9]

Similarly, this book, specifically chapters 8 and 9, focuses on the "perspective" of the interpreter as he or she encounters *Perpetual Peace*. The interpreter's consciousness—"his whole mode of conceiving things" as Mannheim says—when he or she examines a text on the subject of international political theory is in many ways shaped by the historical, social, and political currents of a given age. The book asserts that this Mannheimian "perspective" conditions and influences his or her interpretation of the text.[10] Additionally, the larger patterns that I argue have emerged reflect the "perspective" of a number of interpreters at work during well-defined historical stages. The book submits that this is a plausible way to account for the variety of competing interpretations that have arisen over the past century and one-half, especially when it is understood that all interpreters were reading similarly translated texts of *Perpetual Peace* through the entire period in question. Though the language of the text remains the same through time, the meaning of the text changes shape with time.

Perpetual Peace: *Textual Interpretations* Under Consideration

In completing a broad interpretive history of this kind, it is important to set out which interpretations are under consideration in development of the argument. Generally speaking, the book examines English-language interpretations of Kant's *Perpetual Peace* completed from 1845 to the year 2003. The majority of these interpretations were written by Anglo-American scholars and commentators who consider the treatise in a variety of books, academic articles, book reviews, and even prefaces and introductions to translations of the text. It is necessary at this stage to say a few words about those interpretations that are not considered in the book and the reasons for their exclusion.

First, as stated earlier, Kant's *Perpetual Peace* was published in the year 1795. We are told that it initially sold fifteen hundred copies,[11] was readied for a second edition in 1796, and translated into the English and French shortly thereafter.[12] While given greater attention by scholars since the publication of F.H. Hinsley's enduring analysis of it in *Power and the Pursuit of Peace* (1963), it had been discussed by historians, international lawyers, and peace advocates, as well as those writing within the relatively new field of academic International Relations and the somewhat older field of Political Science, long before Hinsley's well-known work reached the bookshelves.

Importantly, there have been translations of the treatise into a number of languages over the years and my research has discovered commentary on the piece, however more prevalent since the end of the Cold War, in tongues as varied as French, Spanish, Italian, Japanese, and even Croatian, as well as the original German. While it is assumed that the latter offer discerning textual analyses in their own right, in order to delimit the project and to avoid the morass of linguistic difficulties that might easily follow from an expansive interpretive history of this kind, I have deliberately chosen to focus the lion's share of my research efforts on scholarly commentary about *Perpetual Peace* written in the English language. Such a preference, however befitting to a book written within a discipline whose origins are predominantly Anglo-American, is in no way intended to slight well-developed interpretation of Kant's popular treatise in these additional languages.[13] Indeed, there are several instances throughout the following chapters where such interpretations are discussed as points of comparison or as examples of interpretive consistency (or inconsistency) across linguistic and geographic boundaries.

Second, Kant's writings on international relations are relatively few in number, written mainly during the later part of his life, and have sometimes been criticized by scholars for their supposed lack of seriousness stemming from rather suspicious remarks Kant made about them. For example, Hannah Arendt remarks that Kant "called some of [his political writings] a mere 'play with ideas' or a 'mere pleasure trip.'"[14] And in reference to the "ironical tone of *Perpetual Peace*," which Arendt deems "by far the most important of them," she says not to take "too seriously" the treatise he once called in a letter to Kiesewetter (October 15, 1795) little more than "'reveries.'"[15] Still, well-respected authors note their "lasting influence" on the discipline of international relations.[16] Because of Kant's important later writings on international relations, Howard Williams and Ken Booth recently stated that the German known most for his critical and moral philosophy "has a justifiable claim to be the first comprehensive theorist of world politics."[17] They give much of the credit for contemporary academic interest in Kant's writings on international relations to Martin Wight and his influential work *International Theory: The Three Traditions*. According to Williams and Booth, Wight "was the first modern theorist of international relations to take Kant's work seriously."[18] Specifically, *Perpetual Peace*, of all of Kant's works on politics and international relations, has received the most attention from contemporary scholars for its visionary proposals and the relevance it is held to have for present-day international politics. Indeed, Wight remarks, "Kant's essay on *Perpetual Peace* was perhaps the ripest fruit of his philosophy" and "the most illustrious example" of writings by "some of the greatest political philosophers . . . fascinated by the problems of international relations."[19]

While there is ample evidence of Kant's unpublished reflections on the subject of international relations from 1764 to 1768 and from 1773 to 1789,[20] the most influential published writings occur even later in his life from 1784 to 1797. The following are four essays written by Kant during this later period: *Idea for a Universal History with a Cosmopolitan Purpose* (1784); *On the Common Saying: This May be True in Theory but It Does not Apply in Practice* (1793); *Perpetual Peace* (1795); and *The Metaphysics of Morals* (1797). All wrestle with the same issues Kant confronts in *Perpetual Peace*.

Some of the scholarly commentary and interpretation discussed in the book attempts to discern the meaning of Kant's international theory through a comparative analysis of all the works just mentioned. In its treatments of these accounts, however, the book carefully isolates commentary on *Perpetual Peace* from the discussion of Kant's other writings on international relations. Only occasionally are the latter considered. This is because the book is not an exposition on the history of Kant's general international theory based on an analysis of interpretations of all his works on the subject. The principal focus is on *Perpetual Peace*—a treatise Chris Brown recently called "the first genuine masterpiece of international political theory."[21]

PART 1

Kant's *Perpetual Peace*: An Introduction to the Text, Interpretations, and Patterns

CHAPTER 1

The Textual Hooks of Interpretations

Introduction

The object of chapter 1 is to introduce the reader to the text of *Perpetual Peace*. More specifically, this chapter explores which parts of the text are of greater (or lesser) consequence to interpreters in their attempts to decipher what this complex and intricate treatise proposes. The more pivotal parts of the text are introduced in connection with a general summary of the interpretations that refer to them. This presentation of the original Kantian text coupled with a summary of representative interpretations from each of the four historical periods under consideration, permits easier entry into the detailed analysis of individual interpretations that follows in arguments for the existence of patterns in parts 2 and 3 of the book. Table 1.1 summarizes each of the Articles of Kant's treatise and is provided here for the convenience of the reader.

Interpretations from the Mid-Nineteenth Century to the End of World War I

Chapter 2 argues that interpretations written from the mid-nineteenth century to the end of World War I assert that *Perpetual Peace* calls for a significant restraint on state sovereignty through establishment of a centralized authority above the level of states. A number of these interpretations focus almost exclusively on one portion of the text of *Perpetual Peace* in coming to this conclusion. Though references are made to different Articles in the text

Table 1.1 *Perpetual Peace*: The articles of Kant's treatise

The Preliminary Articles of a Perpetual Peace between states	
First Preliminary Article	No conclusion of peace shall be considered valid as such if it was made with a secret reservation of the material for a future war
Second Preliminary Article	No independently existing state, whether large or small, may be acquired by another state by inheritance, exchange, purchase, or gift
Third Preliminary Article	Standing armies will gradually be abolished altogether
Fourth Preliminary Article	No national debt shall be contracted in connection with the external affairs of the state
Fifth Preliminary Article	No state shall forcibly interfere in the constitution and government of another state
Sixth Preliminary Article	No state at war with another shall permit such acts of hostility as would make mutual confidence impossible during a future time of peace
The Definitive Articles of a Perpetual Peace between states	
First Definitive Article	The civil constitution of every state shall be republican
Second Definitive Article	The right of nations shall be based on a federation of free states
Third Definitive Article	Cosmopolitan right shall be limited to conditions of universal hospitality
First supplement: on the guarantee of a Perpetual Peace	Perpetual Peace is guaranteed by no less an authority than the great artist Nature herself
Second supplement: secret article of a Perpetual Peace	The maxims of the philosophers on the conditions under which public peace is possible shall be considered by states, which are armed for war

and some interpretation carried out on text within those Articles, what *Perpetual Peace* ultimately does for these interpreters is based substantially on a small section toward the end of the Second Definitive Article.

Accordingly, the most quoted and frequently referred to passage by interpreters that discuss the text of *Perpetual Peace* during this historical period is the following:

> There is only one rational way in which states coexisting with other states can emerge from the lawless condition of pure warfare. Just like individual men, they must renounce their savage and lawless freedom, adapt themselves to public coercive laws, and thus form an international state (*civitas gentium*), which would necessarily continue to grow until it embraced all the peoples of the earth.[1]

This passage is recognized by a number of interpreters from this period as definitive proof that *Perpetual Peace* requires the sovereignty of each state to be relinquished. To these interpreters, the applicable solution to the problem of war between separate states is understood to be the formation of a centralized authority capable of enforcing laws above the level of states.

It is important to note that interpreters working during this historical period use different terms when referencing the portion of the text just quoted. As used in Nisbet's translation, the terms "international state" and "*civitas gentium*" are seen in interpretations during this time. Additionally, terms like "universal state," "state of nations," and "republic universal" are encountered as well. The potential shades of difference between these terms are not of significant concern to advancement of the general argument. In the context of the interpretations under study, each term can be generally described as a centralized authority existing above the state level. While there is little discussion of the political, judicial, and/or military components of this authority (indeed most interpreters neglect this detail not out of inattention to the entirety of the treatise but simply out of respect for the text, which avoids it as well), there is general agreement on the coercive character of its laws assisted by the institutionalization necessary to their enforcement. Most certainly, such an authority restricts state sovereignty. Of the few interpreters during this period who describe Kant's proposal as a "federal union," "universal federation," or "federation of the world," the key point to recognize is that they continue to view the text as one in favor of a peace proposal above the state level.

Of related significance, there is interpretive uniformity on the subject of Kant's alternative to the conception of the international state by interpreters writing during this period. Directly after the oft-quoted passage mentioned earlier, Kant asserts the following:

> But since this (the international state or *civitas gentium*) is not the will of the nations, according to their present conception of international right (so that they reject *in hypothesi* what is true *in thesi*), the positive idea of a *world republic* cannot be realized. If all is not to be lost, this can at best find a negative substitute in the shape of an enduring and gradually expanding *federation* likely to prevent war. The latter may check the current of man's inclination to defy the law and antagonize his fellows, although there will always be a risk of it bursting forth anew.[2]

While contrasting language within the Second Definitive Article exists, it is most strikingly evident in Kant's discussion of the nature of the organization necessary to establish peace. The two apparently conflicting passages quoted so far provide the interpreter with much to consider and debate. However, chapter 2 argues that in a majority of interpretations during this period, there is very little inquiry into the characteristic features of Kant's "negative substitute"—the "gradually expanding federation." Indeed, most do not even mention the proposed alternative (or offer any textual analysis of it), even though many passages within *Perpetual Peace* refer to this pared-down surrogate for instituting peace. The interpreters working during this period are more persuaded by the first passage, which discusses the international state.

Undeniably, for such a short treatise, *Perpetual Peace* has much to say: six specific Preliminary Articles with generous commentary coupled with three Definitive Articles considering everything from the appropriate constitution for each state, to theories of international organization, even to the right of strangers to be treated with hospitality upon their arrival to a foreign territory. This would seem to offer ample material for an eager interpreter. Instead of analyzing in detail the conflicting passages within the Second Definitive Article, much less the relationships between all three of the Articles, most interpretations from this period are satisfied with a focus on one passage. Furthermore, there is very little mention within these interpretations of the subsequent two supplements to the treatise wherein Kant discusses the complex role that nature plays in the establishment of peace and the need for a secret "Philosopher's" Article.

As such, in comparison to the more involved textual analysis by interpretations written during the alternative three historical periods under consideration, this summary of the first collection of interpretations may seem rudimentary. Unfortunately, there is not much more to be said at this point.

Simply stated, interpretations during this period (which I argue in chapter 2 reveal the first phase of Pattern One) read little else into *Perpetual Peace* than the following avowal: Kant's text specifically endorses a peace proposal above the state level wherein the sovereignty of each state is reined in by a centralized authority with the "teeth" to enforce its own laws.

Interpretations from the End of World War I to the Mid-Twentieth Century

According to chapter 3, what emerges from those interpretations completed from the end of World War I to the mid-twentieth century is an understanding that the text of *Perpetual Peace* requires the surrender of some sovereignty by each independent state to a wider federation. For almost all interpreters writing during this period, a federation, not an international state, becomes the ideal toward which nations should work to achieve. Finally, as will be seen from an examination of the full range of interpretations completed during this period in chapter 3, there is a clear tendency by these interpreters to liken this federation to the League of Nations founded immediately after World War I.

The broader argument to keep in mind as detailed issues of the text are addressed in chapters 2 and 3 is that interpretations from both of these periods under study read the text as favoring peace proposals above the state level. Importantly though, each set of interpretations presents a somewhat different idea of how much sovereignty is to be transferred to this authority.

The principal passage of interest to interpretations completed during this period has already been stated. Though rarely ever mentioned within interpretations from the earlier era, Kant's concept of "an enduring and gradually expanding federation" as a "negative substitute" for the "positive idea of a world republic" becomes the primary textual anchor of this collection of interpretations.[3] Within these interpretations, there is a noticeable lack of focus on the "one rational way" Kant has offered to prevent future war between states.[4] These interpretations more clearly commit themselves to passages like the one above that bolster support for the alternative suggestion mentioned earlier. This alternative suggestion is that Kant's ideal in the Second Definitive Article is a federation, not an all-powerful international state. These interpreters appear more cognizant of and ultimately persuaded by statements within the Second Definitive Article that focus on the term "federation" and offer logical reasons for embracing it instead of an international state in their efforts to decipher Kant's real solution to the problem of war.

For example, Kant begins the Second Definitive Article with the "initial assumption" that if the Second Definitive Article is concerned entirely with the right of nations, the concept of it "only makes sense if there are independent nations."[5] The second explanation related to this is more involved than this simple "assumption" and worth quoting here. Kant remarks:

> People who have grouped themselves into nation states may be judged in the same way as individual men living in a state of nature, independent of external laws; for they are a standing offense to one another by the very fact that they are neighbours. Each nation, for the sake of its own security, can and ought to demand of the others that they should enter along with it into a constitution, similar to the civil one, within which the rights of each could be secured. This would mean establishing a *federation of peoples*. But a federation of this sort would not be the same thing as an international state. For the idea of an international state is contradictory, since every state involves a relationship between a superior (the legislator) and an inferior (the people obeying the laws), whereas a number of nations forming one state would constitute a single nation. And this contradicts our initial assumption, as we are here considering the right of nations in relation to one another in so far as they are a group of separate states which are not to be welded together as a unit.[6]

These are intuitive reasons for initially rejecting the international state in the context of his Second Definitive Article.

He later follows these with a more cogent argument regarding the relationship between the internal constitutions of states and a potential world constitution to be imposed on them from the outside. He states, "while natural right allows us to say of men living in a lawless condition that they ought to abandon it, the right of nations does not allow us to say the same of states."[7] This is because "they already have a lawful internal constitution, and have thus outgrown the coercive right of others to subject them to a wider legal constitution in accordance with their conception of right."[8] Kant suggests here that it is illogical for a state, which already possesses an internal constitution, to be subject to an external one as well.

Finally, Kant's rather critical remarks about the kind of constitution necessary to the founding of an international state end with a positive averment that suggests again his commitment to federation. He explains that "peace can neither be inaugurated nor secured without a general agreement between the nations; thus a particular kind of league, which we might call a *pacific federation (foedus pacificum)*, is required."[9] Different than the goal of a "*peace treaty (pactum pacis)*" which is to terminate *one* war (the pacific federation) would seek to end *all* wars for good."[10] While the primary aim of said federation may be to create the conditions of a permanent peace, Kant reluctantly closes the Second Definitive Article with this admonition: "(the federation) may check the current of man's inclination to defy the law and antagonise his fellows, although there will always be a risk of it bursting forth anew."[11]

The above paragraph's accent on quotation may seem excessive (and, as is shown in chapter 3, such passages are rarely referred to directly in interpretations during this period). Still, it is helpful to identify *in toto* the selections of the original text from which the interpreters may generally draw in coming to their conclusion that a less formidable federation, not an all-powerful international state, is what the text requires. These passages, more specifically, their focus on federation coupled with reluctance to embrace the argument for an international state, give shape to the principal passage most frequently alluded to by interpreters working during this period. From this, these interpreters read into *Perpetual Peace* a desire to curb state sovereignty through establishment of a federation with certain positive powers, albeit one where less sovereign authority is ceded to it than a world state would require.

Finally, and given much greater attention within the contextual arguments of chapter 3, one of the characteristics shared by nearly all interpretations completed during this period is the tendency to view the League of Nations as the institutional manifestation of Kant's model federation they understand to be proposed in the Second Definitive Article. One interpretation, in particular, explains that "at least six of the famous Fourteen Points are anticipated" by *Perpetual Peace*.[12] More precisely, the term "league," considered separate from its "League of Nations" label above, is not employed as an interpretive term of art clarifying the proposed Kantian federation until interpretations begin to surface after World War I.[13] However preliminary the thought, both of these potential examples of language used in elucidation of the text are arguably interrelated and reflect, once again, this series of interpretations shift away from understanding *Perpetual Peace* as advocating something similar to an international state and toward the view that the Kantian ideal in the text is something analogous to a federation where sovereign power is distributed more evenly between its central organizational feature and the assembled political parts. Their interpretations on this issue, as is shown in chapter 3, are entirely consistent.

Interpretations from the 1950s to the Early 1980s

The collection of interpretations written from the 1950s to the early 1980s makes the fullest use of the text available in *Perpetual Peace*. Thus far in this introduction to text and interpretation, little has been written about the Preliminary Articles, the First Definitive Article requiring the civil constitution of every state to be republican, the Third Definitive Article concerning the limitation of cosmopolitan right to conditions of universal hospitality, or the First Supplement and its discussion of what, in fact, guarantees perpetual peace. While the First and Third Definitive Articles[14] are important to this set of interpreters, the Preliminary Articles and the First Supplement (together with the Second Definitive Article) are crucial to their account of what the text recommends.

The argument presented in chapter 4 is that interpretations completed between the 1950s and the early 1980s understand *Perpetual Peace* as a text that views the sovereign state as the fundamental unit through which peace will be achieved. These interpretations offer a reading of the text, which advocates peace proposals at the state level. Concerning specific textual hooks, it is not uncommon to see the principal passage of interest to interpretations completed between the end of World War I and the mid-twentieth century in interpretations written during this new period. Still, there is one final excerpt from the text of the Second Definitive Article, which receives a significant amount of attention from interpreters during this period and is generally not discussed by interpreters during either of the earlier periods. As a provision of textual support for the collection of interpretations completed between the 1950s and the early 1980s, it is as influential as any.

Upon affirming that "peace can neither be inaugurated nor secured without a general agreement between the nations [in the form of] a particular kind of league . . . call[ed] a *pacific federation (foedus pacificum),*" Kant attempts once more to describe, however general, the nature of the pacific federation in question.[15] He states, "This federation does not aim to acquire any power like that of a state, but merely to preserve and secure the *freedom* of each state in itself."[16] Though certainly in different degrees, both sets of interpretations already introduced above understand peace to be a consequence of an institutional restraint introduced above the state level.

The collection of interpretations from this period, however, places special emphasis on Kant's claim in this passage that peace must be established through the continued freedom of the sovereign state, not on its limitation. Kant closes this excerpt with further remarks that seem to encourage this new interpretation. He writes:

> It can be shown that this idea of *federalism*, extending gradually to encompass all states and thus leading to perpetual peace, is practicable and has objective reality. For if by good fortune one powerful and enlightened

nation can form a republic (which is by its nature inclined to seek perpetual peace), this will provide a focal point for federal association among other states. These will join up with the first one, thus securing the freedom of each state in accordance with the idea of international right, and the whole will gradually spread further and further by a series of alliances of this kind.[17]

At last, "If the concept of international right is to retain any meaning at all, reason must necessarily couple it with a federation of this kind," what Kant has called, immediately before this sentence, "a free federation."[18]

Focusing on language like "association of states," "alliance (of states)," "securing the freedom of each state," and "free federation" from the excerpts above, interpretations from this period sense a genuine commitment to the preservation of state sovereignty in the Second Definitive Article. Such language conveys the notion of an ultimate separateness of states. An "association" or an "alliance," even a "free federation," directs this group of interpretations away from the institutional character of the proposed international authority prevalent in the first two groups of interpretations and toward a loosely bound and dissoluble collection of independent states where peace is insured by the workings of nature upon them and their eventual adoption of republican government.

For the first time, the term "voluntary," never mentioned in the Second Definitive Article of Kant's translated tract, is used throughout interpretations of the text to indicate the unforced process through which separate states freely choose to band together. Rarely if ever is the phrase "coercive laws" used in interpretations from this period.

Finally, for these interpreters, any limited organizational structure that might develop would not possess the powers over states interpretations completed during the first and second periods suggest. Though to different degrees, there are "teeth" in the international authorities accepted by both phases of Pattern One. This is clearly not the case with the first (or second) phase of Pattern Two. The general reading of the text offered by this new group of interpreters suggests the locus of authority and law within the international system remains with and between the independent state(s).

In addition to text within the Second Definitive Article, it is not uncommon for interpreters during this period to consider the six Preliminary Articles as further evidence for their claims.[19] The titular headings of the Articles are presented here as follows:

1. No conclusion of peace shall be considered valid as such if it was made with a secret reservation of the material for a future war.

2. No independently existing state, whether it be large or small, may be acquired by another state by inheritance, exchange, purchase or gift.
3. Standing armies (miles perpetuus) will gradually be abolished altogether.
4. No national debt shall be contracted in connection with the external affairs of the state.
5. No state shall forcibly interfere in the constitution and government of another state.
6. No state at war with another shall permit such acts of hostility as would make mutual confidence during a future time of peace.[20]

Several of these interpreters note that the Second, Third, Fifth, and Sixth Preliminary Articles all appear to "assume" the continued existence of the independent state. Furthermore, there is selected commentary below each Article, which suggests, with ever greater discernment, the logic associated with the preservation of the sovereign integrity of the state.

Most applicable, Kant explains in the commentary to the Second Preliminary Article that "a state, unlike the ground on which it is based, is not a possession (patrimonium). It is a society of men, which no-one other than itself can command or dispose of. Like a tree, it has its own roots, and to graft it on to another state as if it were a shoot is to terminate its existence as a moral personality."[21] He further states in the commentary to the Fifth Preliminary Article that "the interference of external powers [in the constitution and government of another state] would be a violation of the rights of an independent people . . . Such interference would be an active offense and would make the autonomy of all other states insecure."[22] Finally, in the closing section of the Preliminary Articles, Kant distinguishes between those Preliminary Articles that ought to be introduced at once (Articles One, Five, and Six) and those that permit some delay in their execution (Articles Two, Three, and Four). He explains, "The latter need not necessarily be executed at once, so long as their ultimate purpose (e.g. the *restoration* of freedom to certain states in accordance with the second article) is not lost sight of."[23]

Essentially, interpretations from this period find in the headings and commentary of the Preliminary Articles a clear link to its interpretive position on the Second Definitive Article. This position reveals the sovereign state as the fundamental operational unit through which international peace will be achieved. With no coercive legal mechanism above the separate states to guarantee peace, this new collection of interpretations relies on Kant's central idea based in the First Supplement to achieve the same goal. Exhibiting a grand faith in "the great artist *Nature* herself (*natura daedala rerum*)," interpretations from this period extract from this textual anchor of the First

Supplement the route through which peace can be attained within and between independent states.[24] Yet, as Kant quickly asks, "how does nature guarantee that what man *ought* to do by the laws of his freedom will in fact be done through nature's compulsion, without prejudice to the free agency of man? The question arises, moreover, in all three areas of public right—in *political, international* and *cosmopolitan right.*"[25]

Like most social contract theorists of his era, Kant is initially concerned with the formation of a civil constitution or *political right.* Through what he calls the "mechanism of human inclinations," nature wakes reason from its own slumber so that the latter might overcome the former.[26] Neighboring peoples, indeed their multiplicity of rational human wills "so admirable in [themselves] but so impotent in practice," are driven by internal dissent and external conflict created from their conflicting and self-seeking inclinations bestowed by nature to collectively form separate protective states under law.[27] Thus, *political right,* in the ultimate form of a republican constitution, is achieved by the phenomenal pulse of nature arousing dormant human reason.

Nature does not stop, however, at the domestic level. As to *international right,* which "presupposes the separate existence of many independent adjoining states," it also prevents the inclination of each newly formed and presumably not yet republican state among these from attempting to dominate the rest through universal despotism.[28] Via the barriers of linguistic and religious difference that nature imposes, intermingling between states is thwarted. This nature-induced separateness of states and the consequent avoidance of one state's will to "universal despotism which saps all man's energies and ends in the graveyard of freedom" creates a peace that is "guaranteed by an equilibrium of forces and a most vigorous rivalry."[29]

In cases of both *political* and *international right,* the natural mechanism of phenomenal conflict inherent in relations between men and the separate states constructed from them necessarily achieves peace. Yet just as nature separates to foster peace, so too does it unite to fulfill the same objective under *cosmopolitan right.* By the same motivation of mutual self-interest supplied by nature, "the *spirit of commerce* sooner or later takes hold of every people, and it cannot exist side by side with war."[30] Here, peace results again from the natural condition, not the moral potential, of humanity privately functioning within independent states united for common economic purposes.

The First Supplement is a most influential part of the text for interpreters writing during this period. While the Preliminary Articles may solidify the independent state as the primary actor under interpretations from this period, the First Supplement guarantees peaceful relations between such states in the long run. Essentially, and certainly allied with the Preliminary Articles, these two provisions yield further textual support to the view advanced by these interpreters that the Second Definitive Article embraces the sovereign state as the way to peace. Placed within the contextual framework of chapter 4, the defense of state sovereignty becomes the defining feature of interpretations completed between the 1950s and early 1980s.

Interpretations from the Early 1980s to the End of the Twentieth Century

In chapters 5–7, I argue that interpretations written from the early 1980s through the end of the twentieth century explain that *Perpetual Peace* views the sovereign republican state as the channel to peace. Like those interpretations written between the 1950s and the early 1980s, these also read the text as favoring peace proposals at the state level. To avoid repeating passages and meanings already clarified in Pattern Two, Phase One above, it is sufficient to submit in this summary that Pattern Two, Phase Two's understanding of the Second Definitive Article rests on excerpts within it that, through analysis and interpretation, reveal positions centered on the sovereign republican state as the channel to peace. The distinction between these two sets of interpretation that makes them worthy of division concerns the special weight and specific textual analysis this final group of interpreters give to the First Definitive Article. For them, what Kant spells out in a particular section of the First Definitive Article becomes the crucial ingredient in the grand peace proposal offered by *Perpetual Peace*.

First, for this final group of interpreters, Kant's "negative substitute," or from other passages, his "alliance," "league," or "free federation," is properly understood as a collection of independent states with republican constitutions committed to the rule of law, the separation of legislative and executive powers, and full representation of the body politic. On the surface, this conception is not so different from interpretations that reveal Pattern Two, Phase One. Yet there is a subtle change that occurs. Related to the formal thrust or a priori claims of his moral theory, Kant states within the First Definitive Article that "The republican constitution is . . . pure in its origin (since it springs from the pure concept of right)."[31] With their focus on the First Supplement (and the role that nature plays in the practical establishment of peace), this reading of the First Definitive Article is normally sufficient for Pattern Two, Phase One interpreters.

For Pattern Two, Phase Two interpreters, however, the passage immediately following the above provides the practical reason, for them not any less important than the formal, for states to adopt a republican constitution. Not only is the establishment of the republican constitution right in theory, but similar to the role that nature plays, "it offers a prospect of attaining the desired result, i.e. a perpetual peace" as well.[32] Kant responds lengthily with the following reason why:

> If, as is inevitably the case under this constitution, the consent of the citizens is required to decide whether or not war is to be declared, it is very natural that they will have great hesitation in embarking on so dangerous an enterprise. For this would mean calling down on themselves all the miseries of war, such as doing the fighting themselves, supplying the costs of the war from their own resources, painfully making good the ensuing devastation, and, as the crowning evil, having to take upon themselves a burden of debt which will embitter peace itself and which can never be paid off on account of the constant threat of new wars. But under a constitution where the subject is not a citizen, and which is therefore not republican, it is the simplest thing in the world to go to war. For the head of state is not a fellow citizen, but the owner of the state, and a war will not force him to make the slightest sacrifice so far as his banquets, hunts, pleasure palaces and court festivals are concerned. He can thus decide on war, without any significant reason, as a kind of amusement, and unconcernedly leave it to the diplomatic corps (who are always ready for such purposes) to justify the war for the sake of property.[33]

Pattern Two, Phase Two interpreters are far more likely to accept the above passage (and the practical reason offered within for adopting the republican constitution) as the text's primary solution to the problem of war.

Finally, for Pattern Two, Phase Two interpreters, implicit in the quoted excerpt is the relationship between states with republican, representative government and their peaceful propensities toward each other. This, as well, becomes a pivotal theme of Pattern Two, Phase Two interpretation. Again, it does not go unrecognized in both phases of Pattern One or Pattern Two, Phase One. The important point is that this theme, and its logical complement that states without representative governments are more likely to be warlike with each other, receive far less interpretive emphasis than is evident in Pattern Two, Phase Two. Essentially, and really for the first time, *Perpetual Peace* is understood to be a treatise with full textual support for the idea that domestic politics determines international politics. As Pattern Two, Phase Two interpreters sense the "statist" orientation of the Second Definitive Article, they see the potentially belligerent relationship between separate states overcome by Kant's practical argument in the First Definitive Article. The overall thrust of Pattern Two, Phase Two interpretation recognizes, to a much greater extent, the primary importance of the First Definitive Article, specifically the practical reason for its adoption.

Conclusion

To conclude, however less frustrating *Perpetual Peace* may be to read and understand than Kant's other works, this chapter should have made clear that his popular text is still involved and complex. Upon a first reading, the text may seem to contain contradiction after contradiction. Here Kant says an international state is needed, there a federation, or there simply an association of sovereign states. As has been briefly shown here, interpreters emphasize different portions of the text as more or less consequential in coming to their conclusions as to what peace proposal(s) the text ultimately endorses. This chapter has sought to introduce this notion and has hopefully provided a sound basis from which to explore, with greater specificity, the full range of interpretations over past years necessary to the formulation of my argument that two distinct patterns of interpretation have arisen.

PART 2

The Articles of *Perpetual Peace*: Peace Proposals Above the State Level

CHAPTER 2

Pattern One, Phase One: Reining in State Sovereignty

Interpretations from the Mid-Nineteenth Century to the End of World War I

Introduction

It is the primary purpose of this chapter to advance the argument that close analysis of individual interpretations written during this historical period reveals the first phase of an interpretive pattern of Kant's *Perpetual Peace*. Study into each textual interpretation is critical to a full and fair explication of the book's thesis. This approach seems best suited for exposing general similarities between interpretations to effectively advance the argument of pattern formation. It is important to remember that not all interpretations that reveal a particular phase of a pattern exactly mirror each other. If they did, then this whole exercise would be too immaculate. The idea behind the argument for patterns is simply that a majority of interpretations over a specific historical stretch tend toward similar analysis of the text in question. I argue that it is possible to tease from these similar particulars a pattern of interpretation.

As introduced in chapter 1, the common thread running through these interpretations is the view that *Perpetual Peace* calls for the restriction of state sovereignty through the formation of a centralized authority above the state level as an effective solution to the problem of war. Based on a singular focus on one particular passage from the text of *Perpetual Peace*, a number of interpreters refer to Kant's authority as an "international state," "*civitas gentium*," or "state of nations." Others consider it a "universal state" or "republic universal." Still others label it a "universal federation" or "federal union." Finally, there are those who note the warlike ways of independent, sovereign states and suggest Kant's text as a remedy to this ever-present problem because it is, in their view, clearly in favor of the significant limitation of sovereignty. Importantly, a central feature of the first phase of Pattern One is the "reining in of state sovereignty."

Henry Wheaton: An Early British Interpretation

The first English-language interpretation of Kant's *Perpetual Peace* that I consider is from Henry Wheaton's well-known book, *History of the Law of Nations in Europe and America*, published in 1845.[1] After repeating what Kant says in the First Definitive Article, Wheaton begins his commentary by lamenting the fact that "In the existing system of international relations, the state of nature, which has ceased as between individuals, whilst it still subsists as between nations, is not a state of peace, but of war, if not flagrant at least always ready to break out."[2] According to him, this is because the "code expounded by public jurists to nations has never had the obligatory force of law, properly so called, for want of an adequate coercive sanction."[3] To remedy this (and with a passage that mirrors a portion of the text from *Perpetual Peace*), Wheaton suggests Kant's conclusion that "Nations must renounce, as individuals have renounced, the anarchical freedom of savages, and submit themselves to coercive laws, thus forming a community of nations, *civitas gentium*, which may ultimately be extended so as to include all the people of the earth."[4] Without "the guarantee of a special compact having for its object the perpetual abolition of war," Wheaton contends that the Kantian "state of peace must . . . ever remain insecure."[5]

Recalling the introduction to text and interpretations written during this period in chapter 1, it is important to note that nowhere after these remarks does Wheaton question whether Kant believes the submission by numerous states to coercive laws under a larger *civitas gentium* is unrealizable. Indeed, he even quotes Kant in saying that such an "idea . . . is not an impracticable or visionary" one.[6]

Furthermore, the alternative to state submission to public laws enforced by an authority existing above the state level is what Kant refers to as the "negative substitute" of "an enduring and gradually expanding federation."[7] This section of the text, which states that federation is more likely to be accepted by the "will of nations" than the *"civitas gentium,"* is not considered in Wheaton's discussion.[8] Wheaton's conclusion is clear: *Perpetual Peace* is ultimately in favor of the establishment of an authority existing above the level of states whose laws are backed by, as he calls it, "an adequate coercive sanction."[9] This will result in a clear restraint on state sovereignty.

An Interpretation by James Lorimer: A "Stricter Bond of Union" Required by the Text of Perpetual Peace

James Lorimer focuses his discussion on one passage from *Perpetual Peace*. In his *Institute of the Law of Nations* written in 1884, Lorimer quotes the text directly: "Nations must renounce, as individuals have renounced, the anarchical freedom of savages, and submit themselves to coercive laws; thus forming a *civitas gentium*, which may ultimately extend, so as to include all the people of the earth."[10] Like Wheaton, Lorimer does not consider the passage directly following this one which questions the practicality or will of nations to form a *civitas gentium* and suggests instead a "negative substitute of an enduring and gradually expanding federation likely to prevent war."[11] Though he does suggest thereafter that Kant struggled with the "difficulties attendant on this proposal," he makes this remark in the context of another work, namely Kant's *Metaphysics of Law*.[12] Lorimer quotes selected passages from this work[13] then explains in these that "Kant [is] guarding himself, as if by anticipation, against the imputation of desiring to establish a Universal State."[14] Making no reference to *Perpetual Peace* during this discussion, Lorimer clearly sees *Perpetual Peace* as the treatise by Kant most sympathetic to a universal state (and his *Metaphysics of Law* as opting for something far less ambitious). This is probably why he concludes his analysis of Kant's two works with the explanation that, in *Perpetual Peace*, Kant was advocating a much "stricter bond of union" than in the *Metaphysics of Law*.[15] Like Wheaton's, Lorimer's interpretations suggest a similar reduction in state sovereignty.

Independence of the State Questioned in Interpretations by D.G. Ritchie, R. Latta, and Benjamin Trueblood

There follows a stream of late-nineteenth-century and early-twentieth-century interpretation, which continues to rein in state sovereignty in interpretations of Kant's *Perpetual Peace*. For example, David Ritchie, in his 1902 book *Studies in Political and Social Ethics*, offers an interpretation that strongly endorses the notion that *Perpetual Peace* calls for a clear restraint on state sovereignty as the only path to peace. Though brief, his statements on this subject are emphatic. He writes "it is more than a hundred years since Kant wrote his essay on 'Perpetual Peace.' Kant saw quite clearly that there is only one way which war between independent nations can be prevented; and that is by the nations ceasing to be independent."[16] He echoes this statement when he writes the following a few lines later: "The absorption of smaller nations into larger political bodies means the prevention of war within great areas."[17]

As with Ritchie above, Professor R. Latta points out quite clearly the danger Kant sees in nations maintaining their sovereign independence. He first explains that, for Kant, "perpetual peace is an ideal, not merely a speculative Utopian idea, but a moral principle which ought to be, and therefore can be, realised."[18] Yet "realisation of this ideal" will never occur without "honestly facing political facts and getting a firm grasp of the indispensable conditions of a lasting peace."[19]

The political facts of Latta's age are exactly those of Kant's—the sovereignty of each nation in the world is inviolable and unquestioned and to "strive after the ideal [of perpetual peace] in contempt or in ignorance of this condition is a labor that must inevitably be either fruitless or destructive of its own ends."[20] As such, according to Latta, "Kant thus demonstrates the hopelessness of any attempt to secure perpetual peace between independent nations. Such nations may make treaties; but these are binding only for so long as it is not to the interest of either party to denounce them. To enforce them is impossible while the nations remain independent."[21] Thereafter, he directly quotes Ritchie's phrase already excerpted earlier: "There is only one way in which war between independent nations can be prevented; and that is by the nations ceasing to be independent."[22] He too sees *Perpetual Peace* as a text advocating the restriction of nations' sovereign independence.

Also writing during this time period, Benjamin Trueblood explains that "The last years of the eighteenth century gave us Kant's great tractate on 'Perpetual Peace,' in which was uttered for the first time the idea of the federation of the world in an international state built upon republican principles."[23] In another article, he states, "A great international state, coextensive with the surface of the globe, with some sort of government directing the general interests of the race and compatible with local self-government, is the necessary and inevitable outgrowth of the nature of man and of society."[24] Though he mentions in a footnote below this remark that Kant "does not seem, however, to have believed such an [international] state possible," he still maintains in the same footnote that, nevertheless, "Kant was the first to give us the idea of a great international state in *Perpetual Peace*."[25]

Comparison with Interpretation by the German Biographer Friedrich Paulsen

The German biographer Friedrich Paulsen, writing around the time of Latta, Ritchie, and Trueblood, published his book *Immanuel Kant: His Life and Doctrine* in 1898. While interpretations of *Perpetual Peace* written in German are not the subject of this book, it is useful to compare Paulsen's discussion with those English-language interpretations during this period. In his section on Kant's "Theory of Law and the State," Paulsen states that "Everlasting peace was the favorite idea of Kant when he was growing old. The condition of its possibility lies in a universal union of states under just laws."[26] According to Paulsen, Kant believed that "to promote the universal union of states under just laws is a duty, just as it was declared to be a duty to promote the formation of the national constitution."[27]

After these initial remarks, Paulsen seems intent on linking Kantian "Reason" to his interpretation of *Perpetual Peace*. Paulsen's explanation, though lengthy, is worth inclusion. He explains:

> Nor would the aged Kant lend a willing ear to the laudation of clever and unscrupulous politicians. His impressions of the politicians have great similarity with the views expressed by Plato. He describes them as persons who make possible everything impossible, except the dominance of right upon the earth, which they rather regard as something absolutely impossible. He regards them as empiricists lacking in ideas, who see no further than the advantage of the day, but are not able to estimate things in their large relations. In distinction from this, it will remain the permanent task of philosophy to view things from the standpoint of ideas, or as Spinoza would say, *sub quadam* objection of unpracticality. This reproach is often raised against Plato's *Republic*: but ideas are not refuted by vulgar appeal to alleged contradictory experience. Rather experience has to be measured by ideas formed after their pattern. The philosopher should set up an archetype and the task of the politician should be "to bring, in accordance with this, the existing constitutions ever nearer to the highest possible degree of perfection."[28]

To this, Paulsen adds the most relevant paragraph for our purposes:

> Like the idea of a perfect system of laws in a state, the idea of an international union of states united by law, and the consequent substitution of a legal process for violence and war, is a necessary idea of reason, and as such perfectly legitimate. It is the duty of the politician to work for its realization;

the saying "thou canst for thou oughtst" holds not merely in private morality, but also in public matters concerning the laws.[29]

While far from an in-depth interpretation of the Second Definitive Article of *Perpetual Peace*, Paulsen arrives at the conclusion that Kant in *Perpetual Peace* suggests a union of states under law because it is a necessary "idea" of reason and, as such, is something towards which politicians should always work. Yet he further explains Kant's belief that the realization of this idea may come about even without "the good will of the politician."[30] Kant discusses in *Perpetual Peace* the ever-increasing number of evils associated with war, for example, "the evils of present war, the intolerable burdens of preparing for future war, and the paying of debts of past wars."[31] According to Paulsen's reading of Kant, "The increase of these evils will continue to strengthen the impulse to get rid of them. As they have been strong enough to induce savages to submit to the rule of a political constitution, they will also be effective in compelling the states to give up their savage freedom."[32]

In these cases, Paulsen understands the underlying argument of *Perpetual Peace* to be one favoring the sacrifice of the freedom of the state. This, as hopefully is becoming clear, is a similar thread running throughout interpretations during this period. It is interesting to note this developing theme's similarity with both an uncovered German interpretation here and the French interpretation briefly outlined in note 9.[33]

Commentary from Translations of Kant's Perpetual Peace: Interpretations by J.D. Morell, W. Hastie, and Mary Campbell Smith

As was stated in the Introduction, some of the interpretation or commentary on *Perpetual Peace* over the past century and one-half comes from remarks made, whether in introduction or preface, to translations of the text from the original German. The first English translation (since the original translation of *Perpetual Peace* from German into English in 1796) appeared in the year 1884; J.D. Morell was its author.[34] Though little depth of textual analysis is offered prior to the translation, Morell does see the treatise as one in favor of a "method of creating a federal union between neighbouring nations . . . [through] which the end of durable peace can be gradually attained."[35] Recalling Kant's statement from Appendix II that "politics and morality can only be in agreement within a federal union . . . and that the rightful basis of all political prudence is the founding of such a union in the most comprehensive form possible," Morell's former statement (and its similarity to Kant's "comprehensive federal union") certainly suggests a commitment to the creation of a federal union wherein the sovereignty of each state existing within it is necessarily contained.[36]

In what is likely a stronger endorsement of such a "comprehensive" union, W. Hastie explains in the Introduction to his 1891 translation that, according to Kant, "war . . . can only be brought to an end by a better political organization."[37] From this, Kant "expounds and applies . . . the idea of a Universal Federation of the Human Race, in the most original and fertile way."[38]

The textual analysis in Mary Campbell Smith's introduction to her translation of *Perpetual Peace* is much more thorough than Morell's or Hastie's. Though Smith does discuss the other Articles in her Translator's Introduction, she (as with other interpretations during this time) views the Second Definitive Article as the "central idea of the treatise."[39] Distinctively, she is one of the few interpreters during the period that makes reference to Kant's "negative substitute" or federation as a possible alternative to a state of nations. In analysis of the Second Definitive Article, she explains that "the only footing on which a thorough-going, indubitable system of international law is in practice possible is that of the society of nations: not the world republic the Greeks dreamt of, but a federation of states."[40]

Yet even with this remark, Smith notes with an asterisk by the term "world republic" that Kantian "Reason [still] requires a State of Nations."[41] Smith uses the terms world republic and state of nations interchangeably. According to Smith, a State of Nations "is the ideal" in *Perpetual Peace* and "Kant's proposal of a federation of states is a practical substitute from which we may work to higher things."[42] Within her translation, Smith refers the reader to a particular part of the text of *Perpetual Peace* explaining that "Kant seems to speak of a State of nations as the ideal" as opposed to a "federation of nations."[43] This passage has already been singled out by Wheaton's and Lorimer's interpretations. Smith's translation of that passage reads as follows: "For states, in their relation to one another, there can be, according to reason, no other way of advancing from that lawless condition which unceasing war implies, than by giving up their savage lawless freedom, just as individual men have done, and yielding to the coercion of public laws. Thus they can form a State of nations (*civitas gentium*), one, too, which will be ever increasing and would finally embrace all the peoples of the earth."[44] Smith is less convinced that the only entity Kant favors in *Perpetual Peace* is a state of nations. As stated earlier, she acknowledges that a federation, rather than a state of nations, is the more practical option for Kant. Still, she admits that in *Perpetual Peace* the state of nations remains the ideal and, as important, reason requires it as "the surest way to attain peace."[45]

Leonard Woolf and Edwin Doak Mead: Final Interpretations from this Period

The final interpretations of *Perpetual Peace* from this period come to us from Leonard Woolf and Edwin Doak Mead. Woolf's discussion of *Perpetual Peace* is fairly brief but complimentary of the work's ambitious proposals. Speaking initially of the great number of proposals for peace that have arisen over the past several centuries, he notes that "A stream of calf-bound, cloth-bound, paper-bound volumes has for the last 300 years issued from the world's presses containing schemes for the establishment of perpetual peace."[46] Writing this around the beginning of World War I, Woolf states, "The Great War has for the moment caused this stream to run a little fuller."[47] Regarding *Perpetual Peace*, he adds "Of all these projects and schemes and dreams none is more curious and original than Kant's *Zum Ewigen Frieden*."[48] According to Woolf, not only is it "full of political wisdom," it is by "far the most 'practical' work ever written on the subject."[49] After listing the Preliminary and Definitive Articles, he refers to them as the "pillars of the Temple of Perpetual Peace" and notes, "not one is chimerical or utopian."[50] Through them, "Kant has succeeded in laying down the conditions of international relationship and government which would have to exist in order to make perpetual peace possible."[51]

While Woolf acknowledges that *Perpetual Peace* is in favor of "international government," Mead is thoroughly convinced that the text supports the establishment of a world government in his interpretation. In reference to *Perpetual Peace*, he begins quite grandly by stating "It was a remarkable insight of Kant's that universal peace could come only with the republic universal."[52] Without initial explanation as to the structure of this "republic universal," it does not seem a stretch to say that such a "republic universal" would involve the loss of state sovereignty in order to form a single world entity. Based on this single statement, it cannot be determined whether or not he continues to see states in Kant's "republic universal" as existing after its formation (which may more likely be said for other terms from this group of interpretations like "state of nations"). Still, it is difficult to think of a more definitive term than "republic universal" for describing a worldwide governmental authority that will exist above the state level and operate as a clear restraint on state sovereignty.

After a short discussion of the Preliminary articles (where he essentially quotes directly from the text and offers little analysis), Mead begins to offer more evidence in support of the above statement concerning the "republic universal." First, like other interpreters during this period, he sees the second section of *Perpetual Peace* within which exists the three definitive articles as most important to the body of the treatise. He states that the "three great constructive principles are stated in the definitive articles" of the treatise.[53] He then explains Kant's understanding of Nature's role in improving men, the state, and international relationships. Agreeing with Smith and Paulsen above, Mead asserts that Kant "surveys again the course of evolution, with all its struggles and antagonisms, to show that just as individual men, with all their conflicting interests and inclinations, are forced out of a condition of aloofness and lawlessness into the condition of a State, so individual nations are being gradually forced towards arbitration and federation by the sheer dangers and evils of the present disorder, self-interest pointing the same way which morality commands."[54] He also expounds on Kantian "Reason" and "Morality" and the requirements it places on politicians to work toward the ideal of a "republic universal," echoing again earlier words by Smith. He states:

> To the objection of the practical politician, that great reforms theoretically admirable cannot be realised because men are what they are, Kant wisely answers that many have large knowledge of *men* without yet truly knowing the nature of *man*. The process of creation cannot be justified if we assume that it never will or can be better with the human race. Kant's cardinal position is that the pure principles of right and justice have objective reality and can be realised in fact, that it is precisely our vocation to proceed about their realisation as fast as we apprehend them, and that failure to do this is really opposed to nature and is dangerous politics.[55]

Mead concludes his discussion of *Perpetual Peace* by doing what a number of interpreters from this period do. He quotes directly from the text those several lines that often appear in interpretation from the mid-nineteenth century to the end of World War I: "For States viewed in relation to each other, there can be only one way, according to reason, of emerging from that lawless condition which contains nothing but occasions of war. Just as in the case of individual men, reason would drive them to give up their savage, lawless freedom, to accommodate themselves to public coercive laws, and thus to form an ever-growing State of Nations, such as would at last embrace all the nations of the earth."[56]

Mead could have as easily quoted, then discussed the following two sentences after this to demonstrate what seems like confusion in the Second Definitive Article over what the text is proposing:

> But since this is not the will of the nations, according to their present conception of international right (so that they reject *in hypothesi* what is true

in thesi), the positive idea of a *world republic* cannot be realised. If all is not to be lost, this can at best find a negative substitute in the shape of an enduring and gradually expanding *federation* likely to prevent war.[57]

Instead, he understands the genuine position of the Second Definitive Article to be found in the former selection. He never quotes or even refers to the latter excerpt.

Conclusion

To briefly conclude, this chapter has primarily discussed English-language interpretations of Kant's *Perpetual Peace* completed from the mid-nineteenth century to the end of World War I. It argues that these interpretations reveal the first phase of an emerging pattern, which understands the text of *Perpetual Peace* to be in favor of a significant restraint on state sovereignty through formation of a centralized authority above the level of states. Terms like "international state," "*civitas gentium*," "universal state," "world republic", and "republic universal" are often used to describe this authority. Other commentators refer to it as a "universal federation" or "federal union." Importantly, neither Kant nor the interpreters that consider *Perpetual Peace* go into any details about this centralized authority, its political and military components, and so forth. The most that can definitively be said about it is that it will exist above the level of states, diminishing the sovereignty of each through public laws above them that it can enforce.

Finally, several interpretations that significantly contribute to the emergence of this first phase of Pattern One focus almost exclusively on one passage within the Second Definitive Article of *Perpetual Peace* and rarely consider the First, Third, or even the remainder of the Second Definitive Article in their textual analysis. It is difficult to determine whether these interpreters were simply ignoring the rest of the text or were so certain that the proposal for an "international state" or "state of nations" in that passage was of such central importance that discussion of competing claims or secondary aspects of the text was unnecessary. Either way, their frequent focus on this proposal to the exclusion of other alternatives presented elsewhere in the text suggests how pivotal this passage was to their determination of what *Perpetual Peace* ultimately recommends as a solution to the problem of war between states. As for those commentators from this period whose brief interpretations do not quote directly from the text, their interpretations still acknowledge that the prevention of war will occur through peace proposals above the state level.

CHAPTER 3

Pattern One, Phase Two: Sovereignty Curbed

Interpretations from the End of World War I to the Mid-Twentieth Century

Introduction

This chapter discusses English-language interpretations of Kant's *Perpetual Peace* written between the end of World War I and the mid-twentieth century. The common thread running through these interpretations is the view that *Perpetual Peace* requires the surrender of some sovereignty on the part of states to a wider federation. In the sense that both Phase One and Phase Two of Pattern One read the text as requiring a peace proposal above the state level, the latter is not so different from the former. Still, there is a detectable shift in interpretation that occurs from Phase One to Phase Two, which includes the following distinctive components. First, *Perpetual Peace* suggests to almost all interpreters working within this period that the ideal toward which nations should work to achieve peace is a federation, not an international state. Second, it is shown that inter-pretations written during this period rarely if ever consider the passage often referred to throughout interpretations that reveal the first phase of Pattern One.[1] Instead, meanings taken from the text of *Perpetual Peace* by these interpreters rely on a variety of passages, though more precisely on the following passage offered already in chapter 1 but important enough to quote again here:

> Since this [the international state] is not the will of the nations, according to their present conception of international right, the positive idea of a

world republic cannot be realised. If all is not to be lost, this can at best find a negative substitute in the shape of an enduring and gradually expanding federation likely to prevent war.[2]

Most importantly, there is a tendency among many interpreters writing during this period to liken this "enduring and gradually expanding federation" to the first permanent international organization, the League of Nations founded immediately after the end of World War I.

The Ideal Changes: Dwight W. Morrow's Interpretation

According to my research, Dwight W. Morrow completed one of the first post–World War I English-language interpretations of Kant's *Perpetual Peace* in his book, *The Society of States*, in 1919.[3] Morrow focuses primarily on Kant's discussion in the Second Definitive Article. His conclusion is that the text of the Article suggests a federation of states, not a universal state, as the solution to the problem of war between sovereign states. This solution is the ideal toward which all states should work.

For example, in his reading of the Second Definitive Article, Morrow explains that for Kant, "It is to this end (the federation of states) that mankind is advancing. To make many nations into one single State is not only impracticable, but undesirable. It might well lead to despotism and it would ignore the necessity of developing the several national traits."[4] Morrow remarks in another section that "As civilization increases, as men become more and more alike in principles and get more and more of an understanding of one another and of their differences, the final Federation of States will be developed."[5] To this he adds that Kant "describes this ideal at present [to be] unattainable, but still an ideal toward which all men guided by reason must constantly strive."[6] Based on his use of the words "end," "advancing," and "final" in the above quotations from his work, it is clear to him that the ideal expressed in the Second Definitive Article is in fact a federation, not an all-encompassing world state.

The League of Nations' Parallel: Interpretations by Jessie Wallace Hughan, D.P. Heatley, Nicholas Murray Butler, Mehan Stawall, Carl Joachim Friedrich, and R.B. Mowat

As one might expect, there was a stream of scholarly literature that emerged in relation to Wilson's Fourteen Points in 1918 and the subsequent founding of the League of Nations in 1920. Though not particularly comprehensive in their analysis of the full text of Kant's *Perpetual Peace*, these writers did view *Perpetual Peace*, and the idea of an international authority suggested in the Second Definitive Article, as one of the intellectual foundations for the League of Nations. Like Morrow above, these interpreters understand *Perpetual Peace* to favor a federation as the guarantor of a future peace.

According to Jessie Wallace Hughan, writing in 1923, the Second Definitive Article suggests "a federation of free states shall be founded rather than a super-state."[7] Hughan also asserts that, throughout *Perpetual Peace*, "At least six of the Fourteen Points are anticipated, and propositions laid down as to absolutism, armament, war loans, secret diplomacy, self-determination, intervention, methods of warfare, and the League of Nations, which, if followed, would have rendered the events of 1914 an impossibility."[8]

Like many other interpreters, D.P. Heatley, in his 1919 book, *Diplomacy and the Study of International Relations*, hopes to arrive at a Kantian view of international relations through a general study of all his works. As stated earlier, this is the type of analysis with which this book is very careful. Still, he does offer some commentary on *Perpetual Peace* alone. While noting the fact that too much "emphasis has been unduly laid on conclusions by those who cite him [Kant] in their advocacy of a League of Nations," Heatley still understands *Perpetual Peace* to be a text encouraging the formation of a federation of states.[9] In fact, in including a selection from a translation (and unfortunately one he does not reference) where he sets forth what *Perpetual Peace* envisions, he chooses the following quotation: "Every people, for the sake of its own security, may and ought to demand from any other people that it shall join in entering into a constitution, similar to the civil constitution, in which the right of each shall be secured. Thus would arise a League of Nations."[10] Nowhere in Heatley's commentary does he consider the frequently quoted passage from interpretations that reveal Pattern One, Phase One. His final allusion to the text is the simple remark that, for Kant, "international right shall be founded on a federation of free states."[11]

Nicholas Murray Butler also sees the conceptual similarity between Kant's federation and the League of Nations. In his *Path to Peace: Essays and Addresses on Peace and Its Making*, he writes that the "thought of Kant is not restricted to national policy alone."[12] In quoting directly from the text, Butler states, "The public right ought to be founded upon a federation of free states."[13] He then exclaims "There, in a single sentence, is the prophecy of the League of Nations and the function of international law."[14]

Unlike Butler who looks only to the Second Definitive Article, Mehan Stawall sees the resemblance between the ideas of all three definitive articles and the principles of a League of Nations. Stawall refers to *Perpetual Peace* as a treaty and writes, "The 'constitutive' Articles of the Treaty deal more directly with the League of Nations that was then [in Kant's time] only a dream."[15] According to Stawall, "Kant's first requirement for such a League is that every member of it should have a republican form of government . . . and only on the basis of such a League can there be a satisfactory system of international law."[16]

Even as late as 1948, the well-known Harvard scholar Carl Joachim Friedrich likens Kant's treatise to the League of Nations. Yet he comments not only on its similarity to the League, but to the United Nations as well. Friedrich even states, "it is obvious that this [the Second Definitive Article of *Perpetual Peace*] is the keynote of both the Covenant of the League of Nations and the United Nations Charter."[17] Further discussing the world's second permanent international organization, Friedrich asserts that "There can be little question that the Charter of the United Nations in many respects fulfills those conditions which Immanuel Kant had formulated as essential to the establishment of a world-wide organization."[18] Friedrich also acknowledges, "Nor would [Kant] be as disturbed as some among us that the organization turned out to be a league rather than a Union."[19] Appropriate to this comment, Friedrich acknowledges toward the end of his analysis that Kant thought it "wiser to stick to federalism" since a "united government for the world" would most likely "raise the specter of a world-wide despotism."[20] Distinguished from an all-powerful world government, Friedrich recognizes the similarities between the more limited proposals of *Perpetual Peace* and the more limited powers of both the League of Nations and the United Nations.

Finally, in a comprehensive study of the European states system written in 1923, R.B. Mowat remarks in a section devoted primarily to the world's first permanent international organization that "the League had many precursors in the world of thought—[one of which was] Kant's treatise on *Perpetual Peace*."[21] He further states, "the League of Nations offers a reasonable compromise between the sacrifice of independence on the part of the constituent States, on the one hand, and the wielding of universal despotic dominion, on the other."[22] Mowat obviously views the League of Nations (and most probably its intellectual forebear discussed in the Second Definitive Article) as an international institution, which requires the surrender of some independence on the part of member states. As will be shown, this idea (along with the accompanying tendency to liken Kant's federation to the League of Nations demonstrated above) occurs frequently in this collection of interpretations.

I use the terms "accompanying tendency" in the sense that when these interpreters use the term "League of Nations" (and "United Nations" in Friedrich's case), they are not referring to a super-state, international state, or state of nations where state sovereignty is more seriously limited, but to an international authority in which the independent sovereignty of each member is curbed. For example, Thomas Barclay succinctly explains this idea in a 1935 article in the *Contemporary Review*. He writes, "That the League of Nations is not a super-state has been claimed for it, but I cannot regard the acceptance of the dispositions of the Covenant as otherwise than the curtailment of the autonomy of the adherent states."[23] The primary point is that this group of interpreters understand Kant's envisioned federation and the actual League of Nations as international authorities in which members must relinquish some of the their sovereignty. This principal element of interpretations written during this period is far more evident, however, in several of the following interpretations of *Perpetual Peace*, completed primarily in the 1930s and early 1940s.

Sovereignty Curbed: Interpretations by A.C.F. Beales, Waldemar Gurian, and John Bourke

First, A.C.F. Beales, in his historical account of the organized movements for international peace, makes space for brief analyses of several eighteenth-century philosophers whose theories may have contributed to developing peace movements in the late nineteenth and early twentieth centuries. Immanuel Kant and his theories espoused in *Perpetual Peace* are given primary attention. Beales offers a concise review of the treatise, starting with the point that Kant, "as the last of the eighteenth-century philosophers, accepted the new theory of the nation State but rejected the headstrong logic that would enlarge the nation into a Cosmopolis."[24] Unlike many interpreters, Beales sees *Perpetual Peace* as a practical text. He explains that "Kant firmly believed eternal peace to be an unrealizable ideal; therefore his suggestions were more properly concerned with seeking the right road and following it as far as was humanly possible."[25] He further notes, "Kant's *Perpetual Peace* (*Zum Ewigen Frieden*) won him the reproach of being a Jacobin (1795)."[26] He sees "the book," as he calls it, as "falling into two parts—an examination of certain reforms to be undertaken while war still existed, in order to create a public opinion favorable to the abolition of war, and a body of suggestions for the final organization of perpetual peace."[27] With these comments, Beales wishes to present Kant and *Perpetual Peace* as author and text interested not so much in theoretical principle, but practical reform.

Before discussing the Second Definitive Article, he offers background into Kant's domestic political theory:

> Kant agreed with Hobbes that man was by nature selfish and base, but he drew from history the lesson that mankind had risen to a high state of

civilisation through the competition and "mutual antagonism" of individuals "in society," which not only had produced social chaos but also had brought out all man's latent powers, until the chaos had been resolved by the formation of the State.[28]

Beales uses Kant's political theory as a way into his international proposal. He states, "This argument Kant employed similarly to foreshadow an analogous development among States themselves, culminating in a 'federation of free republics.' "[29] After explaining that "By republic, Kant meant any form of government which embodied the liberty and equality of its subjects," he points out that Kant "favoured federation in preference to a World State."[30] Yet if it is clear that Kant did not support one highly centralized super-state as Beales writes, then what does this federation consist of? Many interpreters have struggled with this question over the years, with certainly no help from the text itself. One thing is certain. No matter what interpretation is given in any of the four periods under consideration, it is more likely than not to be just as general as the text itself in the discussion of the concrete attributes of this federation. Yet this is honest interpretation. One thing all interpreters do agree on is that Kant, in the Second Definitive Article, offers little insight into the substance and content of his proposal, be it an international state, a federation, or simply an association of likeminded states. As such, other than interpreting it in one or other of these ways, they are all very careful not to give too many details of its structure.

This is probably why John Bourke is correct in saying that, compared to earlier peace proposals by other thinkers of the seventeenth and eighteenth centuries like the Abbé de St. Pierre, "Kant's scheme [in *Perpetual Peace*] is the first fully to break away from the political conditions of any given time and be based upon universal facts of human nature which do not pass away with the ages."[31] He continues by saying that "for two reasons we must not expect to find in it a programme fulfilling all detailed demands that could be made upon it. It is general in character, an outline, a framework, and does not aim at being more."[32]

Yet even with the admittedly general nature of the proposals offered in the Second Definitive Article in *Perpetual Peace*, there are still relatively clear differences that arise in interpretations over the years. As stated above, an international state or highly centralized federation as important components of Pattern One, Phase One, a less formidable federation as a primary component of Pattern One, Phase Two, or the preservation of state sovereignty as a primary component of both phases of Pattern Two, are all different conclusions of many interpretations written since the mid-nineteenth century.

What is important to note in this context (and in relation to Beales's article) is a central factor that distinguishes the first and second phase of Pattern One. Pointedly, Beales believes that Kant's "Federation would involve 'the surrender of a portion of power in return for participation in a wider, richer, and more secure life.' "[33] This is a very general remark about the nature of Kant's federation yet it comes up time and again, both explicitly and implicitly, in several other interpretations completed in the time period from the end of World War I to the mid-twentieth century. Ultimately, it is why this chapter and the particular phase of Pattern One that is revealed within it is referred to as "Sovereignty Curbed." Accordingly, Beales understands Kant's proposal to involve the "surrender" of some power by the sovereign state to a wider federation. This is somewhat different from most interpretations that reveal Pattern One, Phase One, which envision a more serious restraint on state sovereignty. It is also unlike interpretations completed during the last half of the twentieth century, which suggest that the proposals in *Perpetual Peace* stand for the preservation of sovereignty, not its restraint.

Waldemar Gurian, in his critique of Mortimer J. Adler's book, *How to Think About War and Peace*, briefly echoes Beales's remarks.[34] In speaking of *Perpetual Peace*, Gurian notes, "Kant believed that a curtailment of national sovereignty by a perpetual pact excluding war would make lasting peace possible."[35] He further states, "Hegel rejected this belief, emphasizing that sovereignty of states cannot be bound or limited."[36]

John Bourke's article, already mentioned above, speaks as well of Kant's "(Völkerbund) or federation of nations . . . as one where there must be some surrender of sovereignty on the part of each member state."[37] Though obviously in agreement with the above two interpreters on this important issue, Bourke goes into much more detail than these about the rest of the treatise. While he praises Kant for bringing the issue of the prevention of war to the forefront of his philosophical writings toward the end of his life and briefly mentions four works that deal with the subject, he still chooses to concentrate his interpretive efforts on *Perpetual Peace*. This treatise, he says, "contains the fullest, most independent, and most systematic presentation of Kant's views; and it is upon this that we shall concentrate in considering them."[38] Bourke views Kant in *Perpetual Peace* as "eminently sober and practical, not a visionary or day-dreaming utopian."[39] Still, similar to almost all other interpreters, he is careful to note the general nature of the treatise. He states, "Kant makes no claim to offer a programme, cut-and-dried and complete, for the abolition of war at once, in a lifetime, or in a century."[40]

Unlike interpretations written between the 1950s and early 1980s, many of which view the content of Kant's Preliminary Articles as an argument for the preservation of state sovereignty, Bourke discusses them simply as "preliminary conditions which must first be satisfied before the ideal federation of free republican states can be brought to pass."[41] Bourke senses that Kant, in including these Preliminary Articles, wants to make certain that "each time a war is fought, the period following it shall be less and less a merely negative period, a mere cessation of hostilities, an interval between one war and another, and more and more a positive period in which constructive attempts are made to *establish* peace on a firmer and more lasting basis."[42] With respect to the Preliminary Articles, Bourke says nothing here about their supposed "assumption" of the sovereign state as the sole operational unit through which peace might be established. This, as is shown later, is what commentators writing between the 1950s and early 1980s take from the Preliminary Articles. Instead, Bourke responds, "peace is something which has to be prepared for and *established* with effort, no mere passive state of relief hovering uneasily between a past on which we look back with horror and a future which we view with dazed indifference."[43]

It is apparent to Bourke that the establishment of peace requires the existence of an authority above a collection of separate states. This is why he immediately turns to a discussion of the Second Definitive Article and an organized federation for an answer. As we have seen, Bourke, like Morrow above, has already referred to this federation of free republican states as an ideal.[44] This is characteristic of interpretations written during this time (as the next three interpretations analyzed after this one demonstrate). Yet Bourke is interested in the concrete attributes of this federation too. He follows the discussion of the Preliminary Articles with the comment, "It remains now to inquire what kind of federation it is which Kant here envisages" in the Second Definitive Article.[45] While Bourke believes we may somehow "feel disappointed" with the lack of detail Kant goes into in describing his federation, as has been noted above, "we [still] must not expect to find in it a programme fulfilling all detailed demands that could be made upon it. It is general in character, an outline, a framework, and does not aim at being more."[46] In fact, the most that can be said about it according to Bourke's interpretation is that "there must be some surrender of sovereignty on the part of each member state" within the federation.[47] Though Bourke notes that "we might expect to have found some account in Kant's scheme of the form that this [federation] would take, of precisely what aspects of sovereignty or powers the separate states would agree to forgo to the central authority," he believes it is nowhere to be found.[48] Once again, the most these three interpreters are willing to say about Kant's proposal is that it will involve some limitation of sovereignty through the creation of a federation.

The Ideal is a Federation, not a World State: Interpretations by Jessie H. Buckland and J.F. Crawford

In the Introduction to a 1927 translation of *Perpetual Peace*, Jessie H. Buckland is as clear as Morrow and Bourke in the belief that the ideal in Kant's treatise is a federation. Buckland spends considerable time discussing Kant's moral and political philosophy, which need not be analyzed here. Buckland's understanding of the Preliminary Articles is much like that of Bourke in that he views them simply as "practical" suggestions for the improvement of relations between states after war, not a designation of them as encouraging the entrenchment of the sovereign state.[49] His views on the Second Definitive Article are relatively sparse though quite telling. In his textual analysis, he states that in terms of Kant's treatise, "Since each state is a sovereign state, no common authority over all states can be set up, and there can be no compulsion, as in the case of the individual, to leave the state of nature and to become part of a world state."[50] He further notes, "If we can't aim at the establishment of a common authority to which all states must submit, the only ideal consistent with freedom is that of a federation of free States."[51]

Like Buckland, J.F. Crawford has written an earlier 1925 article that also marks the end, goal, or ideal of Kant's proposal as a federation of states. Though he primarily discusses Kant's *Idea of a Universal History with a Cosmopolitan Purpose* in his analysis, he does offer several comments on *Perpetual Peace*. Crawford first refers to the Preliminary Articles as "concrete proposals" that, if implemented, would help humanity achieve the "goal" of federation.[52] Nowhere does he remark that they are simply proposals to sustain peace through, and only through, the continued existence of the sovereign state, as will be seen in interpretations written between the 1950s and early 1980s.

Crawford then moves to the Second Definitive Article where he quotes directly from the treatise stating, "The law of nations shall be founded on a federation of free states."[53] His comment exactly after this quotation is that "This is not so much a condition of the goal [meaning perpetual peace] as the goal itself."[54] He also asks earlier in the treatise, in a more general discussion, "Does Kant regard the goal of world federation as actually attainable?"[55] When coupling these comments with his further remark that "Kant is so sensitive to the deadening effects of too widely centralized a government that he rejects a world state in favor of a federation," it is clear that Crawford understands the Kantian ideal to be a federation, not a world state.[56] Yet this federation is not just an ideal for Kant according to Crawford. Crawford explains that in the realm of "methods and practical details . . . a federation of states is all [Kant] is willing to endorse."[57]

A Concluding Interpretation by A.C. Armstrong

The final interpretation from this period to be reviewed is by A.C. Armstrong. Published in 1931, Armstrong's article is devoted entirely to Kantian philosophy on peace and war. While he offers a very in-depth analysis of Kant's views on international relations, he does so through an examination of all his texts, not just *Perpetual Peace*. Still, it is fairly easy to distinguish Armstrong's comments that specifically relate to *Perpetual Peace*. Furthermore, they generally resemble all of the above interpretations and thus further the argument for the existence of a second phase of Pattern One. In fact, Armstrong's interpretation has aspects of most of the key elements of interpretations from this period.

Armstrong begins his look at Kant's thought with the comment that there have been those over the years who view Kant as "proposing the destruction of independent nationality . . . in favor of a world state [or Voelkerstaat]."[58] Armstrong then clearly states that this "argument is of course a misinterpretation."[59] This is why he later explains that "Much more frequently, therefore—and this may be called its standard designation by Kant—it is described as a *Voelkerbund*" or a "federation of free states."[60] He concludes that this "federation" is a "federal organization of the several states, or a group of neighbor states, in substitution for the world-state, which has been found impracticable."[61] Yet Armstrong still takes from the text the notion that the original position of states is a "lawless condition."[62] And though a substitution of a world state is not the answer as claimed above, there should occur a "substitution of the federal relationship of nations in place of their original lawless condition."[63]

Armstrong also notes this "federal organization" as part of the "Kantian programme, then, distinctly includes the elements of an international league."[64] Yet according to Armstrong, this organization "transcends the provisions of the Kellogg Pact and parallels the plan of the League of Nations more nearly than that of any other of the later movements for the furtherance of peace."[65] While Armstrong does believe that the "present League is more closely knit together in its organization, as, it should probably be added, it is more complexly framed, than the *Bund* which Kant had in mind," he does see "the federal idea [as] central in his thought."[66]

Conclusion

In conclusion, this chapter argues that textual interpretations of Kant's *Perpetual Peace* found in the period between the end of World War I and the mid-twentieth century have similar themes running through them that reveal a particular phase of Pattern One unique to this specific historical period. The second phase of Pattern One that emerges recognizes Kant's text as one that proposes the formation of a federation in which the sovereignty of each member state is curbed. This federation is an ideal toward which all states should work to achieve. Conceptually speaking, it is also understood as similar to the idea and certain concrete components of the League of Nations founded in 1920 and, in one example offered, the United Nations founded in 1945. Finally, the textual anchor of the term "federation" is found in a variety of passages throughout the Second Definitive Article, though discussion of it in the one principal passage already stated is what interpreters from this period refer to primarily. All of these elements demonstrate a relative shift in the overall understanding of Kant's *Perpetual Peace* that occurs in the movement from Phase One to Phase Two. Still, both phases recognize that the text suggests peace proposals above the state level.

PART 3

The Articles of *Perpetual Peace*: Peace Proposals at the State Level

CHAPTER 4

Pattern Two, Phase One: In Defense of State Sovereignty

Interpretations from the 1950s to the Early 1980s

Introduction

In this chapter, the argument is made that the first phase of a new pattern emerges from interpretations completed between the 1950s to the early 1980s. These interpretations view Kant's *Perpetual Peace* as a text that endorses the sovereign state as the essential unit through which lasting peace will be achieved. The continued freedom and independence of the state, not its restriction, is what this collection of interpretations suggests.

Frequently, interpretations during this period acknowledge that Kant may have favored a confederation, free federation, association, or alliance of states in *Perpetual Peace*. Still, the interpreters that use these terms always describe such entities as voluntary, loosely bound, and ultimately dissoluble. This is because their reading of the text demonstrates that the sovereignty of the state is not to be compromised, regardless of what kind of international entity may potentially develop.

Finally, this series of interpretations tends to be grounded in more than just the text of the Second Definitive Article. One encounters examination and review of the Preliminary Articles, the First Supplement, and even, to some extent, the Third Definitive Article much more frequently in interpretations written during this period. In support of the claim that the text of the

Second Definitive Article of *Perpetual Peace* champions the preservation of state sovereignty, interpreters from this period look to all of these selections in asserting their position.

Besides the focus on broader portions of the text, interpretations during this period offer considerably more substance and analysis of *Perpetual Peace* than most of the interpretations discussed in chapters 2 and 3. This is certainly evident in what I would argue is the defining interpretation of this period, written by F.H. Hinsley in his 1963 book *Power and the Pursuit of Peace*. While I generally analyze interpretations of the text in chronological order, I think it is more instructive to consider Hinsley's 1963 work first. Clearly, it is most representative of interpretations written during this time, discussing all the core elements of interpretations that I argue reveal Pattern Two, Phase One. As such, an introductory review of it will provide an easier entry into further discussion of the other textual analyses.

F.H. Hinsley's Influential Interpretations

Hinsley initially states in his chapter on Immanuel Kant that the philosopher "took over Rousseau's conception of the international state of nature [as] 'a state of war'" and that therefore posited that "'the state of peace must be founded.'"[1] Upon delving into the text of the Second Definitive Article, Hinsley is not ready to say that Kant's solution to this problem of the state of war between nations is the same as Rousseau's or the Abbè de St. Pierre's. He states that Kant's "detailed exposition . . . in *Perpetual Peace* constitutes a complete departure from their organisational proposals."[2]

More importantly, Hinsley then begins his key analysis of what he believes Kant is proposing in *Perpetual Peace*. Thoughts on this theme essentially occupy the entire chapter. He calls Kant's and Rousseau's idea of an international state of nature and the resulting state of war between states a "predicament."[3] But according to Hinsley, in *Perpetual Peace*, Kant "did not suppose the way out of the predicament [to be] a merger of the separate states."[4] Hinsley obviously sees Kant as favoring the coming together of individuals in a state to avoid the state of war between them and thus to further their most basic interests in survival. Yet he also believes that the international state of nature poses a different problem for Kant. Interpreting the text, Hinsley asserts that though "individuals must combine to survive, states, by their very nature, could not. It was no more logical to hope to solve the international problem by the supersession of the states than it would have been logical to try to end the civil state of nature by the abolition of individuals."[5] He ends this discussion by exclaiming that the above is the "dominant theme in *Perpetual Peace*."[6]

In reaching this first conclusion, Hinsley relies primarily on Kant's statements in the Second Definitive Article. There Kant likens states to individual men which "live in a state of nature . . . [and therefore] for the sake of security can and ought demand of the others that they should enter . . . into a constitution, similar to the civil one, within which the rights of each could be secured."[7] Yet as we have already discussed in chapter 1, the next step toward a single state of nations that would seem the logical response to the international state of nature is both a "contradiction" since "nations already have a lawful internal constitution, thus outgrowing the coercive right of others to subject them to a wider legal constitution" and impracticable because it is not the "will of the nations according to their present conception of international right."[8]

From this, Hinsley concludes the first section with the comment that Kant "accepted the continuing independence of states . . . as morally right."[9] He explains that "Just as [Kant] derived the right to freedom of the individual from the dictates of the moral law, so he derived the right to freedom of the state—the route to and the guarantee of the freedom of the individual— from the same moral law."[10]

Hinsley then turns to the Preliminary Articles for analysis and support of his claim that *Perpetual Peace* stands for the preservation of state sovereignty. Interpretations that reveal both phases of Pattern One discuss the Preliminary Articles on occasion, but mostly in passing, and never in support of their separate positions on the text. Hinsley quickly points out even before his discussion of their impact that "These articles not only assumed the autonomy of the state but sought to strengthen it."[11] Furthermore, Hinsley disagrees with the majority of those who understand the Preliminary Articles to be little more than preliminary conditions that must be "fulfilled" before the Definitive Articles can be offered with the goal of "establishing" peace. He states that " 'the preliminary articles of perpetual peace between states' [are] a statement of the law of nations as it ought to be—and thus of Kant's solution—and not, as has often been assumed, as a statement of the preliminary progress that must be made before the work of establishing peace could be begun."[12] He clearly sees the Preliminary Articles as part of Kant's prescription and therefore integral to what he is advocating. As such, his statement that these articles not only assume, but also seek to strengthen, the sovereign state makes more sense.

His emphasis is on the Second, Third, and Fifth Preliminary Articles. After generally summarizing all the articles, wherein he emphasizes Kant's constant use of the word "state" and the consistent connotation it receives from him as an independent and sovereign entity,[13] he turns to Kant's commentary directly below each of the above three articles in support of his interpretive claim. First, he notes Kant's statement in the Second Preliminary Article that "A state is not a possession like the soil . . . It is a society of men which no one but themselves is called on to command or dispose of. Since, like a tree, such a state has its own roots, to incorporate it as a graft into another state is to take away its existence as a moral person and to make of it a thing."[14] Second, he notes that the Third Preliminary Article "demanded the abolition of standing armies because they 'threaten other states with war' and were 'the causes of wars of aggression,' but argued that 'the case is entirely different where the citizens of a state voluntarily drill themselves and their fatherland against attacks from without.' "[15] Finally, Kant refers to the Fifth Preliminary Article where he says, "No state shall interfere by force in the constitution and government of another state" as such interference would constitute a "trespass on the rights of an independent people and an actual offence which . . . would tend to render the autonomy of all states insecure."[16]

While Hinsley offers little analysis of each section presented, he implies in all of these that Kant is demonstrating his commitment to the independent state. This is especially true in regard to the Second and Fifth Preliminary Articles. First, Kant describes the state as a moral person and essentially says it is contradictory to "incorporate it as a graft into another state or take away its existence."[17] The creation of an international state like that discussed in several interpretations that give rise to Pattern One, Phase One would certainly undermine Kant's notion of the state as a moral person whose independent existence would obviously be compromised by a larger state "incorporating it as a graft into it." Second, the very basic noninterventionist position Kant takes in the Fifth Preliminary Article may come under attack even in a Pattern One, Phase Two–like federation. Finally, Hinsley maintains, "in a concluding paragraph to the preliminary articles, Kant even demanded that states which had lost their independence should have it restored."[18] He turns once again to the Second Preliminary Article but this time to a different section. Here, Hinsley notes Kant's acknowledgment that, in comparison to the First, Fifth, and Sixth Preliminary Articles, which "should be introduced at once," the "execution" of the Second Preliminary Article may be "delayed."[19] Yet Hinsley then quotes Kant as saying this delay does not mean that "The restitution . . . to certain states of the freedom of which they have been deprived . . . must be indefinitely put off."[20] Once again, Hinsley's examination of the text reveals to him, however general, Kant's commitment to the independence of the state.

While Hinsley clearly reads into the Preliminary Articles Kant's support of the inviolable sovereignty of the state, he is just as convinced that this position reveals itself in the Third Definitive Article. In comparing it to the Preliminary Articles, Hinsley states, "Even more remarkable for its emphasis on the independence of the state was another of the definitive articles—the third—in which Kant introduced the notion of 'the Cosmopolitan or World Law.' "[21] Since the Third Definitive Article has barely been mentioned thus far, I offer a quick summary of the text involved in this interpretation. The article pronounces in its titular heading that "Cosmopolitan Right shall be limited to Conditions of Universal Hospitality."[22] According to Kant, "Hospitality means the right of a stranger not to be treated with hostility when he arrives on someone else's territory."[23] Kant goes on to say, "He can indeed be turned away, if this can be done without causing his death, but he must not be treated with hostility, so long as he behaves in a peaceable manner in the place he happens to be in."[24]

Hinsley's reading of the above goes as follows. First, in commenting on the title, Hinsley says, "It is not for nothing that generations of commentators have been puzzled by [it]."[25] He further states, "They have had difficulty in reconciling it with their assumption that he advocated the merger of states."[26] The main point, according to Hinsley, is that "It asserted the right of all men to seek their freedom in as many separate states as natural conditions required—and especially in those backward areas where the state had not yet developed."[27] Hinsley understands Kant to be saying that separate states exist and will continue to exist. As such, cosmopolitan right will always be limited according to this reality.

While Hinsley seems to creatively read into the Preliminary Articles and the Third Definitive Article Kant's support of the independent state, his interpretive position is much more persuasive in his analysis of the Second Definitive Article. Beyond what has already been explained above in reference to it, Hinsley attempts to uncover what Kant actually means by all the different phrases he uses to describe his proposal for peace in the Second Definitive Article. Hinsley asserts, "we must now establish what was Kant's conception of the 'federalism of free states.' "[28] He recognizes that Kant uses this term to describe his proposal in the Second Definitive Article and, like all interpreters, he tries to pin down what Kant is suggesting. As was explained in earlier chapters, this has never been an easy task for interpreters as Kant was very general in his formulations. Still, Hinsley is otherwise convinced and confident that Kant did not favor an international state or federation that restricted state sovereignty in any way.

In Hinsley's analysis to follow, it is very easy to notice the interpretive shift from the broader components of Pattern One discussed in chapters 2 and 3 to the ideas and meanings presented in this instructive interpretation. While this shift is detected through Hinsley's novel focus on the Preliminary Articles and Third Definitive Article, it is even more evident in his discussion of the Second Definitive Article that interpreters from the earlier two periods focus on exclusively.

Though it is not clear if he researched them, Hinsley would seem to have little confidence in interpretations that reveal the first phase of Pattern One. He initially states, "Everybody knows that [Kant] did not advocate world government or the complete but less universal merger of states: he explicitly rejects this solution."[29] In a later book, he says to those earlier interpreters that explained Kant's text in this way that they simply "misunderstood Kant's entire argument."[30]

Showing little sympathy with this Pattern One, Phase One component, Hinsley seems just as skeptical about interpretations that reveal Pattern One, Phase Two. He states that "because of his use of such phrases [federation, federalism, etc.] most people firmly believe that he advocated international federation in our modern sense of the term as the only alternative."[31] He emphatically states, "This is not the case."[32] According to Hinsley, "[Kant] derived these phrases from the word *foedus* and used that to mean 'treaty,' which is what it still means [and therefore] he was envisaging the replacement of the existing imperfect, customary international law by a structure of international society based on a treaty between independent states."[33]

Hinsley clearly believes that Kant in *Perpetual Peace* is as likely to dismiss a federation that exists as an institutionalized authority above the level of states as a world state. His reasons for this interpretive position are as follows:

[Kant] was as much opposed to it [federation] as to world government because of his insistence that the state, like the individual, could not part with its freedom. The individual must impose the state on himself in order to remain free. In the same way "free federation" for Kant was what the state must impose on itself *while remaining free.*[34]

Though Hinsley does admit that a "league or international organization" may arise incidentally from Kant's very limited proposal, he asserts that "voluntary acceptance as continuing independent nations of a rule of law" will not be "backed up by international organisation or physical force."[35] This is because, in the final analysis, "Kant insisted that some other solution must exist—that international peace must be based on and obtained through the freedom of the state—because he took the doctrine of state sovereignty and autonomy to its logical conclusion."[36]

Importantly, Hinsley does not budge from this interpretive position in books he writes in later years. In his 1966 book, *Sovereignty*, he remarks, "We shall acquire, indeed, a renewed respect for the percipience of Immanuel Kant who, in the 1780s and 1790s, spelled out clearly the message that peace could now be founded only on self-imposed improvement in the conduct of the independent sovereign state."[37] Ten years after his first textual analysis of Kant's treatise in *Power and the Pursuit of Peace*, Hinsley published his 1973 book *Nationalism and the International System*. Here, he notes that "Kant . . . rejected the programme for improving the international system by amalgamating states, or by imposing international political organisation upon them."[38] Instead, Hinsley continues to suggest, "For Kant, even more decisively than for Bentham, a treaty agreement between sovereign states was the only means by which the international system might be improved."[39]

Yet this bare-minimum solution, which Hinsley is convinced Kant endorsed, presents obvious problems. The notion of a rule of law in the form of a treaty between independent states is a nebulous one. If states remain independent with only a relatively abstract and unenforceable rule of law between them, then that order presumably created by a federation or world state that may be in a position to enforce the rule of law would seem to be reduced to anarchy in a context of separate, autonomous states pursuing their own external affairs without any checks on their actions.

Even Hinsley admits this problem. He first states, "Kant's dilemma here was the same as that which had faced Rousseau."[40] He goes on to say that if "There could be no lawful international order without an international public law," then "it was not easy to see how there could be an international public law without an international political system."[41] Still, Hinsley firmly believes that Kant was pressing for the development of an international public law that, in effect, "would do the work of an international political system."[42] Clearly, Kant was differentiating "international law as it was from the rule of law as it should be."[43] What he was ultimately "propounding," according to Hinsley's 1973 book, "was not a federation in our sense of the term, but collaboration between states under an improved law of nations."[44] While hope for an improved rule of law between separate states may sound too idealistic to place the goal of the prevention of war in, it should be clear by now that Hinsley does not believe Kant favored anything more than this prescription in the Second Definitive Article of *Perpetual Peace*.

Hinsley is not convinced that the proposal Kant offers in the Second Definitive Article is the only thing that will "guarantee" perpetual peace. Importantly, in one of the first examples of this, an interpreter of the text looks to material beyond the Preliminary and Definitive Articles in attempting to come to terms with what Kant believed would bring about peace. According to Hinsley, "[Kant] analyzed what he thought would produce peace in 'the first addition' to the articles of *Perpetual Peace*, entitled 'On the guarantee of perpetual peace.' "[45] Hinsley (and, as will be argued, other interpreters from this era) considers the "First Supplement: On the Guarantee of a Perpetual Peace" as a "supplemental" avenue.[46] At least in the way Hinsley understands it, the Kantian notion of an improved law of nations and the role it plays in producing peace is in fact "supplemented" by this section of the text.

In the First Supplement, Hinsley views Kant as placing his hopes for peace in " 'the great artist nature . . . as [her] mechanical course evidently reveals a teleology: to produce harmony from the very disharmony of men even against there will.' "[47] This rather complicated idea has already been spelled out elaborately in chapter 1. In Hinsley's case, he does little more than summarize the text of the Supplement (as I have done before). Still, a brief look at his review of the text is helpful. In the first instance, " 'nature creates the disharmony [between men] and the dispersal [of men] in order to force men to use their better qualities [e.g. reason] for overcoming its dangers.' "[48] This "process," as Hinsley calls it, involves the following three areas: " 'constitutional law, international law and cosmopolitan or world law.' "[49]

First, in constitutional law, nature leads humankind toward the formation of a civil constitution by instilling selfish propensities in individuals, which, when opposing each other, " 'impel them to submit themselves to compulsory laws and thus bring about the state of peace in which such laws are enforced.' "[50]

Second, in international law, Hinsley comments, "Nature's purpose in the international field is rather to preserve the separate states and to utilise their conflict [as it does in its relation to and influence on human beings]."[51] Nature utilizes the means of language and religion to differentiate peoples and prevent them from coming together. Such differences, coupled with the already evident selfish inclinations of individuals, " 'occasion the inclination towards mutual hatred and the excuse for war.' "[52] This separating mechanism also brings people and states closer together through the " 'the balancing of these forces in a lively competition (which would not occur under an amalgamation of states in a despotism which leads to the graveyard of freedom).' "[53] Just as men and states remain independent and free, so they will grow closer together and toward mutual agreement on the principles for a lasting peace because of their separateness from each other brought about by nature. It is thus not the transcendence of the collection of sovereign states through establishment of an all-powerful international state, but the competitive tendencies between states that will, paradoxically, bring about peace.

Finally, according to Hinsley, this "balanced competition would thus find its ultimate expression in the cosmopolitan or world law."[54] Under this broad topic, Kant insinuates that the ever-present commercial instinct of humankind does much to prevent war because it cannot exist with it. Though nature does separate states through differences in language and religion, it also unites them under cosmopolitan law through the " 'spirit of commerce which cannot exist with war, and which sooner or later takes hold of every nation [so that] States find themselves impelled (though hardly by moral compulsion) to promote the noble peace.' "[55] In the above three ways, nature, through the mechanism of human self-interest, guarantees peace between separate states.

Hinsley is intent on giving the First Supplement its due. He sees it as an integral part of Kant's treatise, too long left out of discussion and interpretation of the text, and certainly important in understanding how Kant expected perpetual peace to result from the continued existence of the sovereign state with no higher political authority above it to restrict its freedom.

F.H. Hinsley's interpretations of Kant's *Perpetual Peace*, especially his chapter on Kant in *Power and the Pursuit of Peace*, are arguably the most well-known and thorough analyses of the entire text. Two later interpreters referred to it as the "the first close textual analysis of Kant in the Anglo-American strongholds of academic international relations" since *Perpetual Peace* was first written in 1795.[56] Full coverage of its review and analysis, as undertaken above, is crucial to the argument for the existence of a new pattern. Though other interpreters from this period may leave out certain aspects of his analysis of the text in their interpretations, it is certain that he covers nearly all thoughts on interpretation included in their considerations of the text.

Interpretations through the 1950s and 1960s: Frederick L. Schuman, Kenneth Waltz, and Wolfgang Schwarz

In this historical period under consideration, there exists commentary and discussion of the text that predates Hinsley's 1963 book. For example, Frederick L. Schuman in his 1954 book *The Commonwealth of Man* briefly asserts, "Kant's 'articles of *Perpetual Peace*' postulated the independence of all states, nonintervention, and disarmament."[57] Schuman also suggests that the text advocates "more vaguely" some form of collective defense mechanism that operates to protect those independent states existing together in a "loose union, devoted to commerce and to republican constitutionalism."[58] He does not indicate that Kant proposed anything more than the continuing existence of a collection of independent states bound together by similar political institutions and commercial activity.

In a far more significant interpretation of Kant's treatise, Kenneth Waltz writes in his 1962 article "Kant, Liberalism, and War" of Kant's commitment to the sovereign state. He believes it is important to offer this interpretation of the text because there exists so "many misinterpretations of his political philosophy" in the past.[59] Throughout the first two sections of the article, Waltz gives the impression that Kant sees little difference between the state of nature at the civil level and the state of nature at the international level.[60] He explains, for Kant, "The civil state is necessary for two reasons, because men are imperfect and because even good men may fall into dispute and require a legally established mediator. The universal law-state would seem to be necessary for a similar pair of reasons."[61] According to Waltz, "in spite of a number of statements such as the one just quoted, Kant will not accept the 'legal state of Society' on a grand scale, the world constitution 'similar to the civil constitution,' as a solution to the problem."[62] Waltz continues with the comment that "Every time he uses such phrases he quickly adds qualifications that materially change their meaning."[63]

So, Waltz asks, "Why does Kant, after having constructed an argument internally consistent, turn to the conclusion that not [world] government but a voluntary organization is the solution to the problem of war?" Here Waltz answers the question in an almost identical way as Hinsley. He sees two reasons why Kant does not carry the domestic analogy to its logical conclusion.

First, according to Waltz's reading, "States already have a legal constitution; it would be illogical to place them under another. Individuals in a condition of nature have a right to compel others to join with them to form a state. The right of a state to demand that other states submit to the rule of law is not comparably strong."[64] As such, Waltz refers to Kant as "a non-interventionist liberal, in contrast to Mazzini and Woodrow Wilson," because "As a matter of right, no state can interfere with the internal arrangement of another."[65]

The second reason Waltz believes Kant "sh[ies] away from a world state [is that] he fears that such a state, once achieved, would be a greater evil than the war it is designed to eliminate."[66] This is because it potentially "could become a terrible despotism, stifle liberty, kill initiative, and in the end lapse into anarchy."[67]

Following from his argument that a world state is not Kant's answer, Waltz then must offer an alternative, knowing full well that Kant was indeed interested in offering some kind of a solution to prevent future wars in *Perpetual Peace*, not simply a descriptive analysis of war and peace. According to Waltz, Kant "hopes states may improve enough and learn enough from the suffering and devastation of war to make possible a rule of law among them that is not backed by power but is voluntarily observed."[68] Similar to Hinsley's analysis above, Waltz views Kant's proposal as suggesting the "internal improvement of states and [improvement in] the external rule of law" between them.[69] Yet it is the external rule of law that is entirely "voluntary" and "dependent on the perfection" with which the internal improvement of states "is realized."[70] From this, it is easy to conclude that, like Hinsley, Waltz understands the text to place its faith entirely in the sovereign state as the avenue to peace. Nowhere in his article does he mention that the text suggests states should part with some of their sovereignty as has been argued when discussing interpretations that reveal both phases of Pattern One. Hinsley's and Waltz's arguments lay the foundation for the interpretive shift that begins to occur in the 1950s and 1960s.

Detailed interpretations of *Perpetual Peace* by Hinsley and Waltz, well known throughout the International Relations community, do provide the core material in the argument for a new pattern during this historical period. Still, it is important to note that throughout the 1960s and 1970s, other writers considering the text of *Perpetual Peace* offer interpretations very consistent with those of Hinsley and Waltz. Their analysis of the text offer even more support to the argument that a clear interpretive shift occurs during this time period.

Wolfgang Schwarz published an article in 1962 called "Kant's Philosophy of Law and International Peace."[71] In discussing this topic, he is equally as interested in Kant's *Metaphysics of Morals* as he is in *Perpetual Peace*. Still, he does offer some commentary on the latter. While Schwarz outlines the Preliminary Articles in summary form like Hinsley, he does not mention that their very existence "assumes" the autonomy of the state.

Where he seems to agree more with Hinsley is in his brief discussion of the Second Definitive Article and the First Supplement. He refers first to the three Definitive Articles as "the positive conditions of international peace."[72] His focus then turns to the Second Definitive Article. Because of "difference of language, of 'religions,' and the ineffectiveness of laws over great distances," he suggests Kant is not in favor of a "world state."[73] Like Hinsley, he takes the above reasons for this position from the First Supplement. Instead of a world state, he looks to " 'the surrogate of the covenant of civil society, namely, free federalism.' "[74] Once again, the implication that Schwarz gives is that states will "freely" and "voluntarily" enter into agreement with each other on the principles of peace, though not sacrifice their independence in doing so. Finally, in such an atmosphere where states retain their sovereignty, it is not a world state or federation that guarantees "the lawful order of peace," but for Schwarz (as with Hinsley), "'the great artist nature.'"[75] It is only through nature that the "'dint of discord among men'" can bring "'concord even against their will.'"[76] Schwarz's analysis appears to fall in line with certain general elements of interpretations from this period discussed thus far.

Comparison with a German-Language Interpretation Written by the Noted Author Karl Jaspers

As in the prior chapters, it is helpful to compare translated interpretations from other languages (primarily German) with English-language interpretations written during the same period. Here, in his book *Philosophy and the World* published in the same year (1963) as Hinsley's *Power and the Pursuit of Peace*, Karl Jaspers presents a thorough interpretation of *Perpetual Peace* strikingly similar to Hinsley's.

Jaspers lists only the First, Fifth, and Sixth Preliminary Articles as relevant and of "lasting significance."[77] Interestingly, these are the ones that Kant explains must be "executed at once."[78] Though he does not openly state that the Preliminary Articles support the inviolable nature of the sovereign state, his comments under the Second Preliminary Article certainly imply the same. Immediately below his restatement of the article whose title reads "No state shall interfere by force with the constitution and government of another state," he writes:

> That is to say, when a state is rent by internal dissension, this is the struggle of an independent people with its inner disease. As long as this strife is not settled, outside intervention by force would violate the autonomy of this people and state, thus jeopardizing the autonomy of all states.[79]

With these remarks, it is clear that Jaspers understands Kant to respect the autonomy of each existing state, which includes the right of peoples living therein to determine their own political affairs. Any intervention from the outside would violate this autonomy and neutralize this right.

The above discussion of the Second Preliminary Article actually goes hand in hand with Jaspers' view that Kant relies entirely on the internal improvement of states to achieve peace between them. This is expounded most clearly for him in the First and Second Definitive Articles. In his commentary on the First Definitive Article, Jaspers notes, "Only states governed under law can live in perpetual peace with one another. They alone have developed so strong a sense of legality that the consciousness of right may ultimately come to be reliable, even without powers of compulsion."[80] The First Definitive Article calls for the civil constitution of every state to be republican. According to Jaspers, in reference to the word "republican," Kant "does not mean a *form* of government (as the democratic, aristocratic, monarchic ones), but a *manner of government*."[81] It is stated that the "manner of government opposed to the republican is the despotic."[82]

Jaspers then asserts that, for Kant, the republican constitution is characterized by three important ingredients: first, "the legally established freedom guaranteeing the rights of man—rights which do not depend upon majorities"; second, "the separation of powers"; and third, "the system of representative government, tied to free elections."[83] In its very essence, "The basic idea of the first definitive article is that a reliable rule of law—and a reliably peaceful codification of the law by the popular will—can be achieved only under a republican kind of government."[84] Jaspers believes the text suggests that the achievement of the rule of law within states is the only way to achieve lasting peace between states. He explains, "Lasting peace, too, is possible only among states governed in the republican manner; for this alone creates the common premises of lawful community."[85]

Jaspers believes Kant's understanding of the achievement of the rule of law within a state in the First Definitive Article is integral to a clearer view of Kant's positions in the Second Definitive Article. This leads Jaspers to the remark that "The Second Definitive Article does not call for a world state, nor for a universal government."[86] Furthermore, and contrary to elements of Pattern One, Phase Two, it does not even call for a "league of nations" with some "coercive power."[87] First, the reasons he offers in favor of Kant's supposed rejection of the world state stem from a reading of the text similar to those of Hinsley, Waltz, and Schwarz. His primary focus is on the First Supplement. He asserts Kant's belief that "Every state has the lawless desire to achieve 'lasting peace by ruling the whole world, if possible.' "[88] Yet the separation of states that occurs because of differences in religion and language prevent this from happening. In fact, this historical situation, though first leading to war, ultimately produces harmony and a movement toward federalism. Such a voluntary federalism, through constant "balancing . . . in the liveliest competition" that occurs from states remaining entirely independent within it, is preferable to a super-state where "despotism brings peace in a graveyard of freedom."[89] Jaspers' primary point is as follows:

There is one ineradicable difference between civil and international law— the peace among the citizens of a state is kept by the laws of the state which has the power of compulsion; peace between different states can be established and kept legally but only without powers of compulsion.[90]

Jaspers believes that "lasting peace is possible only within a state structure."[91] His final comment is that there are two choices for Kant: "either the peaceful calm of a world state, in which freedom is bound to be stifled by despotism, or a state of free development toward peace by means of law, at the continuing risk of war."[92] For Jaspers, "Kant chose the second way."[93]

Through the 1970s: An Interpretation by F. Parkinson and W.B. Gallie's Major Contribution

Like Hinsley, F. Parkinson in his 1977 book *The Philosophy of International Relations* is one of the first interpreters of *Perpetual Peace* to suggest Kant's primary position in the Second Definitive Article is to advocate not an international state or formidable federation, but simply a treaty between independent states, each under the rule of law. As Parkinson puts it, "what was required now [for Kant in *Zum ewigen Frieden*] was a *foedus pacificum* (a treaty for peace)."[94] Further, Parkinson quotes Kant from the final paragraph of *Perpetual Peace*: " 'It may well be said that this treaty for universal and eternal peace constitutes not only a part, but the final objective in its entirety of law within the confines of common sense.' "[95] Knowing now what Parkinson believes Kant advances in *Perpetual Peace*, it is equally important to consider what he rejects.

First, according to Parkinson, "a world state was dismissed by [Kant] on practical grounds as compromising too large an area to cope effectively."[96] He then skeptically refers to this reason for rejection as "pretextual" and falls in line with other interpreters from this period by offering, as he says, Kant's "real basis for objection which consisted in a denial of a right of states to demand union with other states on the analogy of individuals expecting other individuals to join them in a state for the common benefit of all."[97] Furthermore, in the context of the Second Preliminary Article, which Parkinson discusses briefly, the interpreter reads into the article the dangers Kant sees in merging existing states together based on the latter's conception of the "new type of state."[98] Such a state, "making its first appearance in the French Revolution, possessed genuine organic qualities on the analogy of the human being."[99] Different to the ways "lawyers attribute personality to a state by way of a legal fiction," Kantian states "were living organisms in a real biological and psychological sense."[100] As such, Parkinson asserts that "it seemed unnatural, even monstrous to Kant to suggest that the tissues of one state were capable of being grafted on to the body of another state in the expectation that the two might grow together eventually" in the long-term interest of peace.[101] This would obviously have to occur in the creation of a world state and is another reason, however implied, that Parkinson believes Kant in *Perpetual Peace* is against its formation.

Second, and even more radical than some of the above interpreters, Parkinson does not even understand Kant to favor "a confederation based on voluntary agreement . . . as a practical proposition in the short run."[102] The "internal improvement of states," which will ultimately bring "the creation of a liberal-constitutional order within as many states as possible, was to be the basis of all international welfare."[103]

Parkinson would clearly reject analyses of the text offered by interpretations that reveal both phases of Pattern One. His interpretation is very similar to other interpretations found within this historical period. Still, he, and the others before him, are not as complete in their dealings with the text as Hinsley. If there is one interpretation of Kant's *Perpetual Peace* that can match Hinsley's for its thoroughness and attention to detail, it is W.B. Gallie's attempt in his 1978 book *Philosophers of Peace and War*.[104] He devotes twenty-eight pages to Kant's thinking on international relations and focuses almost exclusively on *Perpetual Peace*.

It must be said at the outset that though it is one of the most involved interpretations from this historical period, it does not differ much from the previous interpretations in its approach to the treatise, its particular focus on certain articles, and in its interpretive conclusions. In many ways, Gallie sums up all the ideas presented by interpretations within this period by the following statement. Accordingly, he confidently calls Kant "one of the most steadfast of 'statists' in the history of political thought."[105] Like Hinsley and Parkinson above, Gallie understands Kant as saying that "An international order could be initiated only when certain governments freely abjured their right to make war on each other . . . [and] sought membership within the bond (*foedus*) of mutual non-aggression."[106]

One of the reasons Gallie comes to this early conclusion of Kant as "steadfast statist" is the reading he gives to the Second Preliminary Article. He writes, "Complete non-interference in the internal affairs of every signatory state seemed to [Kant] an essential precondition of faithful adherence, by any sovereign state, to the treaty which he proposed."[107] Gallie pronounces that the text's commitment to the integrity of the sovereign state within this treaty might even seem "fanatical" to some.[108]

Gallie is certain that Kant rejects broad Pattern One conclusions on *Perpetual Peace*. First, Gallie remarks briefly on the readings past interpreters have given to the treatise. He states that, historically, the treatise "has been hailed as a harbinger of world-government, despite Kant's clear rejection of this ideal and his insistence that his project leaves states with all their sovereign rights intact."[109] And just as Gallie disagrees with interpretations that reveal the first phase of Pattern One, so he also disagrees with those that reveal the second phase. Accordingly, He remarks that *Perpetual Peace* has been "frequently cited—although far from correctly—as a notable precursor of the League of Nations idea."[110]

Besides these general statements about past interpretation, Gallie offers more detailed reasons why he believes Kant rejects both world state and federation in *Perpetual Peace*. As regards the world state, though Gallie refers to Kant as a "passionate legaliser" and is aware of his "constant emphasis on the necessity of coercion to sustain the law within any established state," he also is very careful to note that despite this, Kant is "equally emphatic that the idea of coercion, to sustain an international order, is both logically and practically an absurdity."[111] Gallie uses the phrase "peace-by-empire" to describe the world state and asserts that such entities "do not solve the problem of inter-state relations, they merely replace it by a situation of large-scale tyranny within which, by definition, specifically inter-state conflicts do not arise."[112] The practical problem associated with "large empires" is that they "cannot command deeply based loyalty and support, and invariably break down into component warring groups for which the problem of creating a legal order will arise exactly as before."[113]

Concerning federation, Gallie believes Kant is equally dismissive of it as he is of a world state. "Peace-by-federation," as Gallie calls it, "looks more promising" at first, but in the end is just as "delusive" for Kant as "peace-by-empire."[114] This is because "Any government that genuinely subscribes to the creation of a combined force, capable of imposing peace within the federation, will *eo ipso* be putting itself out of business—the last thing that any government can be expected to do."[115]

Additionally, it seems Gallie does not believe a Pattern One, Phase Two–like federation to be even a possibility. The notion of shared powers between a state and a larger federation it makes up is a delusion. He states, "if the federation is strong enough to enforce peace, it will become in fact a super-state, inevitably overriding the rights of its members."[116] Along these same lines, "if the federation is not strong enough to do this, the inevitable rivalries of its members will pull them back into international anarchy."[117]

According to Gallie, Kant's "rejection of both these positions [world state and federation] puts him into a difficulty."[118] If true to their name (and general description offered of them by interpretations from the first two periods), both world state and federation depend on public coercive laws above the state level to secure and maintain the peace. But as has been demonstrated, Gallie understands Kant to favor only such laws within the state, not between states throughout the text of *Perpetual Peace*. According to Gallie, Kant believes "there is a fundamental asymmetry between establishing and maintaining a just constitution within a state and in establishing and maintaining a just relationship between states."[119]

Gallie wonders how Kant expects to achieve and sustain peace if he rejects both of these solutions. A simple treaty or bond of mutual nonaggression between independent republican states is the primary solution Gallie understands Kant to propose. In the latter part of the interpretation, Gallie elaborates on this solution (and appears to delve into the Second Definitive Article more carefully). Gallie states, "Kant's positive proposal is that states should form a confederation for a strictly limited purpose."[120] This confederation would result from the founding of the envisioned treaty.

As to what this confederation "binds its members to do," Gallie claims that "In *Perpetual Peace* the primary aim is, quite explicitly and unquestionably, the ending of all aggression *between such powers as would sign his treaty of permanent mutual non-aggression*."[121] Treaty members or "signatories must enjoy what Kant calls a 'republican,' i.e., in some degree a representative, constitution" while their union in the form of a confederation "must be of the barest kind, confined to a repudiation of war-like or war-making acts against each other, while the enforcement of laws of common benefit to the signatories must be left to the *particular* state that is most immediately concerned."[122] Importantly, Gallie makes the distinction between *Perpetual Peace*, which he says has the primary and sole aim of "peace *between* the signatories," and his other writings, such as *The Idea of a Universal History* and the *Metaphysics of Morals*, where the primary aim is "to secure peace for the signatories— *from aggression by other parties*."[123] This is a relevant distinction to keep in mind.

In all of these texts, however, Gallie maintains that there is no "teeth" in this confederation to "effectively resist and progressively beat back aggressive outsiders."[124] Most importantly for our purposes, he insists "there is not a trace of it in *Perpetual Peace*."[125] This clarifies what he means by a confederation of the "barest kind" or one formed for a "strictly limited purpose." Obviously, he foresees no international authority and enforcement mechanism above the level of states. The confederation of independent states will exist to preserve peace, however fragile it may be, between members who are obviously unwilling to sacrifice any of their sovereignty to a larger body. Finally, with all of the above commentary in mind, it should now be easy to see why Gallie is the first English-language interpreter since the initial publication of *Perpetual Peace* in 1795 to refer to Kant as a "statist." Gallie, rather convincingly, closes his discussion of this topic with the following thought:

> For this makes it clear that [Kant's] vision of perpetual peace is not of a world kept at peace by a central confederate power, but of a world in which every state manifests its own independence in fulfilling the one job of enforcement which Kant's conception of international law requires.[126]

Though Gallie is less clear than other interpreters from this period in his discussion of the First Supplement, he is certainly as convinced as his colleagues about its integral importance to the body of the entire treatise. Coming to the same conclusion as other interpreters from this time who understand the text to assert that the sovereignty of the state should not be surrendered, he seems just as puzzled by how such a loose bond of sovereign states will stay together and guarantee perpetual peace between them in the face of disagreements and quarrels that will obviously develop. He explains, "Kant's repeated insistence that his proposed confederation would not be an 'international state,' that it would leave its members as sovereign as before, and that it expressly excludes the idea of peace-enforcement, naturally gives rise to the question."[127] And this question, undoubtedly asked before by interpreters from this period, goes as follows: "what else, over and above their recognition of the moral unacceptableness of war, will hold its members together when, inevitably, differences, rivalries and suspicions arise between them?"[128]

First, Gallie is keen to point out that Kant "makes clear in a number of passages he is not offering a foolproof guarantee that his confederation will not break down . . . that it may not be overwhelmed at the outset by militaristic powers which detest any idea or project for perpetual peace."[129] This is obviously natural for a loosely bound collection of neighboring states. As such, Gallie calls the term Kant uses—in this case "guarantee"— "ill-named."[130] Still, he recognizes that the "guarantee" in the form of nature is what *Perpetual Peace* puts forward as the answer to neverending problems resulting from the continuing existence of separate states. As Gallie explains, "It is Kant's way of urging, against those who find in human nature certain immovable barriers to political progress, that these barriers can always also be regarded as necessary challenges or springboards to rational human effort."[131] The "animal" and "inherently egoistic" side of man prompt our "rational capacities" into positive actions.[132] Without them, our rational side, however perfect in itself, would simply lie dormant. On a larger scale, the combination of all the former fusing together to bring violence and ultimately war between people and states, prompts "the better angels of our nature" to work together to end both.

Accordingly, Gallie remarks, "Only as war becomes patently more destructive and more costly, will men be moved to take the first difficult steps towards a permanent peace."[133] Yet even as these steps are taken, and the association of states expands to include more and more states in the attempt to root out war, "backslidings" into violence and war will continue to occur.[134] This is driven by the nature of man and results in very slow progress toward peace.

In the final analysis, Gallie appears more skeptical of the "guarantee" outlined in the First Supplement than other interpreters writing during this period. Still, his interpretation identifies it as the path through which peace will be achieved in the long run. In addition, though he views progress toward peace to be a long and difficult journey, he never sways from his understanding of the text as one that expects the sovereignty of separate states to remain intact throughout.

To be sure, Gallie does not change this position he takes in a later article he writes on the subject of international relations in 1979. Presenting his own arguments this time (instead of analyzing Kant's as he has already done before), Gallie explains that he "accepts in the main Kant's view that the ground of the distinction between these two great fields of political life [home and foreign politics] is to be found in the idea of 'public legal coercion,' which, while indispensable in home politics, has—so Kant maintains— simply no proper application in connection with international problems."[135] As such, Gallie further states that he accepts "the main consequence Kant draws" from this.[136] This is Kant's belief that "the central task of international politics is to establish and maintain, on a purely voluntary basis, an association of states pledged to mutual non-aggression, to the settlement of their differences by arbitration, and to the steady expansion of their membership, simply by the attractive example of their success, until the association includes all existing states."[137] Finally, he reiterates what he has already said earlier about the First Supplement. He states that he accepts Kant's proposition that "international initiatives and achievements along the lines just mentioned are not to be expected until certain 'lower' human interests combine to support the promptings of reason and morality."[138] In all three of these ways, he remains true to his original interpretation, even when he puts forward his own prescriptive claims.

Concluding "Statist" Interpretations from the Early 1980s: Susan Meld Shell and Patrick Riley

Moving into the early 1980s, Susan Meld Shell sounds very much like the aforementioned interpreters, especially Hinsley, in her discussion of *Perpetual Peace*. Like Hinsley, she recognizes the Preliminary Articles as offering unquestionable support for the independence of the state. Though referring to them as "preparatory steps," she sees these articles as "lay[ing] the foundation for peace by asserting the integrity of each individual nation."[139] Thereafter, the Definitive Articles "supersede" these and attempt to "establish cosmopolitan laws grounded in a federation of free, republican states."[140] From this general statement, it is not clear what she means by "federation of free, republican states." Although use of the term "free states" certainly hints at an interpretation suggesting the continued existence of the sovereign state, the term "federation," as we have seen, requires some fleshing out. Her commentary relating to the brief summary she offers above of the three Definitive Articles is helpful.

It is clear to Shell that Kant is not an advocate of a world state. For practical reasons it is "impossible" and would "immediately break apart or collapse into world despotism."[141] Furthermore, the law of nations, which is what Shell understands Kant to be describing in *Perpetual Peace*, "concerns the relations between citizens of different states."[142] As such, "The individual state has a responsibility to its citizens and cannot rightfully be deprived of that sovereignty which they have duly authorized."[143] For these reasons, Shell acknowledges that the way to peace for Kant lies in an "alliance or confederation which preserves the separate sovereignty of every member."[144] Clearly, like Gallie above, Shell does not believe a federation of free states, confederation, or alliance that may ultimately develop will have any "teeth" like the authorities suggested by Pattern One interpreters. Further, in common with other post-1950 interpreters, Shell concludes, "The member-state, unlike the citizen, may withdraw from the union whenever it deems it necessary or just to do so."[145] It has been one of the goals of this chapter to demonstrate that the idea of a voluntary and dissoluble alliance between states is what interpretations from this period suggest.

Finally, Shell agrees with other interpreters from this period when she offers the same answer to the frequently asked question "How can peace be guaranteed between independent states when there is no enforcement power above them such as a world state or powerful federation?" She turns to the First Supplement for the answer. There she explains that in *Perpetual Peace* "History or 'nature's art' emerges in Kant's thought as a substitute on a cosmopolitan scale for that enforcing power which renders feasible the civil state."[146] Her interpretation of the First Supplement differs little from the above so there need not be repetition of the central ideas that interpreters from this period view it as offering. It is important to mention only to demonstrate her belief that it is what the text suggests will guarantee peace. As we have seen, little has been written about the First Supplement in interpretations that reveal both phases of Pattern One. The thought is that in both of these there exists an authority above the state level, which will reduce conflict by reducing sovereignty. In these, nature and history as outlined in the First Supplement seem less important as other mechanisms are in place to perform the same function.

The final interpretation to be discussed from this era is by Patrick Riley in his 1983 book *Kant's Political Philosophy*. Riley uses the Preliminary Articles, the Second and Third Definitive Articles, and the First Supplement to demonstrate that *Perpetual Peace* indeed is in favor of "preserving substantial state sovereignty."[147]

First, Riley asserts, "far from undercutting the notion of state sovereignty," the Preliminary Articles of Kant's *Perpetual Peace* "actually reinforce it."[148] After listing all of them, he specifically mentions the Second Preliminary Article, which indicates, "Like a tree, an [independently existing] state has its own roots, and to graft it on to another state as if it were a shoot is to terminate its existence as a moral personality and make it into a commodity."[149] Also, Riley turns to the final section of the Preliminary Articles where Kant speaks of which articles need or need not be executed at once and notes here that "Kant even insisted that, in principle, states which had lost their freedom (e.g., Poland) should have it restored."[150]

After this brief foray into the Preliminary Articles, Riley acknowledges that the Third Definitive Article is "Even more remarkable for its emphasis on the independence of the sovereign state."[151] In the Third Definitive Article, Kant writes that world law or "cosmopolitan right shall be limited to conditions of universal hospitality."[152] Simply on this statement alone, Riley contends that "This extreme limitation on world law indicates very plainly that Kant meant to preserve substantial state sovereignty."[153]

His interpretation of the Second Definitive Article is fairly standard for interpreters during this period. He sees Kant offering two primary reasons for rejecting the state of nations in this article. He focuses first on Kant's statement that a "state of nations contains a contradiction" since many nations "would, in a single state, constitute only one nation" and the concern of this article is with "the rights of [separate and independent] nations towards each other."[154] Second, Riley briefly discusses Kant's idea that states are in a different position than humans in a state of nature. As Riley explains, states are not "under the same obligation to leave that condition as 'natural' men."[155] As states already have "internally a legal constitution . . . [they] have outgrown the coercion of others who might desire to put them under a broadened legal constitution."[156]

From these two reasons, Riley is persuaded that Kant "seems to say that a world organization must be worked out in terms of sovereignty, in terms of a free federation of *corporate* bodies voluntarily obeying international law, and not a world law for individuals."[157] Once again, we see an interpreter from this era convinced that a reading of *Perpetual Peace* suggests that the sovereignty of the state is not to be abandoned in the pursuit of peace.

And finally, if in fact the existence of separate states is not to be overcome in the interests of a stable and enforceable peace, then the rule of law grounded in the republican government of each separate state and the guarantee offered by nature will ultimately have to bring it about. Riley sees the thrust of the text and its goal of establishing peace as reliant on Kant's "historical view that nature's purpose for man was the extension of reason and reasonable conduct in the species as a whole through conflict."[158] Furthermore, "a series of clashes" resulting from this natural conflict "would ultimately (though very late) bring states into new and more rational relations in which international good conduct would be voluntarily accepted."[159]

Conclusion

In conclusion, consistency between interpretations over a period is what strengthens the argument for patterns. As much as any, the interpretations written between the 1950s and early 1980s are remarkably similar in their outlook. This is even more surprising when one considers the attention to textual detail of interpretations found during this period, especially when compared to earlier ones where less text is analyzed and shorter, more general interpretations given.

There is a clear interpretive shift that occurs between those interpretations of Kant's *Perpetual Peace* written from the mid-nineteenth to the mid-twentieth century and those written from the 1950s to the early 1980s. For the first time, interpreters begin to focus more seriously on text outside the Second Definitive Article in their interpretations. Through discussion of the Preliminary Articles, the Second and Third Definitive Articles, and the First Supplement, the central theme running through all interpretations is Kant's acceptance of the sovereign state as the vehicle through which peace will be achieved. Unlike both phases of Pattern One, where peace is understood to be established through a centralized authority above the state level, this historical period and the interpretations of *Perpetual Peace* that reveal this new Pattern view the text as defending state sovereignty. Clearly, the first phase of Pattern Two understands the text to recommend peace proposals at, not above, the state level.

Furthermore, though Pattern Two, Phase One suggests that the sovereign state may at some point come to exist within an alliance, association, confederation, or free federation of politically likeminded states, each state will join voluntarily with the option to withdraw surviving in perpetuity. There will be no "teeth" in any of these modes of international organization that may develop and they will only exist to help preserve the sovereign independence of each state. Finally, Pattern Two, Phase One understands peace between independent states and their peoples to be guaranteed not by a centralized authority above them, but by the external forces of nature and history working upon and through them.

CHAPTER 5

Pattern Two, Phase Two: State Sovereignty Preserved I

A New Interpretation Takes Shape in the Early 1980s

Introduction

The final historical period within which Kant's *Perpetual Peace* has been utilized, takes us, and pattern formation, up to the present day. The last interpretation within this period given consideration comes from Harold Kleinschmidt's *The Nemesis of Power*, published in 2000. The first within this period is by Michael Doyle, a leading "liberal peace" theorist, in a well-known 1983 article entitled "Kant, Liberal Legacies and Foreign Affairs." Like F.H. Hinsley's 1963 interpretation, Doyle provides us with a pivotal textual analysis of *Perpetual Peace*, the influence of which is seen throughout this final historical phase. The article's originality, exclusive focus on *Perpetual Peace*, and the idea and empirical proof of an ever-expanding zone of peace among liberal, sovereign states that it sets forth, make it an interpretation crucial to the development of themes in this chapter and in chapters 6, 7, and 9 to follow.

There are more interpretations of Kant's treatise written during this short time span than in all other periods I have researched. In fact, the extraordinary number of important interpretations requires a discussion and analysis of them in three separate chapters. Why so many interpretations? Clearly, *Perpetual Peace* has experienced a surge in popularity over the past two decades among academics in the fields of Political Science and International Relations. This is most likely a result of Doyle's influential work on liberal peace theory and his use of Kant's *Perpetual Peace* as its intellectual foundation. *Perpetual Peace* is now recognized as one of the first Enlightenment-era essays to demonstrate, theoretically, the relationship between domestic republican government and international peace. While this claim did not go unnoticed during the century after publication of the work, it began to receive more attention as the twentieth century progressed. It finally was put to an empirical test for the first time in 1964 (though little recognition of it within Political Science and International Relations circles occurred until the early eighties).[1]

Though these initial studies reasonably proved the generalization, there was no mention of *Perpetual Peace* as intellectual forebear of the liberal peace phenomenon until Michael Doyle's seminal article on the subject in 1983.[2] Doyle's article was the first in what is now a long line of liberal peace scholarship that hails *Perpetual Peace* as the "source of insight, policy and hope" for "appreciating the liberal legacy."[3] A proliferation of studies on this popular hypothesis followed Doyle's influential article.[4] Like Doyle's, many of these view Kant's ideas in *Perpetual Peace* as theoretical grounding for the liberal peace claim as well.

This chapter focuses primarily on Doyle's notable study along with several other interpretations that take the book's thesis through the 1980s. Doyle's study and its analysis of *Perpetual Peace* influences more thorough-going interpretations of the text written from the first half of the 1990s and discussed in chapter 6. Through analysis of several principal interpretations written from 1990 to 1995, chapter 6 demonstrates that the new trend in analysis of the text begun by Doyle continues into the 1990s. Finally, chapter 7 concludes the study of this period with an exploration of interpretations that, I argue, advance the second phase of Pattern Two through to the end of the twentieth century.

The following three chapters demonstrate that the "statist" interpretation of the text extends from the 1950s through the 1990s across both phases of the pattern. It is clear that a majority of these interpreters recognize the text as recommending peace proposals at the state level. Still, the increased emphasis on the First Definitive Article that these interpreters working after the early 1980s offer, namely a consistent accent on the practical reason offered for adopting the republican constitution as the most important tool for achieving perpetual peace between states, makes this period worthy of division into two phases.

It is also important to note that this seventeen-year time span and the consistent interpretations of the text that can be found within it are necessarily ongoing. Little evidence suggests that the statist interpretation of the text coupled with a greater emphasis on the practical aspects of the First Definitive Article will not continue in future interpretations completed after the year 2000.[5] Though there are enough similar interpretations of the text from 1983 to 2000 to put forth a sound argument for a second phase of Pattern Two, I contend that Pattern Two, Phase Two is still in formation as a new century begins.

The Principal Interpretation

Michael Doyle's Seminal Article on Kant and the Liberal Peace

Before reviewing Doyle's interpretation of Kant's *Perpetual Peace*, it is worth noting his rather bold claim that follows from the empirical part of his study. He states, *"Even though liberal states have become involved in numerous wars with nonliberal states, constitutionally secure liberal states have yet to engage in war with one another."*[6] Though his article is primarily devoted to development of this claim, he is very interested in finding a theoretical foundation for his argument from a notable (and liberal) philosopher. He first writes, "Most liberal theorists have offered inadequate guidance in understanding the exceptional nature of liberal pacification."[7] He dismisses explanations by Montesquieu and others as insufficient. For example, he states that Montesquieu relies entirely on trade and commerce between nations in his explanation of liberal pacification.[8] Doyle remarks that though such "developments can help account for the liberal peace, they do not explain the fact that liberal states are peaceful only in relations with other liberal states."[9] Doyle is obviously more interested in why liberal states are aggressive with nonliberal states, though pacific with other liberal states. He believes that "Immanuel Kant offers the best guidance" in this area.[10] He specifically discusses Kant's *Perpetual Peace* as the one text by the eighteenth-century philosopher that most effectively explores the foundation of the liberal peace.

In his interpretation, Doyle begins by turning to the First Definitive Article. He nearly quotes Kant verbatim when he says that "The First Definitive Article holds that the civil constitution of the state must be republican."[11] Doyle is then interested in sorting out what Kant means by "republican" in this first pronouncement. "By republican," Doyle adds, "Kant means a political society that has solved the problem of combining moral autonomy, individualism, and social order [and a political society] that preserves juridical freedom—the legal equality of citizens as subjects—on the basis of representative government with a separation of powers."[12]

If they choose to discuss it (which many interpretations that reveal Pattern One do not), this is a definition of "republican" that interpreters offer which stays relatively consistent through all historical periods. However, when we look at the reason(s) for adopting a republican constitution (as opposed to the simple definition), the emphasis given by recent interpreters of the text to various passages within the First Definitive Article begins to shift as we move into interpretations from this period.

Kant's pronouncement that "The civil constitution of every state shall be republican" is offered as the initial framework. Immediately thereafter, Kant states, "The republican constitution is pure in its origin (since it springs from the pure concept of right)."[13] As Chris Brown explains (and his full interpretation is discussed later), "The reason that the civil constitution of states should be republican comes out of the general consideration of Kant's moral theory" or similarly, "Republicanism is desirable for its own sake."[14] This is the normative explanation for adopting a republican constitution.

Kant further states that the "republican constitution . . . also offers a prospect of attaining the desired result, i.e. a perpetual peace."[15] This is, in effect, the practical reason for adopting this kind of political constitution. It is what Doyle sees as central to an understanding of the First Definitive Article, indeed the whole of *Perpetual Peace*. Though it may be right in and of itself to promote republicanism within states, it is also desirable since, in the real world, its promotion contributes to prospects for peace between liberal republican states. As Doyle explains, "Kant shows how republics, once established, lead to peaceful relations."[16] Doyle understands Kant's central argument to be that "once the aggressive interests of absolutist monarchies are tamed and once the habit of respect for individual rights is engrained by republican government, wars would appear as the disaster to the people's welfare that he and the other liberals thought them to be."[17] According to Doyle, the "fundamental reason" why is as follows:

If the consent of the citizens is required in order to decide that war should be declared (and in this constitution it cannot but be the case), nothing is more natural than that they would be very cautious in commencing such a poor game, decreeing for themselves all the calamities of war. Among the latter would be: having to fight, having to pay the costs of war from their own resources, having painfully to repair the devastation war leaves behind, and, to fill up the measure of evils, load themselves with a heavy national debt that would embitter peace itself and that can never be liquidated on account of constant wars in the future. But, on the other hand, in a constitution which is not republican, and under which the subjects are not citizens, a declaration of war is the easiest thing in the world to decide upon, because war does not require of the ruler, who is the proprietor and not a member of the state, the least sacrifice of the pleasure of his table, the chase, his country houses, his court functions, and the like. He may, therefore, resolve on war as on a pleasure party for the most trivial reasons, and with perfect indifference leave the justification which decency requires to the diplomatic corps who are ever ready to provide it.[18]

Importantly, it should be noted that this is the only passage of any part of *Perpetual Peace* that Doyle quotes at length. His discussion of the Second Definitive Article, however brief, seems to be informed by his reading of the First. Doyle explains, "Liberal republics will progressively establish peace among themselves by means of the 'pacific union' described in the Second Definitive Article of the Eternal Peace."[19] Like several interpreters discussed in chapter 4, for Doyle, "The pacific union is limited to 'a treaty of the nations among themselves' which 'maintains itself, prevents wars, and steadily expands.' "[20] Doyle's focus here is on the term "steadily expands," which he further emphasizes in italics in another passage. He does not believe Kant expects perpetual peace to come about immediately, or even over a reasonable period of time. He states, "The world will not have achieved the 'perpetual peace' that provides the ultimate guarantor of republican freedom until 'very late and after many unsuccessful attempts.' "[21] During this lengthy period of gradual progress mixed with many failures, the " 'pacific union' of liberal republics [will] '*steadily expand*' bringing within it more and more republics (despite republican collapses, backsliding, and war disasters) and creating an ever expanding separate peace."[22]

It remains to be seen what the nature of this pacific union is for Doyle. His first remark about it suggests what it is not. He states, "The pacific union is neither a single peace treaty ending one war nor a world state or state of nations."[23] The first, Doyle says, is "insufficient," while the second and third are "impossible or potentially tyrannical."[24] Most importantly, for the purposes of this chapter, Doyle then says that "Kant develops no organizational embodiment of this treaty, and presumably he does not find institutionalization necessary."[25] In a footnote below this comment, he states that "[Kant] appears to have anticipated something like a less formally institutionalized League of Nations or United Nations."[26] Finally, he explains, "One could argue that these two institutions in practice worked for liberal states and only for liberal states. But no specifically liberal 'pacific union' was institutionalized. Instead liberal states have behaved for the past 180 years as if such a Kantian pacific union and treaty of Perpetual Peace had been signed."[27]

He finishes the footnote by saying, "This follows Riley's views of the legal, not the organizational, character of the *foedus pacificum*."[28] Doyle is speaking here of Patrick Riley, whose interpretation was analyzed in chapter 4. He believes (as does Doyle) that the establishment of the rule of law within and between republican states is what Kant envisioned in *Perpetual Peace*.

Unlike interpretations that reveal both phases of Pattern One, these two interpreters see no organizational element to Kant's project. They see the text endorsing a peace proposal at, not above, the state level. Furthermore, Doyle is intent on placing Kant within the group of thinkers who believe domestic politics determines international politics. He explains that "representation and separation of powers," both central aspects of the republican constitution, "are produced because they are the means by which the state is 'organized well' to prepare for and meet foreign threats (by unity) and to tame the ambitions of selfish and aggressive individuals (by authority derived from representation, by general laws, and by nondespotic administration)."[29] Doyle is convinced that the mere existence of authoritarian states increases the likelihood of war with other authoritarian states (and liberal states as well). Though he admits that liberal states can be just as aggressive with nonliberal states, he demonstrates with a high degree of empirical certainty that liberal states have behaved quite peacefully with each other over the past one hundred and eighty years. Again, his foundation for the idea of the liberal peace is Kant's First Definitive Article, specifically the "consent of the citizens" passage already quoted. Doyle sees this article and its contents as fundamental to understanding what Kant was promoting in *Perpetual Peace*.

Doyle concludes his section on Kant and *Perpetual Peace* with several telling statements about the nature of relationships between liberal states and liberal to nonliberal states. He first asserts that though "Liberal states have not escaped from the Realists' 'security dilemma,' [defined as] the insecurity caused by anarchy in the world political system . . . the effects of international anarchy have been tamed in the relations among states of a similarly liberal character."[30] While "Alliances of purely mutual strategic interest among liberal and nonliberal states have been broken, [and] economic ties between liberal and nonliberal states have proven fragile," there exists a "political bond of liberal rights and interests [which has] proven a remarkably firm foundation for mutual non-aggression."[31] Finally, he says simply, "A separate peace exists among liberal states."[32] As I have quoted Doyle before, the thinker who he believes "offers the best guidance" in these topics is Immanuel Kant in *Perpetual Peace*.[33]

According to Doyle, Kant "predicts" the ever-expanding pacific union of liberal states whose ties to each other amount to little more than a commitment to republicanism at home, which inevitably translates into a commitment to the expansion of the same political ideal abroad.[34] Still, their relationship to each other as separate republican states is, as Doyle understands the text, a loosely bound togetherness in a "pact of mutual nonaggression" with little "organizational embodiment."[35] This interpretation stands in direct contrast to both phases of Pattern One, and even differentiates itself from those interpretations that reveal the first phase of Pattern Two in the significance it gives to the First Definitive Article and the emphasis it places on a particular passage within that Article.

Subsidiary Interpretations

Analysis of Interpretations through the Rest of the 1980s, Including a Novel Reading of the Text by Leslie Mulholland

The predominant interpretation that leads me to suggest the existence of a separate phase of Pattern Two during this time period does not develop in full until the 1990s. Only then do we see interpretations that strongly resemble Doyle's. After Doyle's, the rest of the 1980s are filled with relatively brief interpretations of the treatise. Some are similar to Doyle's interpretation with its emphasis on the First Definitive Article and the concept of the aggressive nature of despotic regimes compared to the more pacific nature of liberal regimes in their relations with each other. Others sometimes resemble interpretations that reveal Pattern Two, Phase One. Importantly, all interpretations in the 1980s strongly defend a state-centric reading of Kant's treatise, as elaborated in chapter 4. As stated earlier, like Pattern Two, Phase One, the primary component of interpretations that reveal Pattern Two, Phase Two is a statist reading of the text. The component of the latter that distinguishes it is not inconsistent with the former, simply an important addition to it. The point to remember in looking at this first group of interpretations is that they clearly remain in the "sovereignty preserved" category of textual analysis.

Anthony Smith deals primarily with Kant's domestic political philosophy in his 1985 article "Kant's Political Philosophy: Rechtsstaat or Council Democracy?" Still, he does make the brief comment that "On the international plane . . . [Kant] does not call for a social contract on an international scale to enter into a world state."[36] He also offers reasons why he believes Kant thinks this is so. For Kant, according to Smith, a world state "would be conceptually incoherent, impossible from an administrative standpoint, and, even were it possible, would lead to despotism."[37]

Peter Calvocoresi offers a generally similar view to Smith's in his 1987 book *A Time for Peace: Pacifism, Internationalism and Protest Forces in the*

Reduction of War. He understands Kant to "accept collisions between states as a fact of life."[38] Further, he states that Kant "had no use for a superstate but envisioned a system in which states retained their independence and sovereignty but submitted to the overriding authority of law which they themselves freely and collectively would develop and define."[39]

The first interpretation from this period that offers a similar reading to Doyle's comes from Leslie A. Mulholland in a 1987 article entitled "Kant on War and International Justice." Mulholland's first comment relating to *Perpetual Peace* is an observation on the nature of the state as a moral person. Mulholland says it is important to "note that the status of a state as a sovereign power, that is, its right with respect to itself (which would include the right to govern within its traditional territory and hence its right not to be conquered and enslaved) is not an acquired right but a right whereby a state is constituted as a person in the international community."[40] This sets the stage for the state-centric view of Kant's writing this interpreter puts forward. Though Mulholland does pay lip service to Kant's statement that "the voluntary production of a world state [is] 'correct in theory,' " the interpretation ultimately explains that for Kant in *Perpetual Peace* "there is no possible institutional solution to the problem of achieving world peace."[41] According to Mulholland, the solution Kant offers is an "account of the conditions under which states can achieve the rule of law without the use of external coercive institutions."[42] To demonstrate this, Mulholland turns to Kant's concept of republicanism and the First Definitive Article. Importantly, Mulholland spends almost the entire interpretation of the text discussing this and how crucial it is to achieving peace.

First, Mulholland takes from *Perpetual Peace* the quotation that "History offers examples of the opposite effect [to perpetual peace] being produced by all forms of government, with the single exception of genuine republicanism, which, however, could be the object only of a moral politician."[43] From this, Mulholland makes the statement that, for Kant, "republicanism must replace despotism in individual states."[44] Further, "Once this is accomplished, states must voluntarily submit to the rule of law amongst them in a federation of republics and thereby abolish war as a means of resolving disputes."[45] After a long discussion on despotic government and how it is "in principle incapable of voluntary adherence to the rule of law" and therefore, in its relations with other states, always "in principle in a 'state of war' even if there are no actual hostilities or declarations of war," Mulholland begins a thorough discussion of the First Definitive Article.[46]

For Mulholland, "the chief features of a republican constitution" for Kant are "that citizens have freedom to pursue their own ends, private and moral . . . that no subjects have any innate political privileges . . . and that citizens be independent, i.e., have the right to participate in lawgiving, at least through voting for their representatives."[47] Mulholland also points out Kant's insistence on the separation of powers. Accordingly, Mulholland states, "A republican constitution alone represents in its form the united will of the people in the giving and administration of laws."[48]

While Mulholland seems interested in the basic concept of the republic, the interpretation offered then exclaims that "Our chief concern with Kant's contentions regarding the republic . . . is with whether and how the achievement of republican constitutions can help further peace and the rule of law."[49] Mulholland turns to the practical argument Kant makes in the First Definitive Article. Mulholland states that "The practical problem in declaring war in a republic is that since the people suffer the most through the deprivations of fighting, paying the costs of war and rebuilding after a war they would be expected to be cautious in consenting to declare war."[50] However, "In a state run by a despot, there is no need to justify war to the people. Moreover, since a despot need suffer nothing personally by a war even if his side loses, he has no overwhelming prudential reasons to avoid war."[51] This practical reason is also supplemented by the formal, a priori claim that "Only in the case of a republic is there any reason to trust that the authorities will abide by their commitments" because "the general will and the concomitant element of the rights of man have priority as the principle of activity."[52] This, by itself, is enough for Kant to believe that this form of government is the only one that can ever be trusted to commit itself to the rule of law in its relations with other states.

The key point that Mulholland makes is that "Kant's insight into the problem of international law is that there can be no rule of law and no peace unless states can be trusted to commit themselves to law without there being an international executive force to ensure obedience to law through force."[53] This can only happen in liberal republics.

Finally, unlike the organizational aspects from the Second Definitive Article invariably discussed in interpretations that reveal both phases of Pattern One or the historical aspects of the First Supplement focused on in interpretations that reveal Pattern Two, Phase One, Mulholland relies entirely on the execution of the First Definitive Article as the means for achieving peace. None of the other articles or supplements from the text are specifically discussed in this interpretation. Further, and much like Doyle, Mulholland clearly posits a strong relationship between the domestic political organization of the state and the significant influence this has on its behavior in international politics. All of this leads to the argument that, coupled with Doyle's initial interpretation, a somewhat different way of reading the text is beginning to develop during this period.

"What Kant Should Have Said": An Interpretation
by Thomas L. Carson

Thomas L. Carson offers a conventional state-centric interpretation of Kant's *Perpetual Peace* in his 1988 article *Perpetual Peace: What Kant Should Have Said*. In this article, Carson presents himself as a strong advocate of world government with coercive military power over individual states. In one of several passages, he states, "just as nations must maintain an effective monopoly on the kind of coercive power that can be used against individuals, so an international government must maintain a monopoly on military power."[54] As will be demonstrated, Carson does not believe Kant favors world government in *Perpetual Peace*. In fact, he seems disappointed that Kant does not considering his own position.

Carson does discuss the Preliminary and Definitive Articles in his interpretation. As for the Preliminary Articles, he restates them but provides little commentary. In his discussion of the First Definitive Article, he thinks it important to include, as did Doyle and Mulholland before him, the practical reason Kant believes states should adopt a republican constitution. Carson first restates the definition of republicanism Kant suggests, that is, "freedom for all members of society, the dependence of everyone upon a single common legislation, and legal equality for all" and distinguishes between the republican form of government and a democracy, that is, the former requires a "sharp separation between legislative and executive powers."[55] Carson then notes that "In republican forms of government 'the consent of the citizens is required to decide whether or not war is to be declared.' "[56] His commentary on this section goes as follows: "The rationale for making republican government part of a proposal for peace is that since the general populace suffers the burdens and miseries of war, they will be very reluctant to bring these miseries down upon themselves" while "Monarchs and other autocratic rulers do not have the same kind of reluctance to begin wars."[57] Carson then quotes at length a passage from the First Definitive Article, what I have termed the "consent of the citizens" passage. He finally states in another section of the article that "Michael Doyle has proposed a most intriguing defense of Kant's position."[58] Though he does not discuss Doyle's liberal peace idea, it is clear that he thinks implementation of the First Definitive Article and the potential impact on peace that follows it merits consideration.

His discussion of the Second Definitive Article is pretty standard for interpreters of this period. He notes that Kant "takes pains to stress that he prefers a federation of sovereign states to an international state."[59] In his description of this federation, he sounds even more statist. He says Kant's "federation would not interfere in the internal affairs of its member states; it would exist 'merely to preserve and secure the freedom of each state in itself.' "[60] Furthermore, he states that whatever form Kant's federation takes, "it should not [according to Kant] have the power to coerce individual states to do its will."[61]

Additionally, Carson goes through four reasons why Kant rejects the world state as the path to peace. He states the following:

(i) The very idea of a world state is self-contradictory; (ii) that nations and peoples will be unwilling to make the kind of surrender of national sovereignty and national autonomy that would be required of a world state; (iii) that the rights of sovereign states would be violated by the creation of a world state possessing the power to coerce them; and (iv) that a world state would be likely to be despotic.[62]

Even with all of these negative passages and comments about the world state, Carson, unlike most interpreters from the 1950s onward, does suggest that there is one passage in the Second Definitive Article that generally says "if a world state could exercise its authority effectively . . . it would be the best imaginable guarantor of peace."[63] Still, Carson admits that Kant "denies in a later passage" that the world state could exercise its authority effectively so that the federation is all that Kant can ultimately support.[64] His final comment on the text is that "The non-coercive federation that Kant proposes would have no power to prevent individual states from creating armies and using them to begin wars of aggression."[65] Exactly after that, he notes, "It couldn't even compel nations to remain members of the federation."[66] Carson would agree with W.B. Gallie that Kant's ultimate proposal has no "teeth." He obviously sees Kant's recommendation as little more than a voluntary coming together of sovereign republican states.

The End of the 1980s: Interpretations by Ian Clark and Sissela Bok

Ian Clark's 1989 book *The Hierarchy of States: Reform and Resistance in the International Order* "characterizes" Kant and his writings on international affairs as "utopian."[67] Though he devotes an entire chapter to Kant and "the tradition of optimism" (set against Rousseau and "the tradition of pessimism in relation to the international order"), his thoughts on *Perpetual Peace* are relatively few.[68]

The most that can be said of Clark's analysis is that it fits under the category of "sovereignty preserved." He states that though "Kant appears to be following the logic of the domestic analogy, setting the scene for an 'international' social contract," such a global contract "is not Kant's solution."[69] According to Clark, "many people wrongly believe that Kant was advocating world government but this is not the case and he is quite explicit on this point."[70] Clark believes the solution Kant is offering is nothing more than a "league for peace (*foedus pacificum*)."[71] Clark further states, "Kant insists that this league 'will not aim at the acquisition of any of the political powers of a State.' "[72] He refers directly to the commentary of W.B. Gallie in support of his argument when he says that "Gallie is therefore correct to emphasize Kant's position that 'the idea of coercion, to sustain an international order, is both logically and practically an absurdity.' "[73] Finally, Clark notes, "for Kant, 'there is a fundamental asymmetry between establishing and maintaining a just constitution within a state and in establishing and maintaining a just relationship between states.' "[74]

The final interpretation of *Perpetual Peace* completed in the 1980s to be discussed is Sissela Bok's 1989 book *A Strategy for Peace: Human Values and the Threat of War*. Like Clark's above, this is also a brief account of *Perpetual Peace*, though it is similar to Doyle's and Mulholland's in its focus on the First Definitive Article and its emphasis on the continued autonomy of the state. Bok explains that Kant's "plan involved a change, over time, to representative government in as many states as possible."[75] Under Kantian representative government, "freedom and equality . . . would be indispensable for citizens of such states and would enable them to resist being drawn into new wars upon which their rulers were otherwise all too likely to embark."[76] Once again, we see the interpreter focusing on the relationship between unrepresentative government and the belligerent propensities of its rulers. This, I argue, is a primary ingredient of interpretations during the period between 1983 and 2000.

Further, Bok claims that the "federation of free states" formed from these representative governments "would be most likely to promote justice within and between states, while preserving their unique characteristics and freedom vis-à-vis each other."[77] Such a federation would involve "autonomous states joining in submitting voluntarily to laws they had themselves authored."[78] According to Bok, "Kant used a concept of 'autonomy' that the Greeks had applied primarily to states living under self-imposed laws; but he brought this notion of a law freely enacted and imposed upon oneself to bear on . . . the conduct of individuals, of communities or nations in internal affairs, and of a future federation of states."[79]

Bok briefly refers to Kant's categorical imperative when she states, "This self-imposed moral law would enjoin people, singly or collectively [as in a state], to 'act only according to that maxim whereby you can at the same time will that it should become a universal law.' "[80] Bok obviously sees Kant as respecting not only the dignity and autonomy of every individual but the dignity and autonomy of every state. The law that would develop between states would come not from an external source, be it an all-powerful federation or world state, but would begin with the autonomous state imposing a law upon itself based entirely on its internal political structure as a republic.

Conclusion

The principal focus of this chapter has been on Michael Doyle's 1983 study on the liberal peace, which includes one of the most influential interpretations of Kant's text. It also has discussed six subsidiary interpretations of the text completed during the last half of the 1980s. In many ways, the new interpretation offered by Doyle is the pivotal textual analysis of this period. Though relatively brief, the central themes developed in its representation of the treatise show up frequently in interpretations that complete this period and discussed further in chapters 6 and 7 to follow. The First Definitive Article takes center stage as the most important Article of Kant's treatise for Doyle and these interpreters. They make the "consent of the citizens" passage within the First Definitive Article the focal point for peace in their reading of the text and further develop the important theme that domestic politics determines international politics.

CHAPTER 6

Pattern Two, Phase Two: State Sovereignty Preserved II

Into the 1990s, the State-Centric Reading and its Emphasis on the First Definitive Article Solidifies

Introduction

With the end of the Cold War and following Doyle's authoritative study, Kant's *Perpetual Peace* experienced a surge in popularity during the first half of the 1990s.[1] Beyond the proliferation of liberal peace advocates that reference Kant and the text in their various empirical studies during this period, there were a whole host of commentators who more substantively reviewed his text from 1990 to 1995. In fact, this brief five-year time span has the greatest concentration of thorough interpretations of Kant's treatise in comparison with all other periods under consideration. In this chapter, I explore these interpretations in detail and continue the argument initially developed in chapter 5 that the practical reason for adopting a republican constitution outlined in the First Definitive Article becomes one of the most important parts of the text for this group of commentators in their search for what the work ultimately suggests to achieve peace. Considering the relative length of the chapter, I have chosen to divide it into two sections for the convenience of the reader. The principal interpretations discussed first offer the most detailed, comprehensive analyses of the text. The subsidiary interpretations that follow present more concise accounts of Kant's work.

Principal Interpretations

The Interpretive Outlooks of Andrew Hurrell
and Chris Brown

Andrew Hurrell in his 1990 article "Kant and the Kantian Paradigm in International Relations" presents a compelling study of whether Kant is a "statist" or "cosmopolitan" in his writings on international relations. According to Hurrell, the statist paradigm "stresses Kant's explicit and clear-cut rejection of world government . . . the value Kant places on the autonomy of states and his insistence on the importance of non-intervention."[2] Further, "It points to the extent to which progress depends not on grandiose plans for the reform of the state system but on the internal improvement of states and, in particular, the achievement of republican government."[3] "Most crucially," Hurrell explains, the statist paradigm "argues that when Kant speaks of a 'federation of states,' he is thinking only of a loose league of republican states that have come together for the sole purpose of abolishing war."[4] On the other side, the cosmopolitan paradigm emphasizes the universalistic aspect of Kant's writings, suggesting a belief in the importance of overcoming the state system through the establishment of a global government that would insure the rights of a "global society of mankind."[5]

He thoroughly analyzes all four of Kant's works on international relations—*Perpetual Peace, The Metaphysics of Morals, The Idea for a Universal History with a Cosmopolitan Purpose*, and *Theory and Practice*—in coming to the conclusion that "the statist view of Kant is more broadly correct."[6] Most importantly for our purposes, he notes, "In *Perpetual Peace* . . . Kant does indeed reject both world government and a federation with the power to enforce the proscription of war."[7] Hurrell suggests several reasons for this position he thinks Kant is taking in *Perpetual Peace*. First, the establishment of an international state is " 'not the will of nations according to their present conception of international right.' "[8] Second, the civil state already has an internal constitution and thus "it has outgrown the coercive right of others to subject" it to an additional external constitution a state of nations would require.[9] Third, Hurrell points to Kant's comment in the Second Preliminary Article that the state is a "moral personality" or, as Hurrell calls it, an "organic entity" the existence of which would be terminated if it is "grafted onto another state."[10] According to Hurrell, "Kant's fourth and most powerful argument against the idea of an international state is that it is both impractical and contrary to the idea of freedom."[11]

Instead of the world state, Hurrell sees Kant as opting for a " 'federation of free peoples,' i.e., 'a particular kind of league which we might call a pacific federation.' "[12] Importantly, Hurrell explains, "Kant is at pains to underline the need to maintain the independence of states and to uphold a strict principle of non-intervention."[13] He further quotes Kant's statist remark, "This federation does not aim to acquire any power like that of the state, but merely to preserve and secure the *freedom* of each state."[14] His own comment in relation to the Kantian federation is that "the limited pacific federation discussed in *Perpetual Peace* . . . is indeed designed to underwrite international law in such way as to protect the autonomy and independence of the state."[15] Finally, Hurrell states, "The sole purpose of this federation will be to abolish war, although its powers to do so will be strictly limited."[16] "In *Perpetual Peace*," Hurrell concludes that "such a federation appears to Kant to be the limit of what is possible given the constraints of state sovereignty and the importance of state autonomy on the one hand and the need for a lawful framework for international relations on the other."[17]

Yet from where does this "lawful framework for international relations" and the prospects it holds for future peace derive? Hurrell turns to the First Definitive Article for the answer. After recognizing "Kant's belief in the inseparable connection between domestic and international society,"[18] Hurrell explains, "Kant's answer [to the above question] is usually seen in terms of his insistence on the pacific tendencies of republican governments."[19] Hurrell is convinced that, for Kant in *Perpetual Peace*, "the frequency of war is clearly influenced by the character of domestic governments" and that "Kant never tires of denouncing the bellicosity of despots" throughout his treatise.[20] "Republics" on the other hand "will be less inclined to engage in wars . . . because of the power of the citizens to restrain the aggressive tendencies of their leaders."[21] After restating the frequently quoted "consent of the citizens" passage, Hurrell goes on to say that "It is clearly important that the people should directly experience the costs of war."[22]

Hurrell also offers another reason he believes Kant prefers republican government. A liberal state provides the conditions for the possibility of moral progress among individuals within a society. No other form of government does this. Only a liberal state protects the freedom and equality of each individual, which allows him or her to develop as a moral human being. Hurrell believes Kant is in favor of the proposition that "Progress towards perpetual peace is ultimately dependent on the moral progress of individuals."[23] As he says, "By providing the framework within which moral progress is possible, republican government is an essential step on the road to peace."[24] Essentially, Hurrell believes Kant is linking the nature of the individual to the nature of domestic society and presenting to his readers the fundamental influence of both on the condition of international society.

This emphasis on the implementation of the First Definitive Article and the vital role it plays in the production of peace among independent states is a central component of interpretations during this period no less important to Hurrell than to Doyle, Mulholland, and Bok above. Hurrell appropriately comes to the close of his analysis of *Perpetual Peace* with the following comment:

> Kant's concern with the internal arrangement of states need not be seen, as it sometimes is, as subversive of interstate order, but rather as another means of perfecting it. First, because of this belief that peacefully inclined republican states represent the only means whereby a stable system of independent states can be maintained. Second, because of the extent to which constitutional states which guarantee the moral and political rights of their citizens remove an important element of instability and add to the legitimacy of the state system as a whole.[25]

Hurrell's state-centric reading and his reliance on the First Definitive Article as the key medium through which peace will be achieved for Kant in *Perpetual Peace* should be evident by now.

Chris Brown, in his 1992 book *International Relations Theory: New Normative Approaches*, discusses the role of the state for Kant and how this relates to Kant's willingness or unwillingness to accept a world state as the solution to the problem of war. Brown first tells us, "Kant's principles of politics are normative (they tell us what we should do) and based on *Recht*— a word that can only be translated as a mixture of the English notions of law and justice."[26] Later, Brown states that the "role of the state based on *Recht* is, essentially, negative; the state exists to allow free, equal and self-dependent people to find security for themselves and their property" and that is basically it.[27]

Brown then discusses Kant's general concern with war, its devastating effects on the lawful state, and the necessity of the rule of law between states in order to insure the development and stability of the lawful state. Brown suggests, "one way to abolish war would be to abolish states, by creating a single world-state."[28] And according to Brown, this would seem to be the appropriate route for Kant. As he states, "since the role of the state is negative, and the political community is not in itself a source of value, there would seem to be no principled reason why the existing order of sovereign states should be valued" and therefore, no reason why Kant would be against the sovereignty of each state being removed in the interests of creating a world state. Yet even with this logic Brown puts forward, he is still certain that Kant "rejects the notion of a world-state."[29] He summarizes Kant's objections to the world state as follows: "linguistic and religious differences between states" necessarily keep them apart; "princes will not agree to lose their sovereignty"; and "it is doubted whether a world-state would be viable on practical grounds."[30] For Brown then, "since the establishment of a world-state is not the answer, a world without war must be achieved in a world of states."[31]

Without discussing, specifically, the Preliminary and Definitive Articles, Brown seems to have established his statist credentials. His next step is to consider these articles or, as he says, "unpack and contextualise" them.[32] Though he lists all of the Preliminary Articles, he says little of note about each. He simply states that the "six articles are best understood as a set of rules that could, and should, be applied in the absence of perpetual peace."[33] His larger concern is with the three Definitive Articles, which "relate to" and "give content to" the following three legal orders: "a constitution based on the *civil right* of individuals within a nation; a constitution based on the *international right* of states in their relationships with one another; and a constitution based on *cosmopolitan right* in so far as individuals and states, coexisting in an external relationship of mutual influences, may be regarded as citizens of a universal state of mankind."[34]

Brown begins with the First Definitive Article. He does not spend much time on it. Like other interpreters from this period, however, he points out the practical reason for adopting a republican constitution. As he states, "Republicanism is desirable for its own sake, but here Kant adds the important point that a republican constitution will be conducive to peace" as well.[35] The reason he believes Kant thinks this need not be repeated again. Yet his commentary on the "consent of the citizens" passage is different from others above. He does restate the conventional interpretation that "Unlike kings, who treat war as a sport, the citizens of a republic will have to bear the costs of war themselves and for this reason will be naturally peaceful."[36] To this he adds the point that "Kant's republic is not a democracy (which is a variant of despotism)."[37] This is important for Brown as he is aware of "the oft-stated view that democracies are inherently war-like."[38] Understanding that Kant preached republicanism, not democracy, Brown justifies himself in saying such a view "does not touch [Kant's] argument" that republics, not democracies, are peaceful.[39] This is where he parts with Doyle who he thinks "sees liberalism as coming in two varieties—laissez faire and social welfare—neither of which corresponds to Kant's republicanism."[40] Though Brown does disagree with Doyle on this issue, he still calls Doyle's work "suggestive" and says "his picture of an expanding Pacific Union within which war is no longer an instrument of policy . . . is true to Kant's reasoning in *Perpetual Peace*" and that there is "some reason to think that [Doyle's empirical] position . . . is defensible."[41]

Brown sees Kant as preferring the "second-best solution" of a "peaceful federation, initially with a nucleus of republican states but gradually expanding" in the Second Definitive Article.[42] The reasons for rejecting the world state have already been discussed. Brown does say that the "world republic" is an "impractical goal" for Kant but does not distinguish it from the "world-state" he talks of earlier (and says Kant clearly rejects).[43] Finally, Brown understands the Third Definitive Article wherein "Cosmopolitan Right shall be limited to Conditions of Universal Hospitality" to be "far more limited than some modern Kantians would wish."[44]

Defense of the Kantian Theory of International Law: An Interpretation by Fernando Tesòn

Fernando Tesòn's 1991 article, "The Kantian Theory of International Law," defends a liberal theory of international law and its "commitment to normative individualism" against traditional international legal theory's exclusive focus on "the rights and duties of states."[45] He pronounces, "The end of states and governments is to benefit, serve, and protect their components, human beings; and the end of international law must also be to benefit, serve, and protect human beings, and not its components, states and governments."[46] His hope is that some day "the notion of state sovereignty" will be "redefined" so that "the sovereignty of the state" will be "dependent upon the state's domestic legitimacy."[47] The ultimate object of such a redefinition is that the "respect for states" will be "merely derivative of respect for persons."[48] Tesòn believes that Kant is "the first to defend this thesis" and he "reconstructs and examines Kant's theory as put forth in his famous essay *Perpetual Peace*" to support his argument for a liberal theory of international law.[49]

While Tesòn is intent on demonstrating Kant's absolute commitment to international human rights, he is as certain as other interpreters writing during this period that *Perpetual Peace* reinforces the concept of state sovereignty and does not advocate the removal of it to protect these individual rights. Further, in line with these interpreters, he is convinced of the singular importance of the First Definitive Article and sees its primary message as being that "internal freedom at home is causally related to peaceful behavior abroad."[50] As he states more clearly a few paragraphs later, "Kant's originality stems . . . from having been the first to show the strong links between international peace and personal freedom, and between arbitrary government at home and aggressive behavior abroad."[51]

Tesòn goes into little detail in his section on the Preliminary Articles. Other than chastising those "realists" who "use" the Preliminary Articles to support an "interpretation that gives primacy to states and governments over the individuals," his basic point is that these articles "describe the most pressing steps to be taken if we want subsequently to proceed toward the lasting . . . substantive solutions . . . contained in the Definitive Articles."[52] Further, he states that the norms outlined in the Preliminary Articles "are designed to govern the intermediate status of international relations after the lawless state of nature is ended, but before the definitive law of nations is established."[53]

Tesòn's discussion of the First Definitive Article is twenty-four pages long, easily the longest of any interpreters' considered here. It is not necessary to consider every remark made by him about this article. Fortunately, much of his analysis concerns the three principles on which the republican constitution is based: freedom, due process, and equality. His analysis of these is philosophical exposition more than anything else, with the simple goal of locating Kant in the liberal framework of absolute respect for individual rights. Further, he wants to differentiate himself from those like Hinsley who, he claims, "regard the state as deserving respect because it is an autonomous moral being and enjoys sovereignty in its own right" as opposed to his argument that "the moral standing of the state must be anchored" in the three "organizing principles of just republican states."[54] Tesòn understands Kant to be an international theorist who believes that a state is only a "legitimate member of the international community" when it respects these principles for all individuals that live within it. The only constitution that can realize this is the republican.

Tesòn makes the important point that "The requirement of a republican form of government must be read in conjunction with the Second Definitive Article."[55] He states, "Kant asserts that adherence to these requirements [outlined in the First and Second Definitive Articles] will result in an alliance of free nations that will maintain itself, prevent wars, and steadily expand."[56] The operative word used here is "alliance." When we reach the discussion of his interpretation of the Second Definitive Article, it is easier to see why Tesòn chooses this word. Here, he simply says, as I have demonstrated other interpreters from this period have done, that such an "alliance of participant states that protect freedom internally and whose governments are representative" are the only ones that can guarantee peace.[57] He then repeats what he has already said earlier: "Kant for the first time linked arbitrary government at home with aggressive foreign policies."[58]

Tesòn asserts Kant's "central argument" in *Perpetual Peace* "that if people are self-governed, citizens on both sides of any dispute will be very cautious in bringing about a war whose consequences they themselves must bear."[59] This is what Tesòn refers to as Kant's "empirical argument" within the First Definitive Article. I have lately been referring to it, as other interpreters have, as Kant's "practical argument" and both seem interchangeable as they rely on the same "consent of the citizens" passage within the text. Tesòn says that unlike the citizen in a republic, "the tyrant does not suffer the consequences" of a war so "it is relatively easy for a despot to start a war."[60]

Second, "from an institutional standpoint, the separation of powers inherent in a liberal democracy creates a system of mutual controls and relative diffusion of power that complicates and encumbers governmental decisions about war."[61] According to Tesòn, "For Kant, that a multiplicity of decision-makers will participate in decisions to make war is implicit in the notion of autonomy inherent in the republican form of government."[62] Obviously, he sees Kant as supportive of a kind of government that places "institutional limits on power, including the power to conduct foreign relations."[63]

Tesòn offers up two more Kantian reasons, both part of the "empirical argument" why liberal, representative governments are peaceful. He says that in a Kantian republic, "citizens will be educated in the principles of right and therefore war will appear to them as the evil that every rational person knows it is."[64] Finally, and he turns briefly to the Third Definitive Article in this selection, Kantian liberal democracies "foster free trade and a generous system of international movement" that bring people closer together and make war seem costly since it interferes with both.[65] In ending his discussion of the "empirical argument," Tesòn spends several pages strongly defending Doyle's claim that liberal democracies do not go to war with each other. He concludes by saying "The conjecture that internal freedom is causally related to peaceful international behavior is as safe a generalization as one can make in the realm of political science."[66] Admittedly, his endorsement of Doyle's position has little to do with the central concern of analyzing his interpretation of Kant's text. Still, the constant emphasis interpreters working from the early 1980s through the 1990s place on this aspect of the First Definitive Article, that is, the Kantian point that domestic political structure substantially influences relations between states (and Doyle's empirical proof of it), is important to the argument for the existence of a new phase of Pattern Two.

Tesòn also points out the "Normative Argument" made in the First Definitive Article. States should adopt the republican constitution not only because of the peace it brings, but because of " 'the purity of its origin, *a purity whose source is the pure concept of right.*' "[67] Grounding this argument in Kant's categorical imperative from his moral theory, he explains that "The normative argument is addressed to those who rank justice over peace; the empirical argument, to those who rank peace over justice."[68]

Moving to the Second Definitive Article, Tesòn first states that "Most modern commentators . . . agree that Kant did not support world government."[69] In making this statement, he cites Hinsley, Gallie, Waltz, and the French interpreter, Jean-Michel Besnier. His own position on it is very similar. For Tesòn, "Kant's answer . . . to this problem is to propose instead *an alliance of separate free nations, united by their moral commitment to individual freedom, by their allegiance to the international rule of law, and by the mutual advantages derived from peaceful intercourse.*"[70] He then comments that "The global distribution of authority proposed by Kant is thus quite close to the modern international legal system: states have rights and duties under international law, because they represent autonomous moral beings. However, there is no sovereign to enforce them; enforcement is decentralized."[71]

It should be clear that Tesòn understands Kant to prefer a "loose organization of separate states" as the solution to the problem of war.[72] Yet why does he think the text is inimical to a centralized authority above the state level. Tesòn's answer follows: "Kant defended separate states not only because he thought that in this way his proposal would be more realistic, but because he thought that such a loose system was morally justified."[73] Kant seems quite clear on the point that "while world government may be an attractive idea in theory, it carries the danger of degenerating first into a world tyranny and ultimately back into international anarchy."[74] Since Tesòn's main focus is on the freedom of the individual (and he thinks it is Kant's as well), he remarks that "world government presents too great a threat to individual freedom" so that "Liberty is better secured when political power is relatively diluted."[75] Second, Tesòn states that, for Kant, "a system of separate states allows individuals to associate with those that share their same culture, customs, history, and language."[76] He believes this develops and encourages a sense of community, which allows for the autonomy of the individual living within it to thrive. Tesòn develops this argument from Kant's point that differences in language, religion, and culture work to create an " 'equilibrium of the liveliest competing powers' which alone can control the danger of the deceptive peace that despotism [in the form of world government] brings."[77]

As for the Third Definitive Article, Tesòn's main comment further supports the state-centric reading he has given thus far. He states, "Not only does Kant expressly disavow the creation of centralized world government, but the Third Definitive Article, establishing the Cosmopolitan Law, or the rules of free trade and universal hospitality, is inexplicable outside the context of a world of independent nation-states."[78]

Tesòn closes his lengthy but instructive article with the comment that "The community of free nations envisioned by Kant will hopefully expand gradually and maintain itself, as it has done for the past two hundred years, and the aim of perpetual peace will be achieved the moment when the liberal alliance comprises every civil society."[79] This interpreter, however committed he is to the understanding of Kant as normative individualist, still reads *Perpetual Peace* as a statist document. While he does believe that individual freedom and reason come first for Kant, he recognizes that such traits can only exist in a state that adopts the recommendation of the First Definitive Article, that is, the republican constitution. The legitimacy of the state within the international community is entirely dependent upon this. Once the republican constitution is adopted by several states, the alliance of republican states (and an alliance is the most he ever states Kant supports in this treatise) will bring peace between them.[80] The interpretive avenue he takes gives prominence to the First Definitive Article over all others, and understands the Second Definitive Article and its wholesale commitment to the state, in terms of it. Of all the thorough interpretations written during this period, Tesòn's is certainly one of the most clear and complete.

A Thorough Analysis of the Text: Gabriel L. Negretto's Interpretation

Gabriel L. Negretto thoroughly analyzes Kant's *Perpetual Peace* in "Kant and the Illusion of Collective Security," the 1993 Andrew Wellington Cordier Essay in the *Journal of International Affairs*. Negretto does not see any evidence of Kant favoring a world state or strong federation in his most famous text.

Negretto begins with the Preliminary Articles and states that this is where "Kant's absolute rejection of any kind of war of aggression" occurs.[81] These articles are the "necessary conditions for perpetual peace" but are nowhere near as important as the Three Definitive Articles, which Negretto calls "arguably his most important contribution to the philosophy of international law."[82] Though Negretto acknowledges "the importance of the third article," he notes that his analysis is limited to the first and second for purposes of the issue he is dealing with throughout the work—the problems of collective security.[83]

Negretto then turns to a discussion of the First Definitive Article with the statement that "Kant relied heavily upon the idea that European wars were mainly motivated by the greed of governments and statesmen rather than that of peoples."[84] He infers this from the "consent of the citizens" passage quoted directly thereafter. He calls the "consent of the citizens" passage "an assumption" of Kant's and, at least initially, is concerned with the "naive" nature of such a comment.[85] Negretto believes, apart from the text, that "More than once, history has shown that peoples can be as bellicose as their leaders, if not more so."[86] Still, Negretto does agree in the end that "the existence of a republican constitution is not a guarantee of peace *per se*; rather, it is only a form of government that renders *less likely* the initiation of offensive wars for the purpose of advancing the ruler's political ambitions."[87]

Negretto calls "The establishment of a federal system . . . the most controversial aspect of his project."[88] Though he does acknowledge that, for Kant, "states—like individuals—must abandon the state of nature if they desire peaceful coexistence," he does not see Kant as suggesting anything more than an "alliance . . . described as a confederation of free and independent states, rather than a federal state."[89] He also refers to Kant's suggestion, borrowing a phrase from another book on Kant, as "a pact of collaboration among states . . . where the efficacy of the pact of peace does not hinge on the existence of a coercive power above individual states."[90]

Negretto also adds an interesting twist, augmenting his already state-centric interpretation. He quotes directly from Lewis White Beck's 1963 translation: " 'This league does not tend to any dominion over the power of the state but only to the maintenance and security of the freedom of the state itself and of other states in the league with it, without there being any need for them to submit to civil laws and their compulsion, as men in a state of nature.' "[91] Negretto's commentary on this quotation is that "Kant foresaw that if the federation were to become so strong as to enforce peace against aggressor states, it could become a super-state, inevitably overriding the rights of its members."[92] After he gives the usual reasons for Kant's rejection of the world state and notes that "there are no 'teeth' in [Kant's] alliance for the prevention of war," Negretto concludes with the comment that "man must act as though perpetual peace were attainable and attempt to create the essential conditions for its attainment: a republican constitution in every state and a league of peace comprised of independent and free nations."[93] He ends his discussion of Kant by comparing the proposals outlined in *Perpetual Peace* with those of the American President Woodrow Wilson. Briefly, he states, "Wilson, like Kant, believed that world peace could only be established through an alliance of democratically governed nations."[94]

Georg Cavallar's Novel Interpretation

The principal interpretations discussed thus far have been reasonably similar, with consistent focus on the First Definitive Article and state-centric readings of the text. One of the few "outliers," as I call them, during this historical period comes from Austrian Georg Cavallar's article "Kant's Society of Nations: Free Federation or World Republic?" In final analysis, Cavallar does not disagree with other interpreters during this period; he only adds an interesting twist to his analysis.

First, like several other interpreters from this period, Cavallar recognizes the important relationship between the First Definitive Article and the Second Definitive Article. As he states, "Kant provides a short sketch of the peaceful, first step towards world peace" through the following passage: " 'For if by good fortune one powerful and enlightened nation can form a republic (which is by its nature inclined to seek perpetual peace), this will provide a focal point for federal association among other states.' "[95] Cavallar claims that "Kant's contention that the 'focal point' for the federation will be a republic links the first and second definitive article together."[96] His subsequent discussion of the First Definitive Article is similar to those discussed so far. He explains, "on two distinct levels . . . peace is fostered by republicanism."[97] At the first level, or as he calls it, the "transcendental" or "a priori" level, the Kantian republic simply " 'by its nature' will adhere to the principle of justice in international relations."[98] At the second level, or as he calls it, the "pragmatic" or "a posteriori" level, "Kant assumes that it is more likely that citizens as colegislators in a republic will refuse to consent to a declaration of war."[99] Cavallar then discusses the difference between "The autocracy with a republican form of government" and "the 'true' republic, the 'representative system of democracy,' " both of which he believes Kant endorses in the First Definitive Article.[100] Importantly though, he sees the former as "merely a transitory stage" toward the latter.[101] It was the representative system of democracy that he favored most, according to Cavallar, because "The actual consent of citizens to a declaration of war requires a representative republic."[102]

Cavallar obviously sees the important and clear role of the First Definitive Article in bringing about peace for Kant. Yet when it comes to the Second Definitive Article, he is less sure of the text and its recommendations. In speaking of all of Kant's writings on international relations, he initially states that he will side with those interpreters who view Kant as embracing a "free federation, with states having the right to leave it whenever they want to."[103] Compared to Kant's other writings, he is even more convinced of Kant's choice in *Perpetual Peace* for a "weaker model of federalism where states do not submit themselves 'to public laws and to a coercive power which enforces them.' "[104] Since I am dealing solely with *Perpetual Peace*, this is the most important point for my purposes. Cavallar lists "pragmatic, legalistic, and moral arguments" for Kant's dismissal of a universal state.[105] Cavallar does not seem impressed with the "pragmatic" argument. While he admits that Kant endorses the idea that the "larger the [universal state] becomes, the more inefficient and counterproductive it tends to be" and that "Nations are too different, in terms of languages as well as religious confessions" to think a universal state possible, he still thinks the "legalistic" and "moral" arguments are Kant's "more important reasons to criticize the universal state than mere prudential considerations."[106]

Cavallar states, "Kant's legalistic argument against an international state with coercive power is twofold."[107] Though "the weaker claim," as Cavallar sees it, the first argument against an international state with coercive power is that it is "inherently self-contradictory."[108] As Kant says himself (here quoted by Cavallar), "The right of nations presupposes that there is 'a group of separate states which are not to be welded together as a unit.' "[109] Obviously then, to Cavallar, "The right of nations only makes sense if there are independent nations."[110] Cavallar believes the second argument is more potent. Unlike individuals in a state of nature, states "have already acquired a 'rightful internal constitution' " and so " 'have thus outgrown the coercive right of others to subject them to a wider legal constitution in accordance with their conception of right.' "[111] According to Cavallar, this "passage makes clear why Kant defends the 'autonomy' of states in the fifth preliminary article."[112] But it is not just the Second and Fifth Preliminary Article that speaks on autonomy's behalf. Cavallar also states that the "second definitive article does not abandon or eliminate the autonomy of states set forth in the preliminary treaty."[113] This "free federation of states" or "league," as Cavallar calls it, "is basically the rule of law among states that remain completely independent."[114] The autonomy of the state, unlike that of the individual, cannot be compromised. His final comment is that "If states have no coercive force over others, then a free federation, not a universal state, is the idea demanded by pure reason."[115]

Cavallar's interpretation fits well within Pattern Two statist analysis of the text. Yet he is one of the few middle- to late-twentieth-century interpreters of the text to confront, what he calls, "A difficult passage in *Perpetual Peace*."[116] This difficult passage is exactly the selection that a number of interpretations that reveal Pattern One, Phase One rely on in their understanding of *Perpetual Peace* as a text in favor of the significant limitation of state sovereignty. Cavallar states, "A confusing passage in *Perpetual Peace*, however, cannot be integrated into [his] explanatory model."[117] The model he has created and is referring to here maintains that all of Kant's writings on international relations after 1793 favor a statist reading of the text.

The only statement of concern for Cavallar in relation to this "explana-tory model" is toward the end of the Second Definitive Article. As Cavallar remarks, "At the end of the second definitive article, Kant seems to argue in favor of the kind of world government that has been criticized before: 'There is only one rational way in which states coexisting with other states can emerge from the lawless condition of pure warfare. Just like individuals, they must renounce their savage and lawless freedom, adapt themselves to public coercive laws, and thus form an *international state*.' "[118] Though he firmly states, "The main body of the second definitive article and its closing section do not fit together," his interpretation and explanation attempts to reconcile the two conflicting arguments he has revealed.[119] He understands Kant to endorse the free federation of independent republics as a first step, but hoped at some time in the distant future, such independent republics would "on their own decide to submit themselves *freely* under *coercive* laws."[120] In doing so, they "would not have to abandon their sovereignty completely."[121] Instead, "The sovereignty of the states over their subjects would remain intact, and would be protected by the world republic" so that "It would limit states' sovereignty only in foreign relations."[122]

In the final analysis, Cavallar's discussion of the Second Definitive Article is, unfortunately, as inconclusive as Kant's text seems to be to the interpreter. While he does develop the idea of a world republic as something republican states might choose to form in the future, he still says at the end of his analy-sis that "the true Kantian endorses a free federation of states."[123] And when he does discuss the world republic, he says that sovereignty in foreign affairs is all that states would have to give up while sovereignty over their own citi-zens would remain intact. It is clear that the continued autonomy of states and the need for all of them to adopt a republican constitution are in the forefront of Cavallar's analysis. His struggle to reconcile this predominant interpretive thrust with an otherwise isolated passage is admirable, but not particularly clear. Still, this interpretation is an interesting "outlier" to con-sider during a historical period where commentators of the text interpret in very similar ways.

The Kantian Worldview: An Important Interpretation by Jürg Martin Gabriel

Jürg Martin Gabriel in his 1994 book *World Views and Theories of International Relations* discusses every Preliminary and Definitive Article in relative detail. After mentioning that the Abbé de Saint Pierre "drafted a complete charter for an international organization" and that this charter was "different from Kant's plan in every respect," he moves into a discussion of the Preliminary Articles.[124] He says that the "preliminary articles indicate what should be avoided" and that "they represent the negative conditions for peace."[125] While he believes the Definitive Articles contain the most important plans for peace, he does offer commentary on the Preliminary Articles.

As for the First Preliminary Article, "No treaty of peace shall be regarded as valid, if made with the secret reservation of material for a future war," Gabriel notes that "Eliminating secret reservations strengthens peace . . . and it constitutes a step away from the realist conception of international politics where peace is but an interlude between wars."[126] Gabriel then mentions that the Second Preliminary Article, which prevents the state from being acquired by another through "inheritance, exchange, purchase or donation" and thus preserves the right of the state to an independent existence, "actually postulates the right of self-determination which, of course, runs counter to the tradition prevailing at that time."[127] As this is a "big step" according to Gabriel, Kant makes sure to note that this Article, unlike the First, need not be "instituted immediately."[128] In the Third Preliminary Article, wherein Kant states that "Standing armies shall be abolished in the course of time," Gabriel makes the important point, and certainly one relevant to this phase of Pattern Two, that despite his aversion to standing armies, "Kant does not call for disarmament" here.[129] Importantly for Gabriel, Kant "rejects pacifism and does not argue that arms create war."[130] In obvious reference to the First Definitive Article, Gabriel notes in his commentary to the Third Preliminary Article that "As will become more evident later on, [Kant] sees social organization as the chief source of war."[131]

Finally, Gabriel explains that "If perpetual peace is to be established it is more important to change the nature of states than to eliminate weapons."[132] These last two points by Gabriel clearly position him as an interpreter (like most post-1983 interpreters) who demonstrates that domestic political organization is important to Kant in *Perpetual Peace* in creating the conditions for peace. As will be seen, he elaborates on this point in his discussion of both the First and Second Definitive Articles. His commentary on the Fourth, Fifth, and Sixth Preliminary Articles is, on the whole, conventional and need not interfere with the more relevant interpretation he offers of the First and Second Definitive Articles.

Gabriel believes the Definitive Articles "contain the positive factors" or as he says "the dos rather than the don'ts" and, more than any other part of *Perpetual Peace*, "are generally known and have made the study so famous."[133] First, he "sums up Kant's view of republicanism" adopted by the First Definitive Article by saying that "it is a state based on the rule of law, on the separation of legislature and executive, on representation and, ideally, on a single ruler."[134] Since "Power is divided and limited in numerous ways and cannot be misused" in Kant's republic, "self-discipline is imposed upon the state and promotes peace."[135] He then notes that "Consent of the governed is particularly crucial" and goes on to quote in full the "consent of the citizens" selection that describes this idea.[136] He explains that "This passage shows how much Kant believes in the potential for reason in man: people are able to weigh the costs and benefits of war, and they come to the conclusion that peace is rational while war is not."[137] Simply put, "If they have a voice in government their views will prevail and wars will end."[138] This, however, is not true of the "absolutist ruler" who " 'is not a citizen . . . and does not lose a whit by the war.' "[139]

Just as Gabriel explores the practical reason for adopting republican government in the First Definitive Article like many before him, so he adopts a view of Kant's suggested federation that definitely aligns him with other interpreters from this time. According to Gabriel, "Such a federation, for Kant, is not a supranational organization or a world state. A world state would contradict the basic objective of his plan, which consists not only in achieving perpetual peace but also in maintaining the sovereignty, independence and liberty of all republican states."[140] Instead of a world state, Gabriel understands Kant to advocate "only a loose and informal alliance of republican states."[141] Furthermore, he says the text "never calls for the creation of an international organization, and he certainly does not use the term 'League of Nations.' "[142] This plainly distinguishes Gabriel's interpretation from those that reveal Pattern One, Phases One and Two.

In the final analysis, Gabriel remarks that Kant "places great faith in the inherent peacefulness of republican government, and in this respect is a typical second-image theorist," using Kenneth Waltz's now familiar category.[143] Not viewing the text as calling for a world state or international organization, Gabriel concludes that the "centerpiece of [Kant's] scheme is an enlightened state image."[144] He ends his discussion of the text with the following comments that are as good as any in summing up the thread that holds together the interpretations within this chapter. Gabriel succinctly writes that "Given the benevolent nature of republican government, the lives of such states are peaceful and order in anarchy becomes possible. Domestic politics determines international politics, the primacy of domestic policy is assured. Republicanism produces a convergence of national interests that guarantees perpetual peace."[145] "Order in anarchy" seems a helpful way to describe a pattern that sees peace achieved at, not above, the state level.

Charles Covell's Statist Reading of the Text

Charles Covell begins his discussion of Kant's *Perpetual Peace* with the assertion that the First Definitive Article and the significance it places on the republican constitution "occupied a very important position in Kant's explanation of how a lasting peace was to be achieved between states in the international sphere."[146] Further, he states, "The idea of the republican constitution was central to Kant's argument in *Perpetual Peace.*"[147] After a general discussion of the nature of liberal republican government for Kant, including its clearly representative aspect and commitment to the separation of powers between the executive and legislative branches, Covell turns to the Preliminary Articles. He lists them without commentary, then discusses the ideas that "inform" them.[148]

First, the Third Preliminary Article, which "called for the gradual abolition of standing armies, looked forward to the principle, widely accepted by statesmen and policy-makers in the contemporary world, that international peace must depend not upon the maintenance of a balance of military power between states, but upon the preparedness of states to give up voluntarily, and on a permanent basis, the means at their disposal to wage aggressive war."[149] In terms of determining whether he adopts a statist reading of the text, Covell offers "another idea informing the preliminary articles, and one which requires special emphasis in connection with the concerns of the present monograph."[150] Covell explains: "This is the idea that the basic institutional element of an international order committed to perpetual peace had to be the institution of the sovereign state."[151]

He then points to the Fifth Preliminary Article, which posits the duty of noninterference. According to Covell, this Article "underlined the respects in which the law of nations must be founded in principles enshrining the freedom and independence essential to the sovereignty of the state."[152]

Covell's statist reading stems not only from his look at the Preliminary Articles, but from the three Definitive Articles as well. As he states most significantly, "Kant's commitment to the principle of the freedom and independence of the sovereign state is everywhere apparent in his statement and explanation of the three definitive articles of perpetual peace."[153] Covell is especially convinced that the Second Definitive Article suggests the requirement of a sovereign state to achieve perpetual peace. He remarks, "It is the second definitive article of perpetual peace which brings out most clearly the value and importance that Kant assigned to the principle of state sovereignty."[154] Covell elaborates further, "it is this article which underlines that Kant did not consider that the founding of an international order committed to lasting peace required the separate states to relinquish the rights and powers which defined their freedom and independence as states."[155] As Kant fully rejected the "international state, or a state of all the nations" according to Covell, so he accepted a federation in its place.[156] "The essence" of this federation "was not an international government structure that compromised the freedom and independence of the states that were its members" but "the general treaty or agreement among the member states through which the federation was brought into being, and then maintained in being in perpetuity."[157]

The distinctive point Covell makes here is that "the treaty establishing the pacific federation possessed the character of the standard treaty in that it involved an agreement between states which actually presupposed their autonomy and independence."[158] One of the final comments he makes on the Second Definitive Article sounds as if it came straight from Hinsley. The following passage certainly establishes, once and for all, Covell's statist credentials:

> For Kant, then, the founding of the law of nations, and hence the founding of an international order committed to perpetual peace, depended not upon the existence of a system of international government, but upon the voluntary acceptance by independent states of a rule of law which could not, as a matter of definition, be enforced or otherwise supported by any institutions whose rights, powers and organizational structure were anal-ogous to those that embodied the sovereign independence of the state.[159]

Subsidiary Interpretations

Brief Analyses of the Text by Daniele Archibugi and Michael Williams

The following concise accounts offer relatively state-centric readings of Kant's text and a focus on the importance of likeminded, homogenous states to Kant's peaceful alliance. Daniele Archibugi, writing in 1992, explains that "For the first time" among many peace projects, Kant's First Definitive Article tells us that "if international peace is to be 'perpetual,' it must imply a homogeneity of the political constitutions of the individual states, the model for which is to be sought in the republic."[160] Archibugi then follows the typical line of interpreters during this period by selecting for direct quo-tation the "consent of the citizens" passage from Kant's text. Archibugi's explanation is that "Since republican government involves the direct partici-pation of citizens in the management of public affairs, it will necessarily be peaceful."[161] As for the Second Definitive Article, Archibugi states that Kant opts for the "diffused model" of international organization and, as such, "supports the existence of both autonomous states and a voluntary con-federation of states."[162] Importantly, Archibugi believes "the truly significant article" of Kant's *Perpetual Peace* is the Third Definitive Article. Yet even under the notion of Cosmopolitan Law, "States continue to enjoy full sovereignty and are invited to voluntarily join an international confederation."[163]

Michael C. Williams, in his article "Reason and Realpolitik: Kant's Critique of International Politics," has equally little to say about *Perpetual Peace*. As far as "Kant's vision" goes for Williams, he is sure that "Each state remains independent" and that "this is not a call for world government."[164] Instead, "each state recognizes the basis for its independence to be its recognition of the rights of other states and their mutual recognition of its own."[165] There will be a "slow but gradual extension of this mutual recognition, beginning with a small number of like-minded states and eventually encompassing the entire globe."[166]

Otfried Hoffe's Biography of Kant, an Interpretation by Jens Bartleson, and a Brief Look at the Eighth International Kant Congress

The German writer Otfried Hoffe has written a 1992 biography of Immanuel Kant. Though Hoffe gives little attention to Kant's international political theory, choosing to focus instead on his more widely known critical, moral, and legal philosophy, he has a few words to say about *Perpetual Peace*. He states, "Kant's essay *On Eternal Peace* thus has the form of a contract describing the legitimacy and principles of the voluntary union of all nations which reason demands."[167] Such a "union, or league, of all nations should not take the form of a world government, which would lead to unfettered despotism."[168] Instead, Hoffe understands the text to suggest, "The league of nations has no sovereign power which would allow it to interfere in a nation's internal affairs."[169] At most, Kant promises "a federation of free nations which all have republican constitutions."[170]

Jens Bartleson, from the University of Stockholm, would agree with Hoffe's assessment. Writing in 1995, Bartleson explains that "the creation of such a federation would anticipate the coming of perpetual peace, but it would not aim to acquire any power or authority over and above each constituent state. It would aim solely to preserve the autonomy of each state, as long as this is compatible with the equal autonomy of every other confederated state."[171] If no coercive power exists above separate states to prevent conflict between them, then according to Bartleson's reading of Kant "the effective realization of this federation depends on the internal perfection of states."[172] Bartleson's understanding of the process by which states perfect themselves internally deserves mention. This explanation, in detail, prefaces the "consent of the citizens" passage:

The will of the state must be brought to coincide with the will of the people through a constitution derived from an original social contract. Sovereignty must be depersonalized and dispersed throughout the entire body politic. Rousseau's general will, which Kant elevates into a principle of reason, must be reflected in public law, permeate political institutions, and provide the touchstone for particular political decisions. Only a constitution derived from an original contract based on the idea of general will can spur the gradual cultivation of men into citizens by means of civic education and political liberty.[173]

Such a political constitution then allows for the rationale behind the "consent of the citizens" passage to work successfully to serve peaceful ends. As Bartleson states exactly before he quotes Kant from this passage: "Only such a state will be inclined to seek peace."[174]

With this next remark by Bartleson, there is no question he falls into line with other interpreters from this period. He states that "Where international right prescribes what ought to be done in relations between states, political right prescribes what ought to be done within states. Taken together, internal perfection and a free federation are necessary conditions of perpetual peace."[175] Like other interpreters from this time, Bartleson integrates the First and Second Definitive Articles through a reading of the text, which understands peace between states to be determined by the internal perfection of states. In essence, the adoption of republican constitution within a group of several states will lead to a voluntary federation of them as peaceful neighbors, though neighbors that maintain their sovereignty and independence vis-à-vis each other.

The Eighth International Kant Congress was held in 1995. Scholars from Western Europe, North America, Eastern Europe, Asia, and Latin America gathered to "commemorate the two hundredth anniversary of the publication of Kant's essay, *Zum ewigen Frieden: ein philosophischer Entwurf (Toward Perpetual Peace: A Philosophical Project)*."[176] After research into several of the Kant Congresses over past years, I discovered very little consideration of Kant's *Perpetual Peace* until this one.[177] Though I will not discuss any of the papers given at the Congress, it is significant enough to note that six of seven interpretations acknowledge that Kant's *Perpetual Peace* is anti–world government and in favor of a voluntary federation of republican states that exists principally to protect the sovereignty of each member.[178]

A Return to the Anglo-American Study of International
Relations: Interpretations by Kenneth W. Thompson
and Cecilia Lynch

Kenneth W. Thompson's well-known book *Fathers of International Thought* includes a small section on Kant and *Perpetual Peace*. After summarizing his metaphysics and moral philosophy, Thompson turns to the First Definitive Article of *Perpetual Peace* to discuss Kant's contribution to political thought. He states that Kant's "first definitive article for a perpetual peace is republican government in nation-states around the world."[179] First, Thompson likens the Kantian state of nature to that of Hobbes's where the "natural condition of men living side by side in nature is a state of war."[180] For Thompson, "to change this condition . . . It is not enough to end hostility."[181] Instead, "the civil constitutions of every state must be republican."[182] Thompson then seeks to explain Kant's reason for choosing a republican constitution over all others and, more specifically, why republican constitutions established across the globe would be more likely to end war. Essentially, Thompson does little more than offer the "consent of the citizens" passage. After quoting from that passage, Thompson then makes the important point that Kant is advocating liberal republicanism, not democracy, as the best possible political option. A representative government with a separation of powers, which is the "only system of government which makes republicanism possible," is far more likely to calm "an inflamed public or assembly" that "can sometimes be more belligerent and uncompromising than a monarchy or aristocratic regime."[183]

Consistent with interpreters writing during this period, Thompson sees the federation of states Kant advocates in the Second Definitive Article as responsible for one, and only one, function—the preservation of the sovereign state. He first explains, "Nations, like individuals in a state of nature, live in fear of one another paradoxically because they are neighbors."[184] "For Kant," the only "way out" is "unambiguously a federation of states."[185] He states that the "aim of such a federation . . . would not be to gain power or coerce individual states" but "simply to secure and preserve the freedom of each state."[186]

Cecelia Lynch focuses very little on the text of *Perpetual Peace*, but offers general commentary about the treatise that is worthy of a closer look. The title of her 1994 article, "Kant, the Republican Peace, and Moral Guidance in International Law," says a lot in itself. Many of the post-1983 interpreters of Kant's treatise readily point out Kant's disdain for democracy and his advocacy of republican, representative government. Still, when giving him credit as the intellectual forebear of the idea of the liberal peace, they never make what would seem to be the more consistent claim if being true to his work is important. This is simply that the intellectual father of the liberal peace should receive his just dessert by reference to his brainchild as the "republican peace." Cecelia Lynch does this in the first instance. As she states in her initial paragraph:

> Not only has Kant's thought provided the underpinnings of one of the major traditions of international law, but there is a groundswell of interest among international relations scholars today in the question of whether contemporary events, particularly the proliferation of republican states and attempts to create them, signal the march forward to the Kantian ideal of republican peace.[187]

Further, she states that "The fashionable return to Kant has done much to demonstrate that domestic factors play a far greater role in decisions about foreign policy than realist analysis has allowed, and that the behavior of certain types of states toward each other does indeed go against the predictions of structural realists."[188]

Though she discusses several aspects of the republican peace after these initial introductory statements and their relationship to Kant's thought, her focus on the text of *Perpetual Peace* is spotty. Regarding the Second Definitive Article, her only remark is that "most analysts now agree that Kant's aversion to despotism would proscribe any such teleology [a world government] and that the most stringent limitation on international anarchy that Kant could envision was a voluntary federation of republican states."[189] The selection she chooses to quote from the First Definitive Article is the ubiquitous salute to the practical reason why representative democracy is the best political system for avoiding war. Before quoting the "consent of the citizens" passage, she comments on Doyle's earlier thesis and remarks that "the most often quoted or paraphrased passage from Kant by contemporary theorists of the liberal peace is the following: If the consent of the citizens is required in order to decide that war should be declared . . . etc."[190] Though she discusses the Second Preliminary Article in connection with Kant's "caution against interventionism," the rest of her essay is general commentary on Kant's moral philosophy and philosophy of history.[191]

Conclusion

This group of interpretations of Kant's *Perpetual Peace*, specifically the principal interpretations discussed above, continues the themes developed in

Doyle's original interpretation into the 1990s. As stated in the introduction to this chapter, a high concentration of interpretations were written during this period and I have argued that a majority of them view the First Definitive Article as central to Kant's solution to the problem of war developed in *Perpetual Peace*. The "consent of the citizens" passage—the practical reason for adopting the republican constitution—becomes crucial to understanding the most important recommendations of Kant's treatise for these interpreters. Further, these interpreters defend a state-centric reading of the Second Definitive Article. Even if they suggest a voluntary federation, association, or alliance of states may develop, they clearly point out that there will be no "teeth" in these entities; the only reason for their existence is to protect and preserve the sovereignty of each state. Interpretations from this period enhance the argument for a second phase of Pattern Two.

CHAPTER 7

Pattern Two, Phase Two: State Sovereignty Preserved III

Accent on the First Definitive Article Through the End of the Twentieth Century

Introduction

This chapter explores a final collection of interpretations of Kant's *Perpetual Peace* and considers a relatively small group of interpreters. It initially discusses the evolution of thoughts on *Perpetual Peace* by three writers who have written about the text more than once since the second phase of Pattern Two began to take shape with the appearance of Doyle's article in 1983. This section of the chapter demonstrates that, within this period under consideration, several writers who consider *Perpetual Peace* a second (or even a third time in one instance) generally stay consistent in their interpretations of the treatise. If anything, they embrace a more state-centric view of the text and place greater importance on the practical reason for adopting the First Definitive Article in their most recent interpretations to date. Their readings of the text offer even greater support for the argument that a second phase of Pattern Two has solidified by the second half of the 1990s. The last half of the chapter closes the analysis of interpretations of *Perpetual Peace* with a discussion of several commentaries on the treatise that have appeared in the last two years, including one by the prominent American political philosopher John Rawls. These carry the argument of pattern formation up to the present.

Evolution of Thoughts on Perpetual Peace:
Interpretations by Howard Williams

Over the past two decades, Howard Williams has published more articles on Kant's international theory than any other scholar in the field of International Relations. Each of his writings focuses primarily on *Perpetual Peace*. As will be shown, Williams's interpretations from 1983 to 1996 become progressively more state-centric.

His first interpretation is from his 1983 book *Kant's Political Philosophy*. In a sense, this interpretation lays the foundation for those that follow, though each interpretation evolves ever so slightly from its predecessor. Here, he covers almost every aspect of the Preliminary Articles, the First Definitive Article, and the Second Definitive Article. In his Introduction to Chapter Ten, which he entitles "Kant's Plan for International Peace: the Highest Political Good and the Highest Moral Good," his analysis begins, much like his contemporary Doyle does, with the following statement: "Kant holds that the problems of internal order within states and the problems of external order amongst states are inextricably linked and, thus, the supposed division between domestic and international politics is an artificial one."[1] This is a key statement found throughout interpretations that reveal Pattern Two, Phase Two and distinguish it from those that reveal Pattern Two, Phase One. Again, its origins are rooted in the emphasis these interpreters place on the practical argument within the First Definitive Article—peace between each sovereign state will result if there is republican government in place within each state. Before discussing his understanding of the First Definitive Article, it is important to consider his understanding of the Preliminary Articles, which clearly begin to establish some statist credentials.

In explanation of Preliminary Articles One, Five, and Six, which must be "applied immediately," Williams remarks that "There is no possibility of building up trust amongst states if leaders are not prepared to honor existing peace treaties, and the sovereignty and independence of other states."[2] Of all the articles, Williams believes the Second Preliminary Article, which states that "No independently existing state, whether it be large or small, may be acquired by another state by inheritance, exchange, purchase or gift," is "the most important of the preliminary articles."[3] He further explains that "This article sets the tone for the kind of international society that Kant hopes to see, namely, one in which the autonomy, as well as interdependence, of states is respected."[4] After quoting directly from Kant's commentary to the article, which essentially describes the historically independent state as "a moral personality" never to be ruled by another state, Williams asserts, "The universally recognized independence of states must be the basis for world peace."[5] His final point regarding the Second Preliminary Article is that "we cannot expect progress at all if the fundamental principle of the autonomy of states is not recognized."[6]

Williams's reading of the Preliminary Articles initially projects a state-centric view of Kant's treatise. Still, he has more to say about the First and Second Definitive Articles, which to a small extent, seems to call into question his commitment to this interpretive outlook. With regard to the First Definitive Article, Williams states, "A republican constitution [required by the article] rests on the assumption that each citizen gives his consent to the actions of the sovereign through being directly or indirectly represented in the legislature."[7] The importance of this is that "The citizen can in a moral sense, therefore, regard all laws as emanating from his will. Equally, he can regard the actions of the executive as susceptible to his control because it can only act within the confines of laws framed by the citizen's representatives."[8] From here, Williams reaches Kant's "consent of the citizens" passage. Williams states that the representative aspect of republican government "in Kant's view, furnishes a powerful lever of control over governments, and curbs their aggressive instincts."[9] As "those who have to bear the brunt of the financial and human costs of war have the power to decide whether or not they wish to prosecute the war."[10]

As Williams begins discussion of the Second Definitive Article, he first notes, "Positive law requires the existence of a sovereign authority to ensure that all illegal acts are justly punished, but Kant's notion of a federation of free states appears to contradict the idea of one sovereign authority."[11] Williams remarks, "He [Kant] puts great stress on the fact that the federation he has in mind 'would not be the same thing as an international state.' "[12] Instead, "Kant's object" in *Perpetual Peace* "is to advocate the gradual coming together of independent nations into one international organization without sovereign powers."[13] This is because "the federation as it develops and grows [should] not be a completely sovereign body, as each nation's need for an identity and independence has to be respected."[14]

Yet Williams makes the further point that "the seeds of an international state can be sown even in an international system made up of sovereign states."[15] He says this because he believes, at least in this first article, that Kant "is both advocating an international state as the ultimate goal, but not advocating it as something to be realized in the immediate or near future."[16] Though he still regards the international state as an "unattainable ideal" for Kant, he says it should be "an objective to put to the back of our minds" when dealing with the treatise.[17]

What is confusing for the reader of his book is that he immediately reverts back to his initial view that Kant "does not place much stress on such organizational initiatives" in his proposals to bring about perpetual peace.[18] Instead, Williams, in the final section of his essay, sounds much like Pattern Two, Phase One interpreters writing during the very recent years before his 1983 publication who rely on Kant's philosophy of history as the ultimate guarantor of peace. Even more interesting is Williams's Footnote 13 where he states that "What F.H. Hinsley says in his book, *Power and the Pursuit of Peace*, is essentially true, namely, that for Kant 'it was no more logical to hope to solve the international problem by the supersession of states than it would have been logical to try to end the civil state of nature by abolition of individuals.' "[19] I do not see how he can successfully weave this clear anti-international state position (along with all others he sets out above) into an interpretation that also seems to see the international state as Kant's ultimate ideal without being contradictory.

Williams's first interpretation of Kant's *Perpetual Peace* is puzzling and, to say the least, a difficult one to fully grasp. To his credit, even Williams does not seem completely confident in his assessment. He refers to his thorough anti–international state reading (gathered from the Preliminary Articles and the Second Definitive Article) together with the pro–international state reading he offers toward the end of his analysis as a "paradox."[20] When we get to his second work on the subject of *Perpetual Peace* in 1992, we see Williams drop the pro–international state reading almost completely. And by the third article, written in 1996, he presents a reading of the text as statist as any this book has discussed so far.

Williams begins chapter 8 of his 1992 book *International Relations in Political Theory* in the same way as his previous interpretation. He explains, "For Kant the problems of internal political order and external political relations cannot be separated."[21] In order to avoid repeating what has already been stated plainly above, it is important to note that this second interpretation is based almost entirely, sometimes even word for word, on the first interpretation. There is no need to revisit his thoughts on the Preliminary Articles in this interpretation. Also, his understanding of the First Definitive Article demonstrates little change of heart as well. In accordance with one of the aims of his book, which is to demonstrate the relationship between classical political theory and political history, he does suggest that the United States constitution more likely resembles Kant's republican constitution than any other.[22] This is because of its representative aspect and the separation of powers that exists between the executive and legislative branches. He additionally states that the "right of declaring war was further enshrined as a power of the congress in the United States in the early 1970s" and that such "a stress on the right of the people would probably meet with Kant's strong approval."[23]

As for the Second Definitive Article, Williams gives almost no attention to his earlier claim that the international state is an ideal toward which all states should move. He explains, "Kant puts great stress on the fact that the federation he has in mind would not be the same thing as an international state."[24] According to Williams, Kant is concerned with the difficulty of ruling such a genuinely large area with one central government and therefore sees such a state as impossible to establish. He uses the example of the USSR in the 1990s where due to "its sheer size the control of the centre over the periphery unavoidably declines."[25] Instead, he is convinced that the sole "object of the [Kantian] federation is rather to safeguard the independence and maintain the security of the individual states."[26] Further, it shall be "without sovereign powers."[27]

Moving to his final interpretation, the first comment that Williams makes regarding *Perpetual Peace* (and it must be acknowledged that this chapter within the 1996 book *Classical Theories of International Relations* is coauthored by Ken Booth) is that "The sufficient factor for Kant [in the determination of peace] . . . is a states-system comprised of states with republican constitutions."[28] This statement encompasses both the First and Second Definitive Articles.

Concerning the First Definitive Article, Williams notes, echoing his former interpretations and the views of many other interpreters during this period, that "Kant saw a close relationship between bad governments at home and aggression in external policy."[29] He explains that unlike the "sharp dividing line between 'domestic' and 'foreign policy' . . . traditionally drawn" in International Relations theory, Kant "emphasises the intimate relationship not only between internal and external in terms of an individual country's foreign policy, but also in terms of the character of the international system."[30]

Still, the most relevant comparison is between Williams's views on the Second Definitive Article in the prior two interpretations and what there is to say here. He first recognizes the similarities between the Hobbesian state of nature and the Kantian state of nature. He remarks, "For Kant, as for Hobbes, the state of nature was one of war."[31] "The response of Hobbes" of course "was for individuals to submit to the Leviathan of the sovereign state, which by definition turned the international arena itself into a state of nature, since the sovereign state and international anarchy are two sides of the same coin."[32] But what does Kant say? What does he recommend to the world to replace the anarchy between states that has resulted? According to Williams, "Given Kant's cosmopolitan perspective with common humanity as his referent, it might have been expected that his recommended global polity would be one of world government."[33] He continues by saying that Kant not only "rejected this" but actually "believed that perpetual peace must be based on free, equal and independent states."[34] Finally, Williams offers a most potent observation, especially in comparison to his original musings on the subject. He states, "In this and in other respects Kant is more statist than his reputation would suggest."[35]

What are we to make of Williams's three interpretations? It could be said that the last one is not his since it was coauthored. This might be a good argument except for the fact that many of his statements throughout the final interpretation follow his former interpretations word for word. The best answer is simply that his thought has evolved over time. It is clear though that his final look at the treatise yields an interpretation quite similar to those already discussed (and those yet to come).

Interpretation through the mid-1990s: Michael Doyle and Charles Covell Revisited

Before examining what Michael Doyle and Charles Covell have to say about Kant's *Perpetual Peace* the second time around (and to determine whether they remain consistent to their previous interpretations), three relatively brief mid-1990s interpretations need to be considered.

At the beginning of his paper on the subject, Wade L. Huntley asserts: "Much recent scholarship has focused upon the apparent absence of war among liberal democratic states—the liberal peace."[36] He goes on to say, "To help explain the phenomenon, many refer to the political writings of Immanuel Kant, and the central role he envisioned for the liberal republic as the foundation for 'perpetual peace.' "[37] Huntley then considers the Three Definitive Articles. Regarding the First Definitive Article, he states, "Kant maintains that the republic, in addition to its domestic merits, also manifests an inherent inclination towards peace."[38] After quoting the "consent of the citizens" passage, Huntley remarks, "Kant clearly contends that republics will not initiate aggressive war."[39]

His next task is to show the important relationship between the First and Second Definitive Articles. In a first attempt, he explains, "To depict the specific circumstances under which republics can be more republican is the principal aim of Kant's second article, calling for a 'federation of free states.' "[40] His view of the First and Second Definitive Articles is similar to many of his contemporaries. He believes that "this federation is possible only among republics, not states of any sort" and that "the extension of the rule of law among states depends upon extension of the rule of law within states."[41] Yet what makes Huntley's interpretation so similar to those that have come before his during this period is the statement that "Taken together [meaning the First and Second Definitive Articles], then, Kant is holding that establishing freedom and the rule of law domestically and internationally are mutually dependent, symbiotic processes—and he is often credited as the first to insist explicitly on this link."[42]

He is just as convinced that Kant "explicitly rejects the idea of a 'world state.' "[43] Instead, "Kant contends that nations can establish the rule of law among themselves without, as people must, an overarching authority."[44] And in what he calls "a key juncture in Kant's argument," he cites Hinsley, Gallie, and Doyle in making the argument that " 'The individual must impose the state on himself in order to remain free. In the same way, free federation for Kant was what the state must impose on itself while *remaining free*.' "[45] Huntley's final point concerning the Second Definitive Article is an important one. He maintains that, for Kant, "progress towards an international rule of law does not necessitate (and in fact contradicts) diminishing the sovereignty of power of separate states."[46] In Huntley's words, "Kant departs far enough from the 'domestic-international' analogy to hold that a rule of law can grow among sovereign states without centralized authority."[47] Once the rule of law in the form of a republican constitution is established within states, "the 'free federation' is 'self-enforcing'—in the same manner (but to a greater degree) as is any republican constitution."[48]

In a 1997 book about Francis Fukuyama's *The End of History and the Last Man*, three authors discuss Kant's view of history in relation to Fukuyama's work. They spend a small portion of a chapter discussing *Perpetual Peace* as well. Compared to the *Idea of a Universal History with a Cosmopolitan Purpose*, the authors state, "In this essay [*Perpetual Peace*], Kant puts more emphasis on the role that states themselves can play in the development of world harmony."[49] They then turn directly to the First Definitive Article. To it they mention, "The first definitive article of the essay on perpetual peace requires states to bring about republican constitutions" and that "By working towards a republican constitution within their states they can contribute to the gradual development of a peaceful world situation."[50] Though they do not quote the "consent of the citizens" passage directly, they make obvious reference to it in the following comment: "Kant believed that republican states based on these principles would incline towards peace with their neighbours because their citizens would no longer be subject to oppressive rule, and because their representatives would have the responsibility for considering whether or not to declare war."[51]

Unlike the *Idea of a Universal History*, which the authors say "relies too much on the accidental and contingent" in efforts to make international progress toward peace, "Here [in *Perpetual Peace*] we have the notion of improved civil states which are able to set an example for other states to follow" as an alternative "mechanism to lead to a more peaceful international order."[52] And how do they say Kant's treatise suggests the achievement of this? Like other interpreters before, peace results from a combined implementation of the First and Second Definitive Articles. According to them, "Kant sees this as coming about through a loose federation of states which have republican constitutions or are developing them."[53]

Finally, Fareed Zakaria, a former Managing Editor of *Foreign Affairs*, makes reference to Kant's writing in a well-known 1997 article in the same periodical entitled "The Rise of Illiberal Democracy." Though it is brief, he does focus on the "consent of the citizens" selection from the First Definitive Article. Zakaria notes, "Kant, the original proponent of the democratic peace, contended that in democracies, those who pay for wars—that is, the public—make the decisions, so they are understandably cautious."[54] His other reference to Kant directly follows this when he explains Kant's dislike of pure democracy and his belief in a representative form of government including "a separation of powers, checks and balances, the rule of law, [and] protection of individual rights."[55] Considering the context of his article, which deals with domestic problems that exist when democracies arrive on the scene without constitutional liberalism as essential partner, it is little wonder Zakaria does not discuss the Second Definitive Article. Still, his mention of the logic behind the "consent of the citizens" passage is suggestive of a relationship between his and other interpretations of this period.

While analysis by these authors of Kant's text is brief, they still place emphasis on those aspects of the text and interpret meanings therefrom in a very similar way to those writing before them in this period. Even more valuable is to look at those interpreters who return to *Perpetual Peace* after some years away from it. Both Michael Doyle and Charles Covell are examples of this and, as will be seen later, their second interpretations of Kant's treatise are very similar to their first.

Michael Doyle's initial comment, from his 1997 book *Ways of War and Peace: Realism, Liberalism, and Socialism*, is that "Kant's states continue to live in international anarchy—in the sense that there is no world government— but this anarchy is tamed and made subject to law rather than to fear and threat of war."[56] After listing the Preliminary Articles and introducing the

First Definitive Article as one that mandates the formation of republican constitution, he explains that the "pacific union" of liberal republics "is neither a single peace treaty ending one war nor a world state or state of nations."[57] Further, as he stated in his 1983 article, Kant "develops no systematic organizational embodiment of this treaty, presumably because he does not find institutionalization necessary."[58]

Doyle stays true to his first interpretation. In fact, he adds little in the way of new insight into the text and presumably is satisfied with his first reading. Importantly though, even after fourteen years, he still recognizes that *Perpetual Peace* stands for the proposition that the autonomous republican state, not a centralized authority above the state, is the primary avenue to peace. Doyle remains one of the founding fathers of liberal peace theory and he consistently acknowledges that his assumptions about this controversial idea rest on Kant's *Perpetual Peace*.

It may seem difficult for any interpreter to offer a more statist reading of *Perpetual Peace* than Covell's first interpretation from 1994. Yet Covell's second interpretation completed in 1998, when looked at carefully, is an even more state-centric reading of the text than his first.

Covell begins with a discussion of the Preliminary Articles where he focuses almost exclusively on the Second and Fifth Preliminary Article throughout the discussion. After explaining that the "second preliminary article of perpetual peace laid down a principle of the law of nations which affirmed the freedom and independence of states," he makes the more important claim, for him at least, that "it is the fifth preliminary article that most clearly brings out that Kant conceived of the law of nations as a body of law that was to work to guarantee the rights of states which were essential to their freedom and independence."[59] Covell then refers to the "principle of non-interference" set forth in the Fifth Preliminary Article as "unconditional and overriding."[60] Finally, Covell states that "Not only did the principle of non-interference laid down in the article serve to guarantee the freedom and independence of states in regard to their internal constitution and government," it also "served to give recognition to the formal juridical equality of states, in the respect that the freedom from external interference it guaranteed to states was a freedom that was to be guaranteed to all states equally and without exception."[61]

While Covell's statist reading begins to take shape with his look at the Preliminary Articles, his understanding of the First and Second Definitive Articles is where it takes hold. As important, he demonstrates the important relationship between the First and Second Definitive Articles. He initially states, "Kant's commitment to the republican constitution, as a precondition for peace among men and states, was qualified by his commitment to what he conceived of as a founding juridical principle of the international order. This was the principle of the freedom and sovereign independence of states."[62] Covell believes his commitment to the republican constitution, however, "occupies a central position in the argument of *Perpetual Peace*."[63] Before offering to the reader the entire "consent of the citizens" passage, he nicely summarizes it in the following way:

> In a state based in the republican constitution, the consent of the citizen-body was required in order to decide whether or not the state should declare war. This consent would be difficult to obtain in such a state, for the citizens therein would not readily opt for war given that they would have to suffer the hardships and deprivations resulting from it. However, the situation was quite different in a state without a republican constitution (i.e. a despotism). For, here, the ruler of the state remained subject to virtually no constraints preventing him from waging war at his own arbitrary will and discretion.[64]

To the idea that domestic politics determines international politics, Covell adds, "it was Kant's view that the establishing of a lasting international peace required a fundamental transformation in the structure of internal domestic political organization existing within states."[65]

This "vitally important feature of [Kant's] international thought," as Covell calls it, relates directly to Covell's understanding of the Second Definitive Article as one that advocates the preservation of the powers of the sovereign state as opposed to their limitation. An established republican constitution within a state necessarily makes it more peaceful, especially in its relationship to other republican states, because of its commitment to the rule of law internally. Such a commitment internally will necessarily lead to a commitment externally, and avoid the necessity of creating a centralized authority above separate republican states to preserve and foster peace. As Covell explains, "Kant's view of the law of nations, as law underwriting the freedom and independence of states, finds its clearest expression in the second definitive article of perpetual peace."[66] As opposed to the "idea of an international state or a world state, where the separate states were to be brought together under a system of international government possessing functions and powers analogous to those which he saw as belonging to government as it was constituted in the civil state," the Second Definitive Article actually called for "a voluntary, progressively expanding association of free and independent states, whose defining purpose was merely to bring a permanent end to war."[67]

All these observations lend credence to Covell's initial claim that "Certainly, Kant's was a more radical view of sovereignty than anything that is to be found in the thought of Hobbes, or in that of Vattel."[68] The sovereign republican state is the foundation for an "international rule of law" that would ultimately develop between likeminded states, enhancing the prospects for peace.[69] The establishment of the republican constitution within the state and the preservation of the freedom and independence of that state vis-à-vis its neighbors is ultimately Kant's counsel in his quest to improve upon the state of international order in *Perpetual Peace*. Importantly, Covell even imagines what Kant would have thought of the world today. He states, "There is no doubt that Kant would have approved of the dedication of the present-day international community to the cause of the rights of men."[70] Still, he makes the all-important point that "Equally, there is no doubt that he would have had misgivings about the erosion of the rights and powers of states and their governments that the concern with the protection of human rights has led to."[71]

Covell's reading of the text is state-centric through and through. Further, the importance he places on the First Definitive Article and its relationship to the establishment of peace need not go unnoticed either. Finally, he does not even hint that Kant might be, from a pure standpoint of reason, in favor of international government and the erosion of state sovereignty. His interpretation fits well with others discussed in the post-1983 interpretive context.

An Important Interpretation by John Rawls in
The Law of Peoples: Perpetual Peace *as Liberal Peace*

John Rawls certainly comes to similar conclusions about Kant's famous treatise as his contemporaries writing during the 1990s. In discussing the principles of his "Law of Peoples," Rawls notes that he will choose to "follow Kant's lead in *Perpetual Peace* (1795) in thinking that a world government— by which I mean a unified political regime with the legal powers normally exercised by central governments—would either be a global despotism or else would rule over a fragile empire torn by frequent civil strife as various regions and peoples tried to gain their political freedom and autonomy."[72]

Several pages on he discusses the liberal peace idea and its relationship to history. Within this discussion, he gives Kant and, specifically, *Perpetual Peace* credit for the "hypothesis" that "armed conflict between democratic peoples will tend to disappear as they approach [the] ideal" of a "*foedus pacificum*."[73] He further states that these "democratic peoples . . . will engage in war only as allies in self-defense against outlaw states."[74] Though he does not mention it, it appears that he is drawing primarily from the First Definitive Article and briefly from the Second Definitive Article in coming to this view. Importantly, and this will play a part in the discussion in chapter 9, Rawls expressly states that "I believe this ['liberal peace'] hypothesis is correct and think it underwrites the Law of Peoples as a realistic utopia."[75]

Rawls's commentary on Kant's treatise is admittedly sparse. Still, he falls into line with the majority of interpreters from this period that see the text as rejecting world government in favor of an association of independent democratic states who consistently avoid war between each other while maintaining their defensive posture towards nonliberal states. Rawls seems generally impressed by the liberal peace hypothesis and sees *Perpetual Peace* as its intellectual foundation. It is important to note the concise comments on this topic by one of the most influential political philosophers of the twentieth century. More importantly, Rawls's interpretation and complementary insight into the liberal peace idea have important ramifications for my analysis in chapter 9.

Harold Kleinscmidt's The Nemesis of Power: A Concluding Interpretation

It seems fitting to conclude this chapter with a recently published book on the history of International Relations theory. Harold Kleinschmidt's *The Nemesis of Power*, published in 2000, discusses a variety of authors and offers generally thorough interpretations of their works. Kant's name is referred to throughout the book and Kleinschmidt devotes several paragraphs to *Perpetual Peace* exclusively. After noting that Kant "explicitly rejected Saint-Pierre's and Rousseau's proposals" (as many within this pattern have done before), Kleinschmidt turns his attention to a brief discussion of the main body of the treatise.[76] He first states that Kant's treatise is in the form of a "hypothetical peace treaty."[77] Via "the First Definitive Article," Kleinschmidt points out that for Kant "peace must be willed explicitly."[78] Further, he explains, "Kant took the view that perpetual peace as a universal condition of international relations was categorically different from partial peace treaties."[79] Kant believed peace treaties that ended wars emerged, as Kleinschmidt says, from "temporary conditions."[80] "Perpetual Peace," as opposed to constantly disregarded peace treaties, can only emerge if the peace established is "universal."[81] Kleinschmidt then goes through the list of Preliminary Articles, which follow from this.

What distinguishes his interpretation from Pattern One and, even further, places his ideas on Kant's treatise properly within the second phase of

Pattern Two is his discussion of the First Definitive Article that follows. Kleinschmidt notes that Kant "further requested a specific domestic condition within each polity, namely that the rule of law should be accepted as the very basis of what he referred to as a 'republican' constitution."[82] Kleinschmidt describes this constitution as one in which "rule was accepted as rule by law and by the consent of the ruled and in which the ruler's competence was confined to the exercise of force against those who chose not to abide by the law."[83] "Consent of the ruled" had another part to play in this proposal as well. Though Kleinschmidt does not directly quote the "consent of the citizens" selection so often emphasized by Pattern Two, Phase Two interpreters, he does explain that "Kant saw in what he termed a 'republican' constitution an essential condition for a lasting peace because he believed that polities with a 'republican' constitution would not develop attitudes of aggression towards their neighbours."[84] Here Kleinschmidt hints at the liberal peace.

More importantly, there is a definite emphasis by Kleinschmidt on the First Definitive Article as the primary textual avenue to peace. Other than a brief remark in another chapter where Kleinschmidt states that Kant "sceptically rejected the idea of world rule," the interpreter barely touches the Second Definitive Article.[85] His only other indirect reference to the Second Definitive Article is developed in terms of the First Definitive Article. Relevant to this, he states that in *Perpetual Peace*, Kant "insisted that 'republican' constitutions were possible only within sovereign territorial polities and urban communities because only in such polities could rule be rule by consent."[86] Because Kant "rigorously adhered to contractualism," Kleinschmidt concludes that Kant "denied that a 'republican' constitution was conceivable for frameworks overarching sovereign polities."[87] Essentially, world "republican" government, in Kleinschmidt's reading of the text, "would be an illegitimate reduction of the rights of the ruled to appoint and sanction their rulers."[88]

As such, Kleinschmidt ends his interpretation on a rather statist note. He understands the main thrust of the text to suggest the preservation of sovereignty within independent states that willingly adopt republican constitutions. Only when this form of constitution is adopted by the independent state is perpetual peace possible. In the end, the "sovereign territorial polity," as he calls it, need not and should not cede any portion of its power away to a larger international body. This would only undermine the original republican constitution, which derives its legitimacy from the consent of the citizens and promotes peace simply by its existence within the territorially defined sovereign state. This is certainly a reading of *Perpetual Peace* that recommends a peace proposal at the state level.

Conclusion

In conclusion, a clear majority of interpretations written during the last half of the 1990s further indicate a shift in textual emphasis to the First Definitive Article, specifically, the "consent of the citizens" passage within it. According to these interpreters' reading of the text, the solution to the problem of war between states is seen as the recommendation of liberal republican government in every state. Interpreters during these years continue to view *Perpetual Peace* as a treatise, which demonstrates the important link between domestic political structure and international conduct. Like their predecessors writing after Doyle's 1983 article on the liberal peace, this last group of interpreters also views the text as the intellectual foundation for this now famous claim.

Furthermore, though the Second Definitive Article is important to these interpreters, they read Kant as saying that it is the implementation of the key First Definite Article, which ultimately determines whether or not peace will someday be achieved between states. Essentially, a state-centric reading of the Second Definitive Article is predominant because the independent liberal republic, not any form of international government above it that might reduce its sovereignty, is seen as the primary vehicle to peace. The end result is a reading of the text wherein the sovereign republican state is preserved and the prevention of war is understood to occur through, not above, such a state. The second phase of Pattern Two has clearly established itself as we enter a new century of commentary on Kant's celebrated treatise.

PART 4

Shifting Hopes, Shifting Patterns

CHAPTER 8

Pattern Formation as a Function of the Rise and Decline of Hopes for Peace Through International Organization

Introduction

In completing an interpretive history of Immanuel Kant's *Perpetual Peace* from the mid-nineteenth to the end of the twentieth century, I argue that two clear patterns are revealed through an analysis of English-language interpretations over this historical period. The first pattern, which develops between the middle to late nineteenth century and survives to the mid-twentieth century, views Kant's treatise as favoring peace proposals above the state level. The second pattern, which develops from the mid-twentieth century and survives through to its end, views Kant's treatise as favoring peace proposals at the state level.

The final two chapters of the book offer a principal and a subsidiary explanation for these patterns. In this chapter, I present the argument that the formation of the two patterns is a function of the rise and fall of hopes for peace through international organization. In brief, the principal explanation for Pattern One is the enthusiasm and hope for the prevention of future wars through international organization, which prevailed from the middle to late nineteenth century to the mid-twentieth century. The explanation for Pattern Two is the loss of faith in international organization as a path to peace that has prevailed from the mid-twentieth century to the present.

In chapter 9, I offer a subsidiary explanation. It considers the steady increase in the number of liberal states in the western hemisphere over the past one hundred and fifty-five years and the affect of this evolving historico-political phenomenon on the minds of interpreters of *Perpetual Peace* living during this time and generally within this geographical space. Importantly, this subsidiary explanation complements the principal explanation presented in this chapter.

The Dream of Peace Through International Organization

During the seven decades from the mid-nineteenth century to the end of World War I, at which time Pattern One emerged and became the dominant interpretation, I argue that there was a general rise in hopes for peace through the mechanism of international organization. This was especially true in Britain where many intellectuals and politicians (especially of the liberal internationalist bent) became very enthusiastic about the possibility of forming a unique world organization that would ultimately work to prevent wars between states. In developing an explanation for the existence of Pattern One, specifically the first phase of the pattern, it is important to contextualize the argument with the acknowledgment that a majority of interpreters writing about *Perpetual Peace* during this period were British.

It is necessary to begin with some historical background to develop this initial argument. Inis Claude, Jr. writes that "Before the nineteenth century, rulers of Europe were so preoccupied with their Sovereign Dignity that they were virtually unable to do anything more at international conferences than argue about questions of precedence and prestige."[1] Yet once the Napoleonic Wars ended, the rest of the century teemed with what Claude refers to as the "great conferences of the nineteenth century."[2] These began with the Congress of Vienna in 1815 that "initiated a series of developments which made it possible to speak of a nineteenth century conference *system* without precedent in the modern world."[3] Unlike those of the eighteenth century, these conferences "contributed notably to the facilitation of serious consideration of problems by the representatives or rulers of sovereign states."[4] Most importantly for Claude, "the political conference system . . . produced the prototype of a major organ of modern international organization—the executive council of the great powers."[5]

According to Claude, the successful experience of the nineteenth-century conference system, which brought on even greater hopes for further international organization, culminated in the Hague Conferences of 1899 and 1907. As Claude writes, "the Hague Conferences...represented the climax of a century of development in which attention shifted more and more to the possibilities of international institutions as instruments of world peace."[6] He believes one of the most significant achievements of the Hague Conferences was their "mark of a new peak in development of collective activity for the purpose of general permanent reform of the system of international relations, as distinct from the purpose of dealing with specific and temporary situations."[7] Differentiating this from the political conference system of the nineteenth century, Claude explains that "More conspicuously than the Concert of Europe, the Hague System was divorced from immediate problems raised by particular wars or disputes and was concerned with international problems in the abstract."[8]

In final analysis, however, Claude is less impressed with the concrete achievements of the two conferences than with the less tangible hopes and promise that they inspired. He states, "The Hague Conferences were notable events in the history of international organization not so much because of their actual accomplishments as because of the conceptions to which they gave expression, the hopes which they dramatized."[9] These hopes manifested themselves in what Claude calls an "urge toward institutionalization" among those thinkers and political activists involved. For the first time, there was generous "attention given to the task of institution-building" within the international sphere.[10] Agreeing with Claude, Clive Archer explains, "Although the Hague Meetings did not prevent the catastrophe of August 1914, they did produce some modest achievements and also pointed the way for the institutional development of organized international relations."[11] Finally, Claude notes that "The statesmen gathered at the Hague...clearly believed they were favored to be the founding fathers of a permanently functioning, efficiently organized mechanism for the maintenance of world peace."[12] As far as the history of international organization goes, this sincere and now realistic hope for institutionalization was something new and unique. Clearly, over the course of the nineteenth and certainly through to the first part of the twentieth century, there developed an ever-increasing enthusiasm for international organization as a method of preserving peace.[13]

Another leading analyst, John Pinder, certainly concurs with Claude. Yet for him, it was not just the general idea of and hope for international organization as a path to peace that successfully made its way into the minds of political leaders and intellectuals during this era. According to Pinder, federal proposals above the state were very much a part of the British intellectual and political context from the mid-nineteenth century to World War I. He notes that "even before 1870, [the British began] to show their capacity for applying the federal principle to the affairs of other states."[14] He further states during the period from the 1870s to World War I, "[British] liberals were the most active in responding with federal proposals to solve international problems."[15]

One of the several British thinkers Pinder discusses to buttress his argument is James Lorimer. Lorimer was Edinburgh Professor of Public Law and the Law of Nature and Nations when he published his well-known two-volume work, *The Institute of the Law of Nations*, in 1884. Pinder explains that this work "clearly took account of the federal principle embodied in the US Constitution."[16] He further sums up Lorimer's main proposal in the following way:

> There was to be a government for international purposes, with a two-chamber legislature, a judiciary, an executive and an exchequer. The government was to dispose of a small standing force and the member-states to disarm to the level required for municipal needs. There would be an international tax, levied by the states, and their internal affairs would be excluded from the scope of central government, save in the event of civil wars.[17]

Hidemi Suganami has also utilized Lorimer's work in his thinking on the subject of the "domestic analogy in world order proposals." He notes that "in Lorimer's view, an international government, embracing the functions of legislation, adjudication and execution was indispensable" to the preservation of order and achievement of peace.[18] Clearly, Pinder and Suganami would both agree that Lorimer's treatise sets forth a peace proposal above the state level. In referring to middle- to late-nineteenth- and early-twentieth-century thinkers on world order, Suganami notes, "before the Great War, many thinkers had advanced arguments based upon it [the domestic analogy]."[19] As Suganami describes it, "the domestic analogy is analogical reasoning according to which the conditions of order between states are similar to those of order within them, and therefore those institutions which sustain order within states should be transferred to the international system."[20] The "institutions" at the state level he speaks of, once transferred, become "institutions" above the state level. Middle- to late-nineteenth-century British and American thinkers like Lorimer and William Ladd, the founder of the American Peace Society, who employ the domestic analogy according to Suganami, also clearly advance peace proposals above the state level in their works.[21]

For the purposes of the advancement of this argument, the brief though important point to take from Suganami's work and Pinder's article is that each (and especially Pinder's) shows that peace proposals above the state were a significant part of the British political and intellectual landscape during the period in which the first phase of Pattern One emerged. Furthermore, Lorimer, the writer referred to by both Pinder and Suganami in their separate projects, actually discusses Kant's *Perpetual Peace* in his important work. Similar to Lorimer's own ideas summarized here, Lorimer also views Kant's text as one in favor of a peace proposal above the state level.[22]

As Pinder states in his conclusion, "By the end of the nineteenth century, the federal idea had indeed made great progress in British thinking" and "it seemed by 1914 that federalism had secured a firm place in British political culture."[23] Little changed during the years of World War I. Another influential British thinker of the time, J.A. Hobson, wrote important works recommending international government in the form of an international federation. David Long writes: "In *Towards International Government* and the Union of Democratic Control pamphlet, *A League of Nations*, Hobson addressed the question of international peace, security and order, and suggested international government as an alternative to the Balance of Power system which, he believed, had been a major cause of the First World War."[24] Long then explains that Hobson's international government would certainly "have extensive powers and functions ceded to it by states."[25] Broadly speaking, Long remarks that "Hobson's proposals for an international government involved extended provisions from arbitration and conciliation and the establishment of an international force."[26] Finally, Long notes that Hobson's "international federation would be a single overarching political structure for the world."[27]

The well-known English writer, H.G. Wells, was also a strong proponent of federation during this time. In September of 1918, Wells contributed a piece to the London *Morning Post* in which he wrote of the importance of controlling the world's armaments. There he stated that "a world control of armaments implies—and there is no good whatever in shirking the fact—some sort of world council, some sort of pooling of the naval, military, and air forces of the world under that council, and a representation of the States of the world thereon to a degree commensurate with their strength and will."[28] Theodore Marburg, the American diplomat and chairman of the foreign organization committee of the League to Enforce Peace, acknowledges that Wells's remarks were clearly "an approach to world federation."[29]

In this wartime context, it is also helpful to briefly consider Martin Ceadel's writings on the British peace movement. Ceadel explains that from

World War I, "the peace movement made a general commitment to supra-nationalism which was to last for over forty years" to the mid-twentieth century.[30] According to Ceadel, the Society for the Promotion of Permanent and Universal Peace (the oldest British peace society founded in 1816), the Union of Democratic Control (the first of the wartime peace societies), the Independent Labour Party (ILP), the journalist and ILP member H.N. Brailsford, J.A. Hobson, and other influential academics, barristers, and politicians such as G. Lowes Dickinson, F.N. Keen and Lord Bryce all "produced numerous declarations in favour of supranationalism" during this period.[31] Though the aforementioned peace societies and distinguished individuals did not all agree on the exact form this international authority would take, the key point for the purposes of the argument is to understand that they all clearly supported some version of supranationalism—something above the nation-state to prevent another war. Furthermore, many of their thoughts, words, and plans were influential in the development of the League of Nations idea.[32]

Another important figure favoring supranationalism and discussed by Ceadel is M. Campbell Smith. Noting that Smith was "the first English translator of Kant's *Perpetual Peace*," he quotes the following passage from the introductory essay to her translation: " 'We are moved to the conclusion that a thoroughly logical programme cannot stop short of the principle of federation. Federal troops are necessary to carry out the decrees of a tribunal or arbitration, if that Constitution is not to run a risk of being held feeble or ineffectual.' "[33] Within the same introductory remarks, Smith also asserts, "it is impossible to ignore a clearly marked tendency towards international federation, towards political peace."[34] Further, she states, "No political idea seems to have so great a future before it as this idea of a federation of the world."[35] I argue in chapter 2 that James Lorimer, whose pro-federation views were summarized earlier in this chapter by John Pinder, takes this same view in his interpretation of *Perpetual Peace*. Consistent with her pro-federation views quoted by Ceadel here, I have argued in chapter 2 that Smith also views Kant's text as one in favor of a peace proposal above the state level.

Like Lorimer and Smith, Leonard Woolf was also familiar with Kant's treatise. Only a year before the publication of his formidable work *International Government*, Woolf had written in the *New Statesman* the following lines: "Kant [in *Perpetual Peace*] has succeeded in laying down the conditions of international relationship and government which would have to exist in order to make perpetual peace possible."[36] In the same article, he also states that *Perpetual Peace* is "full of political wisdom and [by] far the most 'practical' work ever written upon the subject."[37] Peter Wilson notes that the "Woolf-Webb draft convention for a 'Supranational Authority that will Prevent War'...bears a close resemblance to the League Covenant."[38] He further states that "the similarities are striking" and that "in respect of the technical, social, and economic functions of the League, Woolf's influence was [even] more direct."[39] For the purposes of the argument, it is certainly useful to note the probable influences of Kant's *Perpetual Peace* on Woolf's writings, especially the Woolf-Webb plan and *International Government*, and their impact on the development of the ideas and provisions expressed in the League Covenant. Importantly, Lorimer, Smith, and Woolf were three influential British thinkers living within the period in which the whole of Pattern One is manifest, who understood *Perpetual Peace* in broadly similar terms.

To the League of Nations

Once we move into the years following World War I, it is clear that the earlier era of hope, or what Claude calls "the era of *preparation* for international organization," becomes reality with the founding of the League of Nations.[40] Claude refers to this new period as the "era of *establishment* of international organization."[41] The appalling devastation of World War I was fundamental to the transformation of the "era of preparation for international organization" to the "era of establishment of international organization." Gerard Mangone explains, "the very enormity of the world disaster spurred men into a new crusade for an international organization which would promote peace."[42] Claude adds, "the League was, in important respects, the product of the First World War."[43]

The grand hopes for international organization as a way to peace that carried over from the nineteenth century and the Hague Conferences, combined with the acute sense of urgency experienced by influential thinkers during the War years and led to the "Anglo-American enterprise" to draft the Covenant of the League of Nations.[44] Mangone refers to the League as "the first permanent international organization for peace."[45] Archer notes that "The whole League system can be seen as a crucial link which brought together the strands of pre-1914 international organizations and wartime co-operation into a more centralized and systematic form on a global scale."[46] Finally, according to Claude, the new League gave "the modern world" its first ever "taste of institutional centralization" in the international sphere.[47] Never before had "the multi-state system [been] equipped with a central institutional instrument of unprecedented utility."[48]

However delighted the League's proponents might have been over its supposed "institutional centralization" in the form of a permanent Council, Assembly, Secretariat, and Court of International Justice, it was far from a super-state. Still, remarks by Sir Alfred Zimmern, R.B. Mowat, Martin Ceadel, and Mangone do indicate that the League certainly intended to curb the sovereignty of its member-states. Writing about the League during the 1930s, Zimmern notes, "The League, in fact, lies in an intermediate zone between these two extremes (a multi-lateral treaty and a super-state)."[49] "Or, to use a more fitting image," Zimmern remarks, "it swings between these two poles, drawing nearer sometimes to the one, sometimes to the other but never remaining fixed."[50] Speaking generally of its successes, Zimmern states, "It has even exercised authority, controlled the rulers of states and prevented war."[51] Further, Mowat acknowledges, "The League of Nations offers a reasonable compromise between the sacrifice of independence on the part of the constituent States, on the one hand, and the wielding of universal despotic dominion on the other."[52] Ceadel understands the League to be "clearly supranationalist" though "the most limited form of supranationalism."[53] Finally, discussing both the League of Nations and the United Nations, Mangone notes, "Both organizations valiantly attempted to reconcile the virtues of national independence and sovereignty with the patent need for a supernational force to rebuff arrogance and destroy aggression."[54]

Clearly, none of these scholars see the League as a super-state though they all suggest, especially consistent with the second phase of Pattern One, the sovereignty of member-states is to be curbed by this international organization. According to Mangone, curbing sovereignty is exactly what the League did during the notable first decade of its existence. Mangone points to the resolution of the Greco-Bulgarian Crisis of 1925 and the War in the Gran Chaco of 1928 as two shining examples of League success during the 1920s.[55] He explains that "Both the Greco-Bulgarian Crisis dispute and the Bolivian-Paraguay conflict high-lighted a remarkable evolution of international law through international organization."[56] In reference to these successes, Mangone notes that "with rare audacity the new collaborators on international organization struck a blow at the most hallowed pillar of national sovereignty: the unqualified right to declare war."[57] A. Leroy Bennett further comments:

> During the early years of League experience, there were high hopes that the organization could ameliorate tense situations that exhibited the potentiality for erupting into major conflict. The League Machinery was utilized for the hearing of at least thirty disputes during the first decade of its existence, and a majority of these were resolved satisfactorily.[58]

Based on the League's resolution of these conflicts, both of these writers recognize the continued enthusiasm for "international organization as peacemaker" that carried over from the period in which the first phase of Pattern One is revealed into the League of Nations era.

These early successes during the 1920s, however, were shortlived and things began to unravel for the League in the 1930s. Clearly, the Manchurian Crisis and the Italo-Ethiopian War in the 1930s did much to undermine this initial faith in the League as a permanent international organization generally effective at preventing aggression. As the 1930s wore on and another European war appeared imminent, it became clear to most that the League could no longer accomplish what it set out to. Mangone candidly describes the situation of the League and the world's powers in the immediate years after these two failures:

> Whatever the reality of [Japanese and Italian] aggression proved, the fledgling international organization in 1931 and 1936 could not soar beyond its own limitations: the provincialism of the United States, the pessimism of France, the opportunism of the Soviet Union, the conservatism of Great Britain, all shuddered under the ruthless arrogance of Japan, Italy, and Germany while the small states, too, frequently played with callous ambition or petty covetousness.[59]

Still, even with its relative impotence described here, it is important to note that the League was an original experiment in permanent international organization. Not anything as grand as a League of Nations had ever been tried before. Even though the League itself—indeed the first concrete manifestation of hopes for peace through international organization—may not have succeeded, it was not as if hopes for "international organization as peacemaker" were entirely dashed as a consequence of its uneven record.

Bruce Collins explains that during the entire period of the League's existence, through its successes and its failures, a feeling of hope was sustained that some form of organization with institutional authority above the state level could bring peace to the world. He specifically states, "World War I provoked a great deal of experimentation in the effort to create supranational organization. Trying to prevent the slide into further European war in the late 1930s encouraged yet more federalist activity."[60]

Peter Wilson confirms this. He explains that through the "intellectual, organisational and propagandist" activities of the Federal Union, founded in London in 1938, "federalism came to occupy a central place in thinking about European political organization."[61] He notes that the movement attracted "considerable support" from across the political, military, and academic spectra.[62] The British public was also very committed. He writes, "By the spring of 1940, [the Federal Union] had over 8,000 members, in over 200 branches, including branches in France and Geneva" and "organised frequent public meetings, attendance at which sometimes reached 2,500."[63] More specifically, with regard to the intelligentsia, Pinder remarks that there was a "flowering of British federalist literature in the late 1930s and the first period of World War Two, by authors such as William Beveridge, Henry Noel Brailsford, Ivor Jennings, Cyril Joad, Ronald Gordon Mackay, Kenneth Wheare and Barbara Wooton."[64]Pinder also notes other proponents of the federal idea whose writings were influential during this period including Phillip Kerr (Lord Lothian), Lionel Curtis, and Lionel Robbins.[65] Similarly, Wilson explains, "During the 1930s and early 1940s the idea that the institution of national sovereignty was the main villain of the peace received a chorus of approval" from influential British thinkers like Leonard Woolf, Clarence Streit, Lionel Robbins, Friedrich Hayek, and David Mitrany.[66] He notes, "Though there were differences on how it might be done, all were agreed that the sovereignty of states needed to be limited in some way."[67]

Wilson thinks "this view found its most clear expression in the work of Leonard Woolf."[68] By the 1940s, Woolf had come to the conclusion that sovereignty was " 'incompatible with law, order, and peace.' "[69] According to Wilson, Woolf believed "the wings of sovereignty of both the small and the great powers had to be clipped."[70] Further, "Both [the small and the great powers] needed to consent to submit themselves to some form of international government."[71]

As for the others Wilson discusses, Streit thought sovereignty should be "transcend[ed]" if Europe was to have any hope of a future peace.[72] Robbins believed the "right to make war" was "central to the concept of sovereignty" and had to be surrendered. For him, " 'There must be neither alliance nor complete unification, but Federation.' "[73] With his underlying faith in the "interdependence of the modern world," Mitrany was "the most sophisticated critic of state sovereignty" according to Wilson.[74] Importantly, Wilson notes "the central proposition of Mitrany's functional theory" that "sovereignty needed to be transferred from the territorial unit to the functional unit."[75] Finally, Hayek expressed "the need for an international political authority" and thought it even more necessary than an international economic authority.[76] With these five preeminent thinkers in mind, Wilson points out that "the idea of restricting state sovereignty by creating a federal or some other kind of international authority became the dominant idea of the period."[77]

According to Andrea Bosco, it was not just these intellectuals who advocated federal solutions during this time. Bosco explains "not only intellectuals, but also some of the most prominent politicians—such as Chamberlain, Halifax, Churchill, Eden, Attlee, Bevin, Sinclair, and Amery...openly supported the federalist project."[78] Bosco also states that "The major national daily and weekly newspapers—*Times, Daily Telegraph, Manchester Guardian, News Chronicle, Daily Express, Daily Herald, Daily Worker, Observer, Sunday Times*—gave wide space to a lively debate on federalism."[79] Most revealing of all, Bosco quotes Churchill's and Sir John Colville's weighty comments from 1940. He states, "the afternoon of 16 June, a few hours before the French Government accepted the capitulation, Churchill made the famous offer of 'indissoluble union.' "[80] Bosco then offers a telling quote from Churchill's private secretary, Sir John Colville. Colville explained, " 'we had before us the bridge to a new world, the first elements of European or even world federation.' "[81]

Anglo-Saxon political leaders continued to express faith in international organization as the most effective path to peace throughout the war years. Michael Howard begins with the assertion that, if anything, "The failure of the League of Nations to achieve the goal of 'international security' was taken by Anglo-Saxon leaders in World War II as a reason, not to abandon the concept, but to try again."[82] And try again they did according to Claude. Claude supports Howard's assertion with his statement that "The war years were marked by an unprecedented volume of plans and proposals for postwar international agencies."[83] According to Claude, "From non-governmental sources came suggestions ranging from the utopian blueprints of idealistic dreamers to the carefully considered proposals of well-organized groups of experts."[84] More specifically, both the United States and Britain were the primary governmental sources of postwar organizational thinking. Claude notes, "Official consideration of the problems and possibilities of postwar organization was seriously undertaken, particularly in the United States and Britain."[85] Significantly, Claude asserts, "Secretary of State Hull initiated American preparatory work almost immediately after the war began in Europe, and was responsible for the most concentrated and elaborate study of international organization ever conducted by a government."[86]

Claude states, "The climatic event in the long process of building the new world organization was the United Nations Conference on International Organization at San Francisco."[87] Mangone writes of the "high hopes of San Francisco" in the days leading up to the founding of the United Nations.[88] Claude then claims that the fifty-nation conference at San Francisco "was history's nearest approach to a global constitutional convention" and further that "The formal completion of mankind's most ambitious international structure was celebrated on June 26, 1945, with the signing of the Charter."[89] Following all these remarks, Claude concludes that the "establishment of the United Nations represented a renewed effort to achieve world peace through *international organization*."[90] Leland M. Goodrich further asserts that the United Nations was truly intended as a "fresh approach to world problems of peace and security."[91] These scholars indicate that there was a general belief at the time that a second attempt at permanent international organization was not simply meant to advance more limited economic and social goals throughout the world, but to genuinely and powerfully commit itself to the maintenance of world peace and the provision of security.

In America especially during this time, there was a groundswell of individuals and movements in favor of peace proposals above the state level, many of whom thought the United Nations had not gone far enough. More specifically, their efforts were in reaction to the uncertainty and fear that the atomic age inspired. First, Joseph Baratta discusses the interests of nuclear scientists in such proposals:

[The] Advent of the atomic age seemed to many people, particularly Americans, to be a challenge to man that could only be met by the establishment of world federation. The political unification of humanity was no longer a distant ideal but a practical necessity if the world were to be saved. The scientists who had developed the atomic bomb led the political struggle to bring atomic energy under international control. "One World or None" became their slogan. Many of their early position papers looked to ultimate world government.[92]

Baratta adds that Milly Blake, a founder of World Federalists, USA "recalled that people who were inclined to federalism during the war had trusted Roosevelt to take care of the peace. They now became open federalists and were galvanized into action."[93]

Baratta then points out several pro-federalist individuals and groups whose ideas and plans became ever more ambitious and idealistic during the short period between 1945 and 1950. The mood of the times clearly catching him, Mortimer Adler, in *How to Think about War and Peace* (1944), "revised his estimate of when world government would come from 500 years to *five*."[94] The prominent New York lawyer and UN reform advocate, Grenville Clark, "hurried up his plans for a new world constitutional convention like that in San Francisco and assembled a private group of leading internationalists in October 1945 for a conference near his home in Dublin,

New Hampshire."[95] This conference "issued a ringing declaration in favor of a universal federal world government."[96]

Baratta further notes that "Many people who had been preparing for the Senate fight over the UN, such as those in Americans United for World Organization, demanded stronger policies."[97] This prompted Americans United to change their name to Americans United for World Government.[98] He then states that Clarence Streit's Atlantic Union group "began to break up, as members drifted off to stronger, universalist organizations like Americans United or World Federalists."[99] Finally, Cord Meyer, first president of the United World Federalists, writes that "paid-up membership" in the United World Federalists "exceeded fifty thousand" by the late 1940s.[100] He then explains, "At the high tide of our campaign in June 1949, sixty-four Democrats and twenty-seven Republicans in the House of Representatives joined in sponsoring a concurrent resolution which declared the following:

> It should be a fundamental objective of the foreign policy of the U.S. to support and strengthen the U.N. and to seek its development into a world federation open to all nations with defined and limited powers adequate to preserve peace and prevent aggression through the enactment, interpretations and enforcement of world law."[101]

Commenting on Kant's text in the year 1948 during this intense period of interest in peace proposals above the state level, it is no wonder the noted Harvard scholar and UN advocate C.J. Friedrich interpreted *Perpetual Peace* to be in favor of world federalism.

The Nexus

From the mid-nineteenth to the mid-twentieth century, there existed a growing interest, primarily within Anglo-American intellectual and political contexts, in permanent international organization as a potential peacemaker. Hopes that a centralized authority above the state might be a solution to the problem of war began with the great political conferences of the nineteenth century, gained strength during the Hague Conferences of 1899 and 1907, and finally became reality with the establishment of the League of Nations and the United Nations.[102]

It seems beyond doubt that interpretations of Kant's famous text from the mid-nineteenth to the mid-twentieth century are largely a function of this phenomenon. As demonstrated in chapter 1, discussion of international organization pervades the text of *Perpetual Peace*, especially in the controversial and most cited Second Definitive Article. Upward of eight interpreters of the text who comment on the League of Nations, either as supporters or simply as scholarly observers of the League's tenets, interpret Kant's proposals in *Perpetual Peace* as being in favor of international organization, then demonstrate the similarity between his proposals and those of the League of Nations (and one even with the United Nations). These interpreters, including Leonard Woolf, Jessie Wallace Hughan, D.P. Heatley, Nicholas Murray Butler, Mehan Stawall, C.J. Friedrich, R.B. Mowat, and A.C. Armstrong, all wrote during the historical period under consideration. As discussed earlier, the pro-federalists James Lorimer and M. Campbell Smith (and even to a degree, Leonard Woolf) all discuss *Perpetual Peace* during this period and interpret it (similar to their own plans) as favoring a peace proposal above the state level. Finally, considering the intellectual and political contexts of the time in Britain and the United States, it is not surprising that a treatise like *Perpetual Peace* takes on the interpretation that it does. Pattern One, which sees the text as favoring organizational proposals above the state level to prevent war, thus reflects the historical rise in hopes for peace through international organization.

The Decline of Hopes for Peace Through International Organization

During the past half century, there has been a general decline of hopes for peace through international organization. What was once believed by many intellectuals and political activists in the Anglo-American world to be a new and potentially effective way to prevent aggressive wars between states, lost attractiveness and credibility with the outbreak of the Cold War and the beginning of the East–West rivalry. Essentially, hopes that international organization might act as a focal point for the collective maintenance of peace and security were largely shattered from the mid-twentieth century onward. The majority of scholars referred to in the previous section (and a few others not yet discussed) support this position.

First, both Ceadel and Pinder, who recognize British enthusiasm for peace proposals above the state that existed from the late nineteenth to the mid-twentieth century, clearly demonstrate that this did not persist through the last half of the twentieth century. Ceadel initially asserts that from the mid-fifties onward, the British Peace Movement "for the most part abandoned supranationalism altogether."[103] With more detailed analysis, he concludes his essay with the following remarks:

The fifth phase, which began in the mid-1950s, saw the peace movement retreat from the supranationalism to which it had given priority for over forty years. It did so largely in response to the failures of the United Nations, the materialistic, bloc-like nature of the European Communities, and a fear that the issue of nuclear weapons could not be postponed until after the structural reform of the international system. This fifth phase persists today.[104]

Pinder also notes, "far from seeking federal solutions to postwar problems, the British suppressed the memory of their prewar federalist revival."[105] Writing in the early 1990s, Pinder further suggests that "contemporary Britain...does nothing to promote the application of the federal principles more widely in the world."[106]

Also writing during the early 1990s, Long notes that "plans for international government have since fallen out of favour, making Hobson's ideas [in support of federation] appear rather quaint."[107] As stated earlier, Suganami demonstrates that many thinkers set forth arguments based on the "domestic analogy" before World War I through to the creation of the League of Nations. However, he then acknowledges, "in the contemporary (post-World War II) study of international relations, we tend to encounter the critics of the domestic analogy rather more frequently than its adherents."[108] The notion that settled legal and political principles at the state level should be transferred to a level above the state to achieve world order is far less influential today than it once was.

Finally, Wilson writes that after World War II, "Britain's future was seen in terms of continuing to foster the 'special relationship' with America, or in terms of strengthening the bond of the Commonwealth," rather than in European unity or federation.[109] A revival of faith in British sovereignty followed the success of "standing alone" against Hitler.[110] The thought was "if the British state could triumph in wartime it could also triumph in building a prosperous and secure social order in peace time."[111] The result was that "there was no need to surrender sovereignty" to a higher European or international authority.[112] Instead, the opposite was actually true: "To fulfill national objectives, British power and influence needed to be preserved and, if at all possible, enhanced."[113] Wilson concludes the point with the statement that "This marked a significant departure from the assault on national sovereignty which characterized much British political thought between 1938 and 1944."[114]

A similar pattern of thinking was emerging in the United States. Writing in the early 1950s and obviously conscious of the emerging bipolar rivalry between the United States and the Soviet Union, Mangone dismally concludes that only "Five years after the high hopes of San Francisco, the United Nations had been dragged down by the rankling division of the world into two ideologies and two armed camps."[115] The year 1950 marked the North Korean invasion of South Korea. To the American-based United World Federalists movement, flourishing only a few years before, this was the most serious blow to hopes for peace through international organization. Clearly, the North Korean invasion was the key world event, which triggered the end of these hopes for those involved with the movement. Baratta writes:

> The Korean War all but destroyed the world federalist movement. The North Korean invasion was so obviously a case of communist aggression that federalists were hard pressed to maintain that anarchy was the cause of wars. McCarthyism and slurs on federalists' loyalties overwhelmed ordinary members' sense of kinship with all humanity.[116]

Thereafter, Baratta notes, "A mass exodus began from the movement."[117] Besides membership losses, this exodus occurred in the following ways. First, the United World Federalists eliminated their field program and replaced it with a "top-level" approach in 1951.[118] During the same period, the student division all but disappeared.[119] Further, two important publications supporting their efforts were terminated. *Common Cause*, published by the Chicago Committee to Frame a World Constitution, ceased publication when its prominent member Robert M. Hutchins left the University of Chicago.[120] *World Government News* failed the following year because of declining support.[121] Most telling of all, Cord Meyer, who became first president of the United World Federalists during the heyday of its movement in the late 1940s, vacated his position and joined the CIA as an operations officer in the clandestine service in 1951—a strikingly short span of years to go from one extreme to the other and clear evidence that whatever hopes he had maintained in "international organization as peacemaker" were completely dashed by the early 1950s.[122] Baratta notes that Meyer's case was "extreme... but not atypical" considering the times.[123] "It was time," Baratta explains, "to come to the aid of one's country" since "To work for world federation when Russia and America seemed to be locked in a death grip was truly to ignore reality."[124]

Hopes that the establishment of a centralized authority above the state might prevent conflict were clearly beginning to diminish as the 1950s were underway. The idealistic advocates for a world federation more potent than the existing United Nations body were clearly disillusioned. Yet even those more practical and willing to work within the current system were not particularly sanguine about its prospects. For most, the reality of the limited ability of the United Nations to achieve its primary goal of maintaining world peace and security in the face of Cold War rivalry had set in. Writing only a few years later in 1954, Mangone captures the mood of the times with the following remarks: "the UN struggled for eight years, carrying on its mission despite the bitter dregs left by the Second World War, the deep cleavages between the views of the Soviet Union and those of the United States, and the ever-ready cynicism of international politics."[125]

Adam Roberts and Benedict Kingsbury lay initial responsibility for UN failure to preserve the peace on the Security Council veto system and unanimity provision. The maintenance of international peace and security is the primary responsibility of the Security Council. The Five Permanent Members (China, France, Russia, the United Kingdom, and the United States) dominate the proceedings and each retains the power to veto any draft resolution on matters of substance.[126]

Further, Roberts and Kingsbury note that "The veto system privileges a group of five states in a way that is bound to be contentious; and it is widely perceived as having held the UN back from fulfilling its functions in the Cold War years."[127] Claude notes that, with the veto privilege, there was always the "potentiality that the collegium of the powerful might be unable to act at all, either to dominate the world or to save it."[128] Adding support to these claims, Meyer writes in his autobiography, "To me, this veto power was incontrovertible evidence that the major nations intended to retain their complete sovereign independence within the new structure."[129] Meyer goes on to say that "Indeed, in certain respects, the new structure seemed to me even more impotent than the old League of Nations, whose defects Professor Spykman at Yale used to describe with mordant wit."[130]

Roberts and Kingsbury then offer four examples of conflicts that occurred over the course of the period that reveals Pattern Two, Phase One, where the existence of the veto prevented the United Nations from fulfilling its primary role. Existence of the veto meant the Security Council contributed little to the resolution of armed conflicts in which its permanent members were directly entangled—for example, in Hungary (1956), the Suez (1956), Vietnam (1946–1975) and the Sino-Vietnamese War (1979).[131] In the case of the first two conflicts, Michael Howard demonstrates with some historical detail the negative impact of the Security Council veto and the accompanying futility of attempts by General Assembly resolutions to compensate for the divisiveness that resulted from the use of the veto as a Great Power instrument, especially when the United States and the Soviet Union were involved.

Regarding the Suez crisis, France and Britain vetoed any Security Council action over their 1956 attack on Egypt. Thereafter, an immediate cease-fire in addition to the withdrawal of forces from the Suez Canal was called for by the General Assembly.[132] France and Britain then "acquiesced," according to Howard, "less out of any respect for or fear of the united strength of the United Nations than because of the effective economic muscle of the United States."[133] Howard seems to acknowledge that in cases of veto use by lesser powers such as Britain and France, the "persuasive" ability of the General Assembly resolution might, on occasion, be successful at overcoming the veto's usual effectiveness at obstruction. Still, by his quote, it is obvious that he sees its "supposed" accomplishment here as little more than coincidence.

More importantly, when either of the two superpowers was directly involved, he demonstrates the clear weakness of the United Nations system to deal with the conflict at hand. In the case of the Soviet invasion of Hungary in 1956, he notes, "a similar and nearly simultaneous resolution by the General Assembly calling upon the Soviet Union to withdraw its forces from Hungary was ignored, and no action followed."[134] He further claims that "This was not simply because France and Britain were 'persuadable' in a way that the Soviet Union was not." Instead, "It was because in the case of the Soviet Union the UN did not dare to do more than try to persuade, and the Russians knew it."[135]

Howard is convinced that after these two incidents in 1956, the future ahead for the United Nations in its attempts at fulfilling its primary role of maintaining peace and security would be more or less predictable, especially when a conflict erupted in which either of the two superpowers had national interests at stake. He explains:

The lessons of 1956 were clear. First, the UN could take action against "aggression" only if the two great powers were agreed, or if one of them was indifferent; second, there were only two powers who counted. So, for many years, it remained. Whatever resolutions might be passed in the General Assembly, the UN was no more likely to take action against the Soviet Union over, say, Afghanistan than it was against the United States over Nicaragua. Whatever measure of collective security might be created, the superpowers could effectively defy them, and any state enjoying the vigorous support of either could probably do the same.[136]

Even as early as 1956, emerging lack of faith in the United Nations as an effective force for peace was evident. Roberts's and Kingsbury's first passage quoted above takes UN inaction through 1979. Howard continues this line of argument with further evidence of UN intransigence. Here, he notes several more instances of UN inaction during the 1970s and 1980s: "While the UN General Assembly spent countless hours of time and reams of paper discussing grandiose projects for disarmament, no action was taken over such instances of inter-state aggression as Iraq's assault on Iran in 1980, Israel's invasion of Lebanon in 1982, or Indonesia's annexation of East Timor in 1975."[137]

However disillusioned people were with the prospects for peace through international organization from the 1950s through the 1980s, there appeared to be a renewed sense of hope that as the Cold War ended, the United Nations might finally be in a position to achieve what it set out to in 1945. Paul F. Diehl notes, "The prospects for expanding the roles, functions, and powers of international organizations in global governance seemed bright at the beginning of the 1990s."[138] Indeed, even Howard acknowledges effective UN action during the Gulf War. Still, his following comments suggest the unique circumstances of the period and more cynical motives behind Security Council collaboration than enthusiastic agreement on halting aggression. He states:

Only in 1990, confronted with the blatant aggression of Iraq against Kuwait, did the UN take any action, and the circumstances were exceptional. The interests of all major Western powers were involved; the Soviet Union and the People's Republic of China were virtual pensioners of the United States; the great majority of Middle Eastern states were alarmed at the prospect of Saddam Hussein so suddenly and brutally extending his power. For the first time the UN acted as its founders had intended. It is an encouraging precedent, but we would be deceiving ourselves if we thought that such an exceptional combination of circumstances was likely often to recur.[139]

The "encouraging precedent" that Howard believes was established by the Gulf War in the early 1990s was shortlived. According to Diehl, "a series of events underscored the problems and limitations of international organizations as they approached the twenty-first century."[140] Importantly, he explains, "The enhanced ability of the Security Council to authorize new peacekeeping missions did not necessarily translate into greater effectiveness in halting armed conflict or promoting conflict resolution."[141] He then offers examples of conflicts during the 1990s in which the UN either acted and failed or failed to act. He notes, "The UN was largely ineffective in stopping the fighting in Bosnia, could not produce a political settlement in

Somalia, and was too slow to prevent genocide in Rwanda."[142] Writing in the early to middle 1990s, Brian Urquhart would clearly concur with Diehl's 1997 remarks. Urquhart states that "The credibility of the UN is being tested and found wanting in former Yugoslavia, as it was in Angola after the 1992 election. It may be seriously damaged in Cambodia and Somalia."[143] Focusing as well on the Security Council, he asserts that "Many of the Security Council's decisions on conflict resolution at present lack either the legal and political strength to make them respected, or the means to implement them in an effective way."[144] What appeared to be an auspicious time for UN engagement and potential success at deterring conflict immediately following the Cold War never materialized. Urquhart concludes, "After a brief post-Cold War honeymoon, the UN is once again suffering from the inability to enforce its decisions in critical situations, this time without the excuse of the obstacles created by the Cold War."[145]

The above scholars commenting on the United Nations conclude that it has generally failed to carry out its primary objective: the collective maintenance of international peace and security. Several of these same scholars recognize its accomplishments in other areas and I do not argue that the United Nations has not made significant contributions in the economic and social realm or with regard to human rights (or that international organizations, in general, have not proliferated or have not been influential during the twentieth century).[146] However, over the course of the second half of the twentieth century, the period during which Pattern Two is indeed revealed, the history of the UN has been such that faith in permanent international organization as a way to peace and security has clearly subsided. Howard reminds us that the United Nations "has not succeeded in its primary task. It has not created a new world order in which every state derives its security from the collective strength of the whole. It has been able only to reflect the disorders, fears, and rivalries of the world."[147] Peter Wilenski notes that "Through the worst years of the Cold War the UN was no more than a bit player in international peace and security issues: at its worst a propaganda forum, at its best playing a supporting role in the provision of peacekeeping forces once regional hostilities had ceased."[148] He explains that the end result is that "it did not play the role that its founders had anticipated."[149] Finally, writing in the mid-1980s, F.S. Northedge echoes the declining hope in "international organization as peacemaker" with his pronouncement that the failure of the United Nations "raises profound questions about the collective organization of peace through international organization."[150] While international organization continues to thrive, lack of faith in its potential and ability to maintain international peace and security has persisted from the mid-twentieth century to today. The great hope of the Anglo-American world that a permanent international authority might bring perpetual peace no longer inspires as it once did.

The Nexus

The demonstrated phenomenon of ever-declining faith in peace proposals above the state level during the second half of the twentieth century was reflected in interpretations of Kant's *Perpetual Peace* completed during this period. This important treatise, for so long understood as favoring some form of peace proposal above the state, began to be viewed in an entirely different light from the mid-twentieth century onward. Beginning in the 1950s and 1960s, then fully established by the 1980s and 1990s, a second pattern unambiguously replaced the first. Thorough interpretations of the text completed by Hinsley, Waltz, and Gallie (among others) began to change the way *Perpetual Peace* was understood in academic International Relations by the 1960s and 1970s.

Coupling the disappointing record of the League with ever-increasing acknowledgment of the UN's incompetence in the midst of intense bipolar rivalry, there existed for the first time in a long while little intellectual or political enthusiasm for world government, international federation, or international organization as modes of a permanent authority above the state that would maintain peace and security. This coincided with the theoretical reorientation of the discipline of International Relations after 1945. Chris Brown notes, "in the years after 1945, realism became the dominant theory of IR."[151] He further asserts, "Diplomats (and now academics) held views that were realist as the discipline of IR expanded on broadly realist lines."[152] Idealism, and the conventional identification of it with peace proposals above the state level, was replaced by realism's focus on state-centered approaches to peace and security from the 1950s through the 1970s. Reflecting the historical and academic spirit of this period and its alternative approaches to peace and security, Pattern Two, Phase One interpreters analyzed the same translated treatise as their Pattern One predecessors, yet saw the text as favoring the preservation of state sovereignty, rather than its limitation, as the path to peace.

Interpretations stating that Kant's text favored peace proposals "at the state level" as opposed to "above the state level" proliferated thereafter. With ever greater focus on text outside the Second Definitive Article, these interpreters drew from the Preliminary Articles, the Third Definitive Article, and the First Supplement and arrived at a state-centric reading of the full text.

These Pattern Two, Phase One interpreters understood Kant's text to suggest that, ultimately, peace between sovereign states would be guaranteed not by a centralized authority above them, but by the external forces of nature and history working upon and through them.

By the early 1980s, with the state-centric reading already predominant, new emphasis on the practical reason for adopting the First Definitive Article of Kant's text in Doyle's most influential interpretation lead to the development of a second phase of Pattern Two. Still viewing the text as setting forth a peace proposal at the state level, Doyle's interpretation fueled a transformation in understanding exactly *how* Kant thought peace would be achieved between independent states. Simply stated, Doyle viewed *Perpetual Peace* as the textual foundation for the idea of the liberal peace. Since Doyle's well-known empirical study on the liberal peace was published, advanced studies on the idea have proliferated. Kant's *Perpetual Peace* has not been the same since.

Inspired primarily by Doyle's study in the mid-1980s, the liberal peace phenomenon reached its peak in the triumphant years for liberal democracy immediately following the Cold War. The groundswell of interest, especially in America, in the notion that peace between states could be achieved at the state level through the adoption of representative government became extremely influential. Many fervently argued in favor of the proposition while others saw it as historically shallow propaganda. Whether for or against, interpreters looking at *Perpetual Peace* have been affected by the outpouring of liberal peace literature over the last two decades of the twentieth century. The liberal peace phenomenon has clearly influenced the development of a new phase of interpretation. This new interpretive phase, which gathered strength in substance and in numbers through the 1990s, suggested that Kant's most important words were written in the First Definitive Article. These words read that peace between sovereign states would emerge so long as they adopted republican constitutions.

Therefore, the two phases of Pattern Two, with their outright rejection of earlier interpreters' positions that the text favored peace proposals above the state level, became a function of the historical decline in hopes for peace through international federation or world government. Importantly, there was little chance that Pattern One could be sustained with any real credibility or legitimacy considering the international situation post-1950. It is apparent that during the latter half of the twentieth century, with declining faith in international organization as the prescription for peace, hopes for peace shifted to a focus on more state-centered approaches.

Whether adopting the general statist interpretation of Phase One or the more specific liberal peace interpretation of Phase Two, Pattern Two interpreters' view that a state-centric approach to peace was all that Kant envisioned clearly reflected this shift. In essence, the shift in patterns became a function of the shift in hopes.

CHAPTER 9

From the Turmoil of International Anarchy to the Calm of the Liberal Peace

Introduction

Complementing the principal explanation for patterns developed in chapter 8 is a subsidiary explanation that reflects on the steady increase in the number of liberal states in the western hemisphere over the past one hundred and fifty-five years and the affect of this evolving historico-political phenomenon on the minds of interpreters at work during this time period and in this geographical space.

In developing this explanation, I return first to Doyle's 1983 article and discuss his initial conclusions that the drift toward liberal, representative governments over the past two centuries is indeed an empirical fact. Second, while Doyle's belief in the liberal peace that follows from this is admittedly controversial, I argue that it is difficult to disregard the relatively tranquil relationships that have existed between the majority of likeminded liberal states over the past two centuries. Finally, keeping Doyle's arguments in mind, I posit a relationship between the historical ascendancy of the liberal state and interpretation of Kant's *Perpetual Peace*. As part of this final argument, I demonstrate the interplay between this unfolding theme and the explanation offered in chapter 8.

Doyle and the Historical Drift Toward an Ever-Increasing Number of Liberal States

There has been no shortage of friendly colloquy or intense debate on the issue of the liberal peace over the past two decades since it was first widely considered in Doyle's 1983 article "Kant, Liberal Legacies, and Foreign Affairs." Arguments for and against it are passionately held and offered with genuine credibility by either side.[1] Some scholars refer to the liberal peace proposition as "one of the strongest nontrivial or non-tautological generalizations that can be made about international relations"[2] or, even more boldly, as "the closest thing we have to an empirical law in international relations."[3]

There are also those who, as Chris Brown states, "deal harshly with arguments that are based on the proposition that foreign policy behaviour can be related to the domestic structure of states."[4] Brown mentions both Kenneth Waltz's and J.D. Singer's works as representative of this critique. Waltz views the liberal peace argument as narrowly "second image" in *Man, the State and War* and "reductionist" in *Theory of International Politics*.[5] Singer's "Correlates of War" Project is also critical of the liberal peace idea in that it "suggests that involvement in war is a function of position within the international system—broadly, the more important the state, the more wars it has been involved in."[6]

Finally, there are those whose views lie somewhere in between. For example, Williams and Booth are persuaded that there may be a "connection between peace and republican constitutions" but still remark that "the sample is small and the historical conditions advantageous."[7] While disagreements over this controversial proposition persist, one important particular on which most scholars agree, regardless of the position they take on the liberal peace idea, is the following: over the past two centuries, there has been a gradual increase in the number of liberal states across the world.

As stated above, the authoritative study on this topic is Doyle's 1983 article. Within it, Doyle devotes four pages to a detailed table, which demonstrates the growth in the number of what he calls "liberal regimes" over the past two centuries.[8] According to Doyle, the "essential four institutions" that determine whether or not a country is a "liberal regime" are the following: "market and private property economies; polities that are externally sovereign; citizens who possess juridical rights; and 'republican,' representative, government with the latter requiring that the legislative branch have an effective role in public policy and be formally and competitively, either potentially or actually, elected."[9]

Based on this definition, the table he creates illustrates that by the end of the eighteenth century there were only three liberal regimes.[10] From 1800 to 1850, the number increased to eight.[11] From 1850 to 1900, the number increased to thirteen.[12] From 1900 to 1945, the number increased to twenty-nine.[13] And from 1945 to the publication of the article in 1983 the number of liberal regimes increased to forty-nine.[14]

In a separate study, Freedom House, which has monitored the growth of political and civil liberties in countries throughout the world for the past several decades, published in the year 2000 its end-of-the-century *Freedom in the World* survey.[15] On its "Map of Freedom," it placed the number of electoral democracies in 1989 at sixty-nine, the number of electoral democracies in 1994 at one hundred and eight, and the number of electoral democracies in 2000 at one hundred and twenty.[16] The Survey concludes, "In a very real sense, the twentieth century has become the 'Democratic Century.' "[17] Though the methodology in the form of a "Political Rights Checklist" used by Freedom House to determine whether or not a particular state is an electoral democracy is more extensive and detailed than that set out by Doyle above, there is general agreement between the two surveys that the essential requirement is representative government.[18]

These two publications usefully demonstrate the increase in the number of liberal states over the time period of this interpretive history of Kant's *Perpetual Peace*. After a closer look at Doyle's survey, it also appears that the growth in the number of liberal states occurred, generally speaking, in a west to east direction. The three liberal states Doyle includes up to the end of the eighteenth century are the Swiss Cantons, the French Republic from 1790 to 1795, and the United States from 1776 onward.[19] These were the only three liberal regimes in place when Kant made his visionary proposition in 1795 that a gradual increase in states of this kind over a long period would ultimately bring peace between them. Kant's statement in the Second Definitive Article of *Perpetual Peace* is particularly telling. He remarks:

For if by good fortune one powerful and enlightened nation can form a republic (which is by its nature inclined to seek perpetual peace), this will provide a focal point for federal association among other states. These will join up with the first one, thus securing the freedom of each state in accordance with the idea of international right, and the whole will gradually spread further and further by a series of alliances of this kind.[20]

It is not certain whether Kant was referring to the United States or the new French Republic when he made this remark. He was more familiar and excited about the new ideas boiling over in France. Still, he did know about the ideals of the revolutionary movement in the United States. Either way, he predicted a slow and gradual spread of liberal ideas and institutions from nascent and uniquely liberal regimes like the United States and France to the rest of Europe and beyond. Doyle's study appears to confirm Kant's prediction.

Kant also predicted (or at least hoped) that more and more states would, over time, form an "association" with the "one powerful and enlightened republican nation" to create a great and ever-expanding liberal alliance that would "secure the freedom of each state in accordance with international right."[21] As Kant only expected liberal regimes to become part of this new association of states, an alliance possibly similar to the North Atlantic Treaty Organization (NATO) comes to mind when one thinks of a twentieth-century manifestation of Kant's original idea from this section of the text of *Perpetual Peace*.

Within this Kantian liberal alliance, peace not only exists within liberal states because of the establishment of civil society, representative government, and the rule of law, but between liberal states as well. In his study, Doyle boldly states his now rather famous thesis that *"Even though liberal states have become involved in numerous wars with non-liberal states, constitutionally secure liberal states have yet to engage in war with one another."*[22] He further asserts, "No one should argue that such wars are impossible; but preliminary evidence does appear to indicate that there exists a significant predisposition against warfare between liberal states."[23] To prove this, he takes from Melvin Small and J. David Singer's 1982 book, *Resort to Arms*, an extensive table that lists the wars occurring between 1816 and 1980. Of the five hundred and seventy-five wars Small and Singer list, Doyle indicates he is only interested in international wars for the purposes of his argument. As such, in his table, Doyle uses a partial, chronological list of these wars, excluding civil wars and covert interventions.[24] His simple point is that of the one hundred and eighteen international wars in his list that have been fought since 1816, not one has been between two liberal regimes.[25]

Importantly, he does not argue that these liberal regimes have always been peaceful. In fact, they have been as belligerent with nonliberal states as nonliberal states have been with each other. World Wars I and II come quickly to mind as fair examples of this. He only wishes to make the following two points: first, that liberal regimes have generally been peaceful with other liberal regimes over the past two centuries and second (by implication from the list of international wars between mostly nonliberal states he offers) that nonliberal states have been much more likely through the past two centuries to go to war with each other.

Finally, in what looks like anticipation on the part of Doyle of a possible attack by balance-of-power theorists, he makes the important claim that "A liberal zone of peace, a pacific union, has been maintained and has expanded despite numerous particular conflicts of economic and strategic interest."[26] He employs the example of the American Civil War. In it, as he explains, "the commercial linkages between the Lancashire cotton economy and the American South and the sentimental links between the British Aristocracy and the Southern plantocracy (together with numerous disputes over the rights of British shipping against the Northern blockade) brought Great Britain and the Northern states to the brink of war, but they never passed that brink."[27]

Doyle also discusses relations between France and Britain during the twentieth century. He explains, "Despite their colonial rivalries, liberal France and Britain formed an entente before World War I against illiberal Germany (whose foreign relations were controlled by the Kaiser and the Army)."[28] Also, he focuses on Italy's relationship to the Triple Alliance. He states, "During 1914–15 Italy, the liberal member of the Triple alliance with illiberal Germany and Austria, chose not to fulfill its obligations under the Triple Alliance to either support its allies or remain neutral."[29] According to Doyle, liberal Italy "joined the alliance with France and Britain that would prevent it from having to fight other liberal states, and declared war on Austria and Germany, its former allies."[30] Finally, Doyle gives the example of the United States which, "despite generations of Anglo-American tension and British restrictions on American trade, leaned toward Britain and France from 1914 to 1917."[31]

The lessons Doyle takes from his study are several. First, "Statistically, war between any two states (in any single year or other short period of time) is a low probability event."[32] Second, "War between any two adjacent states, considered over a long period of time, may be somewhat more probable."[33] In relation to these two claims, Doyle's point is that "The apparent absence of war among the more clearly liberal states, whether adjacent or not, for almost two hundred years thus has some significance."[34] He seems even more impressed with the fact that liberal regimes, when confronted with world war, always have allied together. To this he says "when states are forced to decide, by the pressure of an impinging world war, on which side of a world contest they will fight, liberal states wind up all on the same side, despite the real complexity of the historical, economic and political factors that affect their foreign policies."[35] I believe Doyle's final comment on this topic finds him at his most convincing. He states:

[H]istorically, we should recall that medieval and early modern Europe were the warring cockpits of states, wherein France and England and the

Low Countries engaged in near constant strife. Then in the late eighteenth century there began to emerge liberal regimes. At first hesitant and confused, and later clear and confident as liberal regimes gained deeper domestic foundations and longer international experience, a pacific union of these liberal states became established.[36]

Doyle's proposition (and the great number of articles it has spawned) has become an increasingly controversial topic over the past two decades in Political Science and International Relations. One noted twentieth-century political philosopher certainly thinks there is merit to it. John Rawls writes in his most recent book *The Law of Peoples* that "The historical record seems to suggest that stability for the right reasons would be satisfied in a society of reasonably just constitutional democracies."[37] He then gives credit to Doyle for discovering this by his remark that "Though liberal democratic societies have often engaged in war against nondemocratic states, since 1800 firmly established liberal societies have not fought one another."[38]

Rawls then goes through a long list of what he calls the "more famous wars of history" and notes that none of them were between "settled liberal democratic peoples."[39] Like Russett and Levy above, Rawls remarks, "The absence of war between major established democracies is as close as anything we know to a simple empirical regularity in relations among societies."[40] Yet even with his considerable support for Doyle's proposition, Rawls still notes historical incidents of liberal states engaging in "covert operations" against "weaker countries."[41] In these instances, Rawls says such actions occurred "without the knowledge or criticism of the public."[42]

In this context and aware of these examples, Rawls supplements his remarks with the statement that "established constitutional democracy" is an "ideal" of which even liberal states sometimes fall short. Only when these states "approach that ideal" will "armed conflict between democratic peoples . . . tend to disappear . . . and they will engage in war only as allies in self-defense against outlaw states."[43] Rawls ends his section entitled "Democratic Peace Seen in History" with the following comment: "I believe this hypothesis [the 'democratic peace' as he calls it] is correct and think it underwrites the Law of Peoples as a realistic utopia."[44]

There are good arguments both for and against the existence of the liberal peace and I do not intend to come out strongly in favor of, or opposed to, Doyle's original claim. As has been shown, a great political philosopher like Rawls certainly sees merit in it along with noted political scientists whose numerous empirical studies have lent it further credibility. On the other hand, there are those who remain skeptical of it, for example, Waltz, Singer, and Williams and Booth, or, even if they are persuaded by the apparent lack of war between liberal states, offer alternative explanations that generally dismiss the theory that the liberal peace is chiefly determined by the domestic political structure of sovereign states.

Above, I have attempted to explore the liberal peace proposition and, based on the arguments and evidence emphasized, it should be clear that I am reasonably sympathetic to it. Concerning Doyle's original claim, however, I make the following more modest assertion: well-established liberal states are less likely to be as belligerent with each other as nonliberal states are in their relations with each other. Another way of stating it is that authoritarian states are as aggressive with other authoritarian states as they are with liberal states. However, long-standing liberal states, though certainly aggressive with authoritarian states, are less likely to be aggressive with other liberal states. In sum, the pacific union of liberal states, gradually spreading from west to east, in fits and starts, and through many liberal gains and losses over the past two centuries, is a relatively recent though seemingly genuine historico-political phenomenon of continuing importance. Though debates on the liberal peace may have died down somewhat recently, discussion of the claim and its intellectual foundation should not become a fading scholarly memory of a few giddy liberals writing in the immediate aftermath of the Cold War.

The Historical Ascendancy of the Liberal State and the Establishment of a Liberal Peace: What does It All Mean?

What does all this mean for writers who interpret a rather ambiguous, perhaps confusing, text like *Perpetual Peace* within a particular geographical, historical, and political context? My argument is that the phenomenon of an ever-growing pacific alliance of sovereign liberal states, in development generally from the time of publication of *Perpetual Peace*, has conditioned the outlook of interpreters considering Kant's work.

First, interpreters working from the middle to late nineteenth century through the early twentieth century (who, according to my research, were primarily British and American) were conscious of and realistically confronted with the historical fact that there existed a large number of nonliberal states. The phrase I used to describe the international situation during this period is the "turmoil of international anarchy." Essentially, the interpreters were aware of the historically belligerent tendencies of nonliberal states and the clear absence of any form of centralized authority above them to control the anarchical situation in international relations present between them.[45] Cognizant of these significant factors, they reasoned that a remedy for the aggressive tendencies of numerous nonliberal states was a permanent authority above them, which would act as a restraint on their sovereignty, specifically their right to make war. With this in mind, they read Kant's text as favoring a solution to the problem of war above the state level. Reading the text of the Second Definitive Article, the interpreter took its rather complex language and viewed it in a way that reflected the general historical and political trend.

More to the point, the Pattern One, Phase One interpretation, outlined in chapter 1, most certainly focuses on one particular passage. This passage states:

> There is only one rational way in which states coexisting with other states can emerge from the lawless condition of pure warfare. Just like individual men, they must renounce their savage and lawless freedom, adapt themselves to public coercive laws, and thus form an international state (*civitas gentium*).[46]

Intellectually encountering this selection from the text when confronted with a large number of illiberal regimes that had proven themselves to be violent toward each other for centuries, influenced the nineteenth- and early-twentieth-century interpreter to conclude that the text offered a way out of this ancient predicament through the formation of a permanent and centralized authority above the collection of separate states.

As has been demonstrated in chapter 3, this line of interpretation changed ever so slightly after World War I. Commentators, many of them proponents of the League of Nations, moved away from a focus on the Pattern One, Phase One selection quoted earlier and began to latch their interpretations to the alternative passage immediately following it. This primary passage (among several others they concentrate on) explains that there should be "a negative substitute [in place of the international state] of an enduring and gradually expanding federation likely to prevent war."[47] This "negative substitute" in the form of a federation seemed to them the better option (or at least the option they thought the text most likely embraced). The interpretive thrust that developed was primarily couched in terms of, as one Pattern One, Phase Two interpreter stated, an authority above the state which required " 'the surrender of a portion of power in return for participation in a wider, richer, and more secure life.' "[48]

Historically speaking, the liberal alliance prevailed against illiberal Germany and Austria and it looked as if a new peace might reign with the founding of the League of Nations. Such an international institution offered, as Mowat says, "a reasonable compromise between the sacrifice of independence on the part of constituent States, on the one hand, and the wielding of universal despotic dominion on the other."[49] Further, the pacific union of liberal states gradually expanded after 1919. From 1900 to 1945, sixteen countries were added to the list of liberal regimes as the total number went from thirteen at the end of the nineteenth century to twenty-nine by 1945.[50] Most of these new additions occurred after World War I. It is clear that the Anglo-American liberal alliance, which also included France, Belgium, the Netherlands, and Denmark as its liberal fringe on the continent, was gradually beginning to solidify itself.

Importantly, the collection of liberal regimes in existence during the interwar period was stronger and with more members than anytime in history. Still, their otherwise peaceful alliance remained relatively loose, under threat, and was a much weaker bond than that which formed after World War II. Germany and Austria, after a brief period of liberalism, returned to illiberalism in 1932 and 1934, respectively, and did more than just threaten the liberal world thereafter.[51] Accordingly, the interpretation of *Perpetual Peace* during the interwar period continued to acknowledge that the text called for peace proposals above the state level, though proposals not as radical as those called for in times before World War I. The interpreter was just becoming aware of the potential of a pacific alliance of liberal states in the Western world, though certainly not aware of it as a secure, well-entrenched idea for a lasting peace just yet.

Recognition of a pacific union of sovereign liberal states swept deeper into the consciousness of the interpreter when the liberal alliance further solidified itself during and after World War II. It was further entrenched by the founding of NATO in 1949. This firm bloc of predominantly liberal states, fully conscious of itself, was aware of the peaceful tendencies between its member states, yet in the defensive position of "cold" war with nonliberal states to its east. This, coupled with the emerging lack of faith in international organization as a path to peace, influenced the decision of the interpreter to introduce a more state-centric view of the text from the 1950s onward.

The key point is that at this stage in history there was recognition by those within the liberal alliance that one certainty in an otherwise uncertain geopolitical world was the existence of peace between liberal states that willingly allied in defense of their liberal institutions and principles. As such, the focus of interpreters during this period shifted to an emphasis on Kantian phrases like the following: "This federation does not aim to acquire any power like that of a state, but merely to preserve and secure the *freedom* of each state in itself along with that of the other confederated states, although this does not mean that they need to submit to public laws and to a coercive power which enforces them, as do men in a state of nature."[52]

Further, the following selection provided the interpreter with a wider array of support for his or her more statist reading of the text of *Perpetual Peace*:

> It can be shown that this idea of *federalism*, extending gradually to encompass all states and thus leading to perpetual peace, is practicable and has objective reality. For if by good fortune one powerful and enlightened nation can form a republic (which is by its nature inclined to seek perpetual peace), this will provide a focal point for federal association among other states. These will join up with the first one, thus securing the freedom of each state in accordance with the idea of international right, and the whole will gradually spread further and further by a series of alliances of this kind.[53]

Focusing on language from this excerpt like "association among states," "alliance (of states)" and the phrase "securing the freedom of each state," Pattern Two, Phase One interpretation began to sense a genuine commitment to the preservation of state sovereignty on the part of the text in the Second Definitive Article.[54] Such language conveyed the notion of an ultimate separateness of states so pivotal to this new pattern's identity. Language like "association of states" or an "alliance (of states)" directed interpretation away from the institutional character of the proposed international authority prevalent in both phases of Pattern One interpretation toward a loosely bound collection of independent liberal states. This is not even to mention Pattern Two, Phase One's new emphasis (discussed in detail in chapters 1 and 4) on the Preliminary Articles, Third Definitive Article, and First Supplement as further evidence of their belief that *Perpetual Peace* stood for the preservation of state sovereignty and the notion that the forces of history and nature acting upon and through independent states would guarantee peace between them in a distant future.

Finally, there was a shift in interpretation that occurred after Doyle's 1983 article, and was firmly established once into the 1990s. Discussed already in chapters 1, 5, 6, and 7, it need only be repeated that the statist view of the text originating in interpretations forming Pattern Two, Phase One, was further supplemented by a new emphasis on the practical reason for adopting the First Definitive Article during this period. These contemporary commentators began to view the most important part of the text to be Kant's suggestion that the representative nature of liberal states decreased the likelihood that such regimes would choose to go to war with each other. They contrasted this unique idea with the implicit claim that leaders of unrepresentative, authoritarian regimes would in fact be much more likely to engage in war with both nonliberal and liberal regimes alike. As such, the interpreters from the mid-1980s through the 1990s saw an ever-expanding liberal alliance of sovereign states as the text's key prescription for peace. During this period of unprecedented liberal optimism, this explanation for such an interpretation is very plausible.

In their remarks on the growing importance of Kant's thinking to International Relations, Williams and Booth acknowledged the following in 1996: "A further state [in this direction of growing recognition for Kant] was reached with the liberal triumphalism at the end of the 1980s, with the collapse of the Soviet Union and the 'victory' of Western democracy and capitalism."[55] It was said, "World politics in important respects seemed to be moving in a 'Kantian' direction."[56] But, as this book hopefully demonstrates, the "Kantian" direction for these and the majority of other interpreters during this period was far different than that espoused by interpreters writing on the same text and similar set of issues a century earlier.

With the alliance of liberal, independent states victorious (and victorious for the "final" time in one influential writer's eyes), the former set of interpreters, witnessing this phenomenon, began to read *Perpetual Peace* as a text in favor of peace proposals at the state level.[57] "At the state level" because they read the text in terms of the very evident "calm of liberal peace" firmly existing between sovereign, liberal states through the 1990s. In such a situation, the more radical "above the state" remedies called for to effectively control the more aggressive tendencies of nonliberal states were no longer necessary in a world determined by an ever-expanding, peaceful alliance of liberal states. The turmoil of international anarchy was overcome by the calm of the liberal peace and the interpretation of Kant's *Perpetual Peace* reflected this historical theme.

Conclusion: The Relationship Between the Principal and Subsidiary Explanations

There is a simple and clear connection between the principal explanation presented in chapter 8 and the subsidiary explanation offered here. First, hopes for peace through international organization, so evident from the mid-nineteenth century to the mid-twentieth century, were also driven by the need to overcome the potentially aggressive ways of predominantly nonliberal states existing in an anarchic international system. Pattern One is a clear function of this.

As demonstrated however, the emergence of an intense and lengthy bipolar rivalry that clearly prevented the United Nations from fulfilling its primary role of maintaining international peace and security meant that hopes for peace through international organization declined from the mid-twentieth century onward. This corresponded, however, with a steady increase in the number of liberal states in the Western world, especially over the course of the second half of the twentieth century, and manifested itself in the establishment of a more formidable liberal alliance. This liberal alliance was the inspiration for the idea of the liberal peace and empirical evidence followed which convincingly suggested that liberal states were far more peaceful in their relations with other liberal states than nonliberal states were with themselves.

International anarchy evident between nonliberal states, the only solution to which was establishment of a permanent, centralized authority above them, was overcome by the historical ascendancy of the liberal state in the West. Further acknowledgment of the liberal peace phenomenon persuasively maintained that peace between liberal states could be achieved without the need of a strong federation or international state. As the second half of the twentieth century unfolded (and especially from the 1980s through the "liberal triumphalism" of the 1990s), ever-decreasing faith in peace proposals above the state level was replaced by a newfound enthusiasm for peace proposals at the state level. Recognition of these significant factors led to the predominance of Pattern Two—a predominance that still exists today.

Epilogue

Within the discipline of International Relations, Kant's *Perpetual Peace* has established itself as a foundational text. The influential treatise is as complex and multifaceted in its proposals as any he composed on the subject. A substantial interpretive history of it needed to be written and it is hoped that this book has contributed to that effort. Yet the effort goes on. It will certainly be of interest to see how *Perpetual Peace* is understood through the next century. As it is translated into more and more languages, views of the text from interpretations written in different tongues will arise and gain influence. An even broader interpretive history may then be in order.

Further, it might also prove fruitful to complete interpretive histories of other influential works similar in content to *Perpetual Peace* and authored by noted classical theorists in the field of International Relations. Perhaps works by Grotius, Hobbes, Rousseau, or Bentham would be valuable to consider. My principal and subsidiary explanations could then be tested against interpretive histories of works written by such figures to see if they apply outside the context of *Perpetual Peace*. This could strengthen their validity as explanatory tools.

Most importantly, in the context of these historical explanations, it will be worthwhile to see whether Pattern Two, Phase Two endures in the interpretation of *Perpetual Peace*. As long as the liberal state continues its ascendancy and the idea of the liberal peace maintains its legitimacy, my argument suggests it will. One of the first notable interpretations of *Perpetual Peace* completed in the new century, by the UN Secretary General Kofi Annan, certainly confirms this phase's continued predominance.

Given as the annual Cyril Foster Lecture at Oxford on June 19, 2001, Annan points out that "Many would associate the idea of a connection between democracy and international peace with the work of Immanuel Kant, whose essay 'Perpetual Peace' was published in 1795."[1] Following exactly the same line as other Pattern Two, Phase Two interpreters, Annan views the First Definitive Article as the pivotal proposal of Kant's treatise. According to Annan, "Kant argued that 'republics'—by which he meant essentially what today we call liberal or pluralistic democracies—were less likely than other forms of State to go to war with one another."[2] "Broadly speaking," Annan states, "the history of the last 200 years has proved him right."[3] Annan continues with the following selection, which mirrors the arguments in favor of the liberal peace:

> During [the past 200 years] there have been many horrible wars, which technology has made more destructive than those of earlier periods. And liberal democracies have played a big part in those wars. But almost always they have fought on the same side, not against each other. Dynastic states have fought each other throughout history—and so have religious states, totalitarian states, and military dictatorships. But liberal democracies have generally found other ways to settle their disputes.[4]

Annan is convinced that independent liberal states are the foundation of international peace and that Kant's work unambiguously endorses this idea. Nowhere in his lecture does he state that Kant's treatise favors international organization, federation, or a world state as the way to peace. This is quite surprising considering his position as UN Secretary General. Pattern Two, Phase Two appears to be in good shape as the new century begins.

Or does it? Annan presented his speech (and his view of Kant's *Perpetual Peace*) several months before September 11, 2001. Times of crisis, particularly a world-historical event like the one that occurred on September 11, 2001, have a way of influencing a shift in patterns. As the arguments in this book have shown, patterns of interpretation, especially those that concern a work as controversial as *Perpetual Peace*, are never static. As such, there will be those who claim that the shocking events of September 11 and their affect on the international system may signal an end to Pattern Two, Phase Two predominance. Is it possible that in a post–September 11 environment we are in the midst of a shift in pattern formation? In the beginning years of the twenty-first century and so close to the date of crisis, it is far too early to tell. Such a hypothesis can only be thoroughly and credibly tested years from now. Still, it is both instructive and intriguing to briefly consult three recent interpretations of *Perpetual Peace*, published after September 11, to gather insight into where the interpretive process may be heading.

In *Kant's Critique of Hobbes*, published in 2003, Howard Williams remarks, "The independence of sovereigns is critical to Hobbes's conception of politics and international politics. Not so for Kant. With Kant the possibility of international law should rest not upon our present lawless condition as peoples, but rather on our future regulated conditions as part of a working federation of states."[5] Williams then quotes the often cited selection of Pattern One, Phase One interpreters: "[So] each nation, for the sake of its own security, can and ought to demand of others that they should enter along with it into a constitution, similar to the civil one, with which the rights of each could be secured. This would mean establishing a federation of peoples."[6] In emphasizing the importance of "cosmopolitan right" to Kant's work, Williams closes his book with the following remarks:

> Where Kant's political philosophy indisputably strikes out in a new direction is in its worldwide scope. Although somewhat foreshadowed in earlier peace plans, such as those of Abbé St-Pierre and Rousseau, and by the cosmopolitan zeal of some of the French revolutionaries, here Kant makes his most telling contribution to political thought. Although extraordinarily far-seeing and ambitious in Kant's day, this cosmopolitan political theory provides us with the most workable and realistic of principles for our present-day condition.[7]

In a brief comment on the relationship between Kant's writings and the events of September 11, Williams notes the following: "The answer to the uncertainties caused by the destruction in New York would seem to lie just as much in the development of one safe worldwide civil society as in the reinforcement of the security and prosperity of the United States itself."[8] With all of Williams's above remarks (and the text he chooses to highlight in *Perpetual Peace*), he sounds much more like a Pattern One, Phase One or Two interpreter than any Pattern Two interpreter discussed in chapters 4–7. Considering Williams's far more state-centric views of *Perpetual Peace* outlined in his and Ken Booth's 1996 essay discussed in chapter 7, it is clear that his thinking on *Perpetual Peace* continues to evolve.[9]

Conversely, Antonio Franceschet, also writing after September 11, presents an interpretation of *Perpetual Peace* very much in line with Annan and other Pattern Two, Phase Two interpreters. Of *Perpetual Peace*, Franceschet initially states, " . . . nearly all progressive change is channeled through the agency of the sovereign (or in this case, the plurality of sovereigns). The non-ideal theory thus enshrines the sovereignty of states as a given foundation of international order, a commitment expressed clearly in 'Perpetual Peace's' preliminary articles."[10] Franceschet continues: "The first two definitive articles of 'Perpetual Peace' rely on the mechanism of the republican sovereign state as the agent of reform."[11] He explains, "Kant *internationalizes* the freedom-promoting effects of republican regimes because he claims they are the only ones capable of pacifying international politics."[12] Like other Pattern Two, Phase Two interpreters, he then proceeds to quote the "consent-of-the-citizens" passage from the First Definitive Article and refers to it as "one of [Kant's] more well known claims."[13]

Of the Second Definitive Article, he notes its advocacy of "the creation of a *confederation* of republican states."[14] According to Franceschet,

> Kant describes the development and form of his peace federation in a way that actually reaffirms the centrality of the (republican) sovereign state as the primary instrument of international reform. In a condition of anarchy, there is ultimately little opportunity or incentive for states to concede or limit their sovereign powers to defend themselves. As a result, a state *qua* state is unlikely to enter into anything more than an extraordinarily loose league.[15]

As was noted in chapter 6, Pattern Two, Phase Two interpreter Jürg Martin Gabriel comments that "Given the benevolent nature of republican government, the lives of such states are peaceful and order in anarchy becomes possible."[16] Like Gabriel, Franceschet is convinced that, for Kant, international reform and order in the international system are possible through the mere existence of a collection of sovereign republican states. He explains, "What this again suggests is that Kant is far more willing to tolerate anarchy among states than among individuals, in spite of his formal understanding of justice."[17] Franceschet concludes:

> After many wars and failed attempts to secure peace, it will require the efforts of "one enlightened and powerful republic" to establish pacific relations with its like-minded neighbors to create conditions favorable to a peaceful confederation. The confederation is ultimately limited, however, by the discrete inclinations and free choices of the sovereigns who have joined. Each member state may finally decide to exempt itself from the whole and, moreover, choose to dissolve the association at any time. If they are true republics, however—and this is obviously a big and important "if"—this voluntary nature of association is not a problem: States will be responsive to the pacific ends of citizens. Kant is very clear that sovereign states, as *representatives* (and mere tools) of their citizens, cannot be transferred to a transcendent suprastate. The confederation he proposes aims only for peaceful relations, not the construction of an "international state."[18]

Franceschet's view here is similar to Hinsley's and Gallie's in its focus on the voluntary nature of Kant's association or confederation of states (and Franceschet actually refers to Hinsley in discussing Kant's commitment to state sovereignty in the international sphere).[19] Further, his interpretation is much closer to Pattern Two, Phase Two interpreters' analysis with its clear emphasis on the First Definitive Article and its view that, for Kant, the sovereign republican state is the sole agent of reform in the international system, not a Williams-like federation that will gradually come to exist above the state level.

In addition, Donald J. Puchala uses Kant's First Definitive Article of *Perpetual Peace* to explain why some analysts believe democracies "refrain from warring among themselves."[20] He notes that "some [analysts] postulate that democratic public opinion is peace oriented and that Kant was correct when he observed that 'nothing is more natural than that those who would have to decide to undergo all the deprivations of war will very much hesitate to start such an evil game.' "[21] He writes, "Immanuel Kant had no problem identifying the historical driver that was moving democratization forward. This was nature itself. A liberal world was foreordained: institutionalizing freedom was the plan of providence."[22] His statements that the First Supplement specifically guarantees "democratization" and that "A liberal world was foreordained" demonstrates a reading of *Perpetual Peace* that clearly reflects the ascendancy of the liberal state.

In closing, while the enormity of the events of September 11, U.S. "unilateralist" responses, and the cracks in liberal democratic relationships, particularly between the United States and European democracies, may influence commentators like Williams to interpret *Perpetual Peace* differently, writers like Franceschet and Puchala continue to read Kant's *Perpetual Peace* as the inspiration for the idea of a long-lasting peace between an ever-increasing number of sovereign republican states. President Bush's recent speech on the necessity of democratic enlargement in the Middle East[23] and his statement in the January 20, 2004, State of the Union that "Our aim is a democratic peace"[24] suggest the continued potency of this idea in international affairs. As such, my principal and subsidiary explanations, which project that interpretation of Kant's *Perpetual Peace* will continue to reflect persistent academic and real world focus on the liberal peace and a similar perception of a decline in hopes for peace through international organization, appear, at least initially, to be on solid ground in a post–September 11 world.

Notes

Introduction

1. Immanuel Kant, *Perpetual Peace*, in *Kant's Political Writings*, ed. by Hans Reiss, trans. H.B. Nisbet (Cambridge: Cambridge University Press, 1970), p. 93 (emphasis added). The majority of text quoted from Kant's *Perpetual Peace* throughout the book derives from this translation. When commentators use alternative translations in their interpretation of the treatise, these are generally noted and any relevant distinctions in language are indicated.

2. Apparently, Kant's Prelude was not clever enough. The publication of *Perpetual Peace* immediately "won him the reproach of being a Jacobin (1795)." A.C.F. Beales, *The History of Peace: A Short Account of the Organized Movements for International Peace* (New York: The Dial Press, 1931), p. 36.

3. Kant, *Perpetual Peace*, ed. Reiss, trans. Nisbet, p. 99.

4. Karl Mannheim, *Ideology and Utopia: An Introduction to the Sociology of Knowledge*, trans. by Louis Wirth and Edward Shils (London: Routledge & Kegan Paul, 1954; first published in England, 1936), p. 237 and p. 238, respectively.

5. Mannheim, *Ideology and Utopia*, p. 240.

6. Mannheim, *Ideology and Utopia*, p. 240.

7. Mannheim, *Ideology and Utopia*, p. 240.

8. Mannheim, *Ideology and Utopia*, p. 240.

9. Mannheim, *Ideology and Utopia*, p. 239.

10. In a short essay discussing Mannheim's thought, E.H. Carr once wrote the following:

   The proposition that thought is influenced and conditioned by the situation of the thinker in time and place had been repeated so often as to become trite and boring. Yet in practice the history of philosophical or political or economic ideas could still be discussed and taught as a self-sufficient entity in which one "school" succeeded another without regard to the social background whose changing character determined the changing patterns of thought. Mannheim labored to show that the history of ideas, like other kinds of history, could not be studied in isolation from the society in which the ideas were born and flourished. (E.H. Carr, *From Napoleon to Stalin and Other Essays* (London: MacMillan Press, 1980), pp. 179–80)

11. Edwin Mead, "Immanuel Kant's Internationalism," *Contemporary Review*, CVII (February 1915), p. 228.

12. W.B. Gallie, *Philosophers of Peace and War* (Cambridge: Cambridge University Press, 1963), p. 9.

13. Chris Brown notes, "the discipline of International Relations remains to this day largely a product of the English-speaking world, although, happily, this may not be the case for much longer." Chris Brown, *Understanding International Relations* (London: MacMillan Press, 1997), p. 22.

14. Hannah Arendt and Ronald Beiner, eds., *Lectures on Kant's Political Philosophy— Delivered at the New School for Social Research, Fall 1970* (Chicago: Chicago University Press, 1982), p. 7.

15. Arendt and Beiner, *Lectures on Kant's Political Philosophy*, p. 7.

16. Andrew Hurrell, "Kant and the Kantian Paradigm in International Relations," *Review of International Studies*, 16 (1990), p. 183.

17. Howard Williams and Ken Booth, "Kant: Theorist beyond Limits," in Ian Clark and Iver B. Neuman, eds., *Classical Theories of International Relations* (Houndsmills, Basingstoke and London: MacMillan Press, 1996), p. 71. While both authors applaud Wight for encouraging scholarly interest in Kant's writings on international relations, they note that Wight "did not serve Kant well" by anointing him "intellectual figurehead of the 'Revolutionist' tradition." Williams and Booth, "Kant: Theorist beyond Limits," p. 71.

18. Williams and Booth, "Kant: Theorist beyond Limits," p. 72.

19. Martin Wight, *International Theory: The Three Traditions*, ed. Gabriele Wright and Brian Porter with an introductory essay by Hedley Bull (Leicester: Leicester University Press for the Royal Institute of International Affairs, 1991), p. 4.

20. Georg Cavallar, "Kant's Society of Nations: Free Federation or World Republic?" *Journal of the History of Philosophy*, 32 (July 1994), pp. 462–63.

21. Brown, *Understanding International Relations*, p. 236.

1 The Textual Hooks of Interpretation

1. Immanuel Kant, *Perpetual Peace* in *Kant's Political Writings*, ed. Hans Reiss, trans. H.B. Nisbet (Cambridge: Cambridge University Press, 1970), p. 105. Because of the initial popularity of the first edition of *Perpetual Peace*, Kant decided to publish a second in 1796. To the second edition were attached two appendices: "On the Disagreement Between Morals and Politics in Relation to Perpetual Peace" and "On the Agreement Between Politics and Morality According to the Transcendental Concept of Public Right." Rarely, if ever, are these referred to by interpreters of *Perpetual Peace*. There are, however, two passages from the appendices that consider issues similar to those discussed in the selection from the Second Definitive Article quoted above that are worthy of note. In the

first appendix, Kant asserts the following:

> The proverbial saying *fiat iustitia, pereat mundus* (i.e. let justice reign, even if all the rogues in the world must perish) may sound somewhat inflated, but it is nonetheless true. It is a sound principle of right, which blocks up all the devious paths followed by cunning or violence. But it must not be misunderstood, or taken, for example, as a permit to apply one's own rights with the utmost rigour (which would conflict with ethical duty), but should be seen as an obligation of those in power not to deny or detract from the rights of anyone out of disfavour or sympathy for others. And this requires above all that the state should have an internal constitution organized in accordance with pure principles of right, and also that it unite with other neighbouring nations or even distant states to arrive at a lawful settlement of their differences by forming something analogous to a universal state. (Kant, *Perpetual Peace*, ed. Reiss, trans. Nisbet, p. 123)

He makes the following point in the second appendix:

> Now we have already seen above that a federative association of states whose sole intention is to eliminate war is the only *lawful* arrangement which can be reconciled with their *freedom*. Thus politics and morality can only be in agreement within a federal union, which is therefore necessary and given *a priori* through the principles of right. And the rightful basis of all political prudence is the founding of such a union in the most comprehensive form possible; for without this aim, all its reasonings are unwisdom and veiled injustice. (Kant, *Perpetual Peace*, ed. Reiss, trans. Nisbet, p. 129 emphasis in original)

2. Kant, *Perpetual Peace*, ed. Reiss, trans. Nisbet, p. 105 (emphasis in original).
3. Kant, *Perpetual Peace*, ed. Reiss, trans. Nisbet, p. 105.
4. Kant, *Perpetual Peace*, ed. Reiss, trans. Nisbet, p. 105.
5. Kant, *Perpetual Peace*, ed. Reiss, trans. Nisbet, p. 102 and Georg Cavallar, "Kant's Society of Nations: Free Federation or World Republic?" *Journal of the History of Philosophy*, 32 (July 1994), p. 467, respectively.
6. Kant, *Perpetual Peace*, ed. Reiss, trans. Nisbet, p. 102 (emphasis in original).
7. Kant, *Perpetual Peace*, ed. Reiss, trans. Nisbet, p. 104.
8. Kant, *Perpetual Peace*, ed. Reiss, trans. Nisbet, p. 104.
9. Kant, *Perpetual Peace*, ed. Reiss, trans. Nisbet, p. 104 (emphasis in original).
10. Kant, *Perpetual Peace*, ed. Reiss, trans. Nisbet, p. 104 (emphasis in original).
11. Kant, *Perpetual Peace*, ed. Reiss, trans. Nisbet, p. 105.
12. Jessie Wallace Hughan, *A Study of International Government* (New York: Thomas Y. Crowell, 1923), p. 156.
13. Though the term "league" is found once in the Second Definitive Article of the 1970 Nisbet translation used here, no English translation that would have been available to this second set of interpreters during the historical period in which

they considered Kant's *Perpetual Peace* included the term in the text. For example, Nisbet refers to "the general agreement between the nations" as a "particular kind of league." Kant, *Perpetual Peace*, ed. Reiss, trans. Nisbet, p. 104. M. Campbell Smith, who translated and interpreted *Perpetual Peace* in the early twentieth century, calls this "compact between nations . . . an alliance of a particular kind." Immanuel Kant, *Perpetual Peace: A Philosophical Essay*, intro. and trans. M. Campbell Smith, pref. Professor R. Latta (Swan Sonnenschein & Co., 1903), p. 134.

14. Of the three Definitive Articles, the text of the Third Definitive Article receives the least attention by interpreters from all four periods under consideration. Still, as is developed in chapter 4, F.H. Hinsley's influential interpretation sees it (together with his understanding of the Preliminary and Second Definitive Articles) as convincing proof of the treatise's commitment to the separation of states. F.H. Hinsley, *Power and the Pursuit of Peace* (Cambridge: Cambridge University Press, 1963), pp. 62–80.

15. Kant, *Perpetual Peace*, ed. Reiss, trans. Nisbet, p. 104 (emphasis in original).

16. Kant, *Perpetual Peace*, ed. Reiss, trans. Nisbet, p. 104 (emphasis in original).

17. Kant, *Perpetual Peace*, ed. Reiss, trans. Nisbet, p. 104 (emphasis in original).

18. Kant, *Perpetual Peace*, ed. Reiss, trans. Nisbet, pp. 104–05.

19. More so than any single interpretation, the influence of F.H. Hinsley's interpretation in *Power and the Pursuit of Peace* (1963) on others during this period is pervasive. As one of the more well-known and helpful representative interpretations from this period, I have chosen in this part of the summary to follow roughly the passages he uses in his discussion of the Preliminary Articles.

20. Kant, *Perpetual Peace*, ed. Reiss, trans. Nisbet, pp. 93–96.

21. Kant, *Perpetual Peace*, ed. Reiss, trans. Nisbet, p. 94.

22. Kant, *Perpetual Peace*, ed. Reiss, trans. Nisbet, p. 96.

23. Kant, *Perpetual Peace*, ed. Reiss, trans. Nisbet, p. 97 (emphasis in original).

24. Kant, *Perpetual Peace*, ed. Reiss, trans. Nisbet, pp. 108–14 (emphasis in original).

25. Kant, *Perpetual Peace*, ed. Reiss, trans. Nisbet, p. 112 (emphasis in original).

26. Kant, *Perpetual Peace*, ed. Reiss, trans. Nisbet, p. 114.

27. Kant, *Perpetual Peace*, ed. Reiss, trans. Nisbet, p. 112.

28. Kant, *Perpetual Peace*, ed. Reiss, trans. Nisbet, p. 113.

29. Kant, *Perpetual Peace*, ed. Reiss, trans. Nisbet, p. 114.

30. Kant, *Perpetual Peace*, ed. Reiss, trans. Nisbet, p. 114 (emphasis in original).

31. Kant, *Perpetual Peace*, ed. Reiss, trans. Nisbet, p. 100.

32. Kant, *Perpetual Peace*, ed. Reiss, trans. Nisbet, p. 100.

33. Kant, *Perpetual Peace*, ed. Reiss, trans. Nisbet, p. 100.

2 Pattern One, Phase One: Reining in State Sovereignty

1. Henry Wheaton, *History of the Law of Nations in Europe and America* (New York: Gould, Banks & Co., 1845), pp. 750–53.

2. Wheaton, *History of the Law of Nations*, pp. 751–52.

3. Wheaton, *History of the Law of Nations*, p. 752.

4. Wheaton, *History of the Law of Nations*, p. 752.
5. Wheaton, *History of the Law of Nations*, p. 752.
6. Wheaton, *History of the Law of Nations*, p. 752.
7. Immanuel. Kant, *Perpetual Peace* in *Kant's Political Writings*, ed. Hans Reiss, trans. H.B. Nisbet (Cambridge: Cambridge University Press, 1970), p. 105.
8. Kant, *Perpetual Peace*, ed. Reiss, trans. Nisbet, p. 105.
9. As a point of comparison with English-language interpretations, it is interesting to briefly consider an 1836 publication by Professor Stapfer of Paris entitled *Life of Immanuel Kant*, translated by Professor Hodge, Library of Useful Tracts, Volume Three (Edinburgh: Thomas Clark, 1836). His comments on *Perpetual Peace* below are few and rather confusing, though there appears to be some similarities with other interpretations from this period. Speaking of Kant in *Perpetual Peace*, Professor Stapfer states:

   > Raising himself to a region, whence he embraces, in one view, the existing relations among nations and individuals, [Kant] discovers and points out the facts and necessities, which must lead men gradually to come out of their present barbarous and destructive state of inquietude; in the same manner as the establishment of social institutions resulted from the union of families, removing the state of nature to guarantee the mutual security of person and property, by creating a central authority, sustained by a force which could not be resisted. Stapfer, *Life of Immanuel Kant*, trans. Professor Hodge, p. 45.

10. James Lorimer, *The Institute of the Law of Nations: A Treatise of the Jural Relations of Separate Political Communities*, Two Volumes (Edinburgh and London: William Blackwood and Sons, 1884), Volume One, p. 225.
11. Kant, *Perpetual Peace*, ed. Reiss, trans. Nisbet, p. 105.
12. Lorimer, *The Institute of the Law of Nations*, pp. 225–26.
13. Lorimer quotes the following from the *Metaphysics of Law* :

   > The establishment of perpetual peace, which ought to be considered as the ultimate object of every system of public law, may perhaps be considered as impracticable, inasmuch as the too great extension of such a federal union might render impossible that supervision over its several members, and that protection to each member which is essential to its ends . . . What we mean to propose is a general congress of nations, of which both the meeting and the duration are to depend entirely on the sovereign wills of the several members of the league, and not an indissoluble union like that which exists between the several States of North America, founded on a municipal constitution. Such a congress and such a league are the only means of realising the idea of a true public law, according to which the differences between nations would be determined by civil proceedings, as those between individuals are determined by civil judicature, instead of resorting to war—a means of redress worthy only of barbarians. (Lorimer, *The Institute of the Law of Nations*, p. 226)

14. Lorimer, *The Institute of the Law of Nations*, pp. 226–27.

15. Lorimer, *The Institute of the Law of Nations*, p. 227.
16. David George Ritchie, *Studies in Political and Social Ethics* (London: Swan Sonnenschein & Co., 1902), p. 169.
17. Ritchie, *Studies in Political and Social Ethics*, p. 170.
18. Kant, *Perpetual Peace: A Philosophical Essay*, intro. and trans. M. Campbell Smith, pref. Professor R. Latta (London: Swan Sonnenschein & Co., 1903), p. VI.
19. Kant, *Perpetual Peace: A Philosophical Essay*, intro. and trans. Smith, pref. Latta, pp. VI–VII.
20. Kant, *Perpetual Peace: A Philosophical Essay*, intro. and trans. Smith, pref. Latta, p. VII.
21. Kant, *Perpetual Peace: A Philosophical Essay*, intro. and trans. Smith, pref. Latta, p. VII.
22. Kant, *Perpetual Peace: A Philosophical Essay*, intro. and trans. Smith, pref. Latta, p. VII.
23. Benjamin F. Trueblood, "The Historical Development of the Peace Idea," Paper presented at the Summer School of Religious History, Haverford, Pennsylvania, June 1900, p. 21.
24. Benjamin F. Trueblood, *The Federation of the World* (Cambridge: The Riverside Press, 1899), p. 3.
25. Trueblood, *The Federation of the World*, p. 3.
26. Friedrich Paulsen, *Immanuel Kant: His Life and Doctrine*, translated from the revised German edition by J.E. Creighton and Albert Lefevre (New York: Charles Scribner & Sons, 1902), p. 355.
27. Paulsen, *Immanuel Kant: His Life and Doctrine*, p. 355. Interestingly, Smith in the Introduction to her translation says nearly the same thing: "It is the duty of statesmen to form a federative union as it was formerly the duty of individuals to enter the state." Kant, *Perpetual Peace: A Philosophical Essay*, intro. and trans. Smith, pref. Latta, p. 60.
28. Paulsen, *Immanuel Kant: His Life and Doctrine*, pp. 356–57.
29. Paulsen, *Immanuel Kant: His Life and Doctrine*, p. 357.
30. Paulsen, *Immanuel Kant: His Life and Doctrine*, p. 357.
31. Paulsen, *Immanuel Kant: His Life and Doctrine*, p. 357.
32. Paulsen, *Immanuel Kant: His Life and Doctrine*, pp. 357–58.
33. The French interpretation referenced is in note 9 earlier. As stated earlier, interpretations of *Perpetual Peace* written in German and French are beyond the scope of this book. Still, the kinship between the two interpretations briefly discussed and English-language interpretations during this period would seem to provide interesting avenues for future research into this particular area of the history of international ideas.
34. Immanuel Kant, *Eternal Peace*, trans. J.D. Morell (London: Hodder & Stoughton, 1884). Morell remarks in the preface that the "1796 translation is no longer to be procured," meaning he believed he was, effectively, bringing the

treatise to the English-speaking public for the first time in many years. Like Morell, I have been unable to locate the 1796 original translation into English or any further English translations between this date and the time of Morell's translation in 1884. This might be one reason why there appears to be fewer English-language interpretations or commentary relating to *Perpetual Peace*, specifically in the Anglo-American context, during the nineteenth century.

35. Immanuel Kant, *Eternal Peace*, trans. Morell, p. vi.
36. Kant, *Perpetual Peace*, ed. Reiss, trans. Nisbet, p. 129.
37. Immanuel Kant, *Perpetual Peace* in *Kant's Principle of Politics*, ed. and trans. W. Hastie (Edinburgh: T & T Clark, 1891), p. XXXVI.
38. Kant, *Perpetual Peace*, ed. and trans. Hastie, p. XXXVI.
39. Immanuel Kant, *Perpetual Peace: A Philosophical Essay*, intro. and trans. Smith, pref. Latta, p. 68.
40. Kant, *Perpetual Peace: A Philosophical Essay*, intro. and trans. Smith, pref. Latta, pp. 68–69.
41. Kant, *Perpetual Peace: A Philosophical Essay*, intro. and trans. Smith, pref. Latta, p. 69.
42. Kant, *Perpetual Peace: A Philosophical Essay*, intro. and trans. Smith, pref. Latta, p. 69.
43. Kant, *Perpetual Peace: A Philosophical Essay*, intro. and trans. Smith, pref. Latta, p. 129.
44. Kant, *Perpetual Peace: A Philosophical Essay*, intro. and trans. Smith, pref. Latta, p. 136.
45. Kant, *Perpetual Peace: A Philosophical Essay*, intro. and trans. Smith, pref. Latta, p. 68.
46. Leonard Woolf, "Review of Kant's 'Perpetual Peace,'" *New Statesman* (July 31, 1915), p. 398.
47. Woolf, "Review of Kant's 'Perpetual Peace,'" p. 398.
48. Woolf, "Review of Kant's 'Perpetual Peace,'" p. 398.
49. Woolf, "Review of Kant's 'Perpetual Peace,'" p. 399.
50. Woolf, "Review of Kant's 'Perpetual Peace,'" p. 399.
51. Woolf, "Review of Kant's 'Perpetual Peace,'" p. 399.
52. Edwin Doak Mead, "Immanuel Kant's Internationalism," *Contemporary Review* CVII (February 1915), p. 226.
53. Mead, "Immanuel Kant's Internationalism," p. 231.
54. Mead, "Immanuel Kant's Internationalism," p. 231.
55. Mead, "Immanuel Kant's Internationalism," p. 231 (emphasis in original).
56. Mead, "Immanuel Kant's Internationalism," p. 232.
57. Kant, *Perpetual Peace*, ed. Reiss, trans. Nisbet, p. 105 (emphasis in original).

3 Pattern One, Phase Two: Sovereignty Curbed

1. To restate, Kant explains toward the end of the Second Definitive Article, "There is only one rational way in which states coexisting with other states can emerge from the lawless condition of pure warfare. Just like individual men, they must

renounce their savage and lawless freedom, adapt themselves to public coercive laws, and thus form an international state (*civitas gentium*), which would necessarily continue to grow until it embraced all the peoples of the earth." Immanuel Kant, *Perpetual Peace* in *Kant's Political Writings*, ed. Hans Reiss, trans. H.B. Nisbet (Cambridge: Cambridge University Press, 1970), p. 105.

2. Kant, *Perpetual Peace*, ed. Reiss, trans. Nisbet, p. 105.

3. D.P. Heatley's *Diplomacy and the Study of International Relations*, discussed below, was also completed in 1919 and includes a brief review of the Second Definitive Article of Kant's treatise. I also discovered a book by the German Mathias Erzberger, *The League of Nations: The Way to the World's Peace*, which was written, then translated into the English in 1919. His reference to Kant, interestingly enough, is brief though worth noting for its similarity to the English-language interpretations of this time. Here, Erzberger is certain that the Second Definitive Article did not endorse a world state:

> Kant, one of the greatest German philosophers, forms, as we see, on a basis of intellectual perception, the same estimate of war, and suggests the same arrangements for its prevention—for example, the greatest possible limitation of war—as did the Popes, the protectors and the embodiment of the Christian moral law. But other prominent Germans, towards the end of the eighteenth century, were concerned with the ideal of peace. Schlegel even suggested an international state, which Kant, in his commentary upon the Second Definitive Article of his Perpetual Peace, rejected. (M. Erzberger, *The League of Nations: The Way to the World's Peace*, trans. Bernard Miall (London: Hodder & Stoughton, 1919), p. 118)

4. Dwight W. Morrow, *The Society of Free States* (New York and London: Harper and Brothers Publishers, 1919), p. 147.

5. Morrow, *The Society of Free States*, p. 145.

6. Morrow, *The Society of Free States*, pp. 145–46.

7. Jessie Wallace Hughan, *A Study of International Government* (New York: Thomas Y. Crowell, 1923), p. 155.

8. Hughan, *A Study of International Government*, p. 156.

9. D.P. Heatley, *Diplomacy and the Study of International Relations* (Oxford: Clarendon Press, 1919), p. 200.

10. Heatley, *Diplomacy and the Study of International Relations*, pp. 203–04.

11. Heatley, *Diplomacy and the Study of International Relations*, p. 204.

12. Nicholas Murray Butler, *The Path to Peace: Essays and Addresses on Peace and Its Making* (New York, London: Charles Scribner's & Sons, 1930), p. 200.

13. Butler, *The Path to Peace*, p. 200.

14. Butler, *The Path to Peace*, p. 200.

15. Mehan F. Stawall, *The Growth of International Thought* (London: Thornton Butterworth Limited, 1929), pp. 204–05.

16. Stawall, *The Growth of International Thought*, pp. 204–05.

17. Carl Joachim Friedrich, *Inevitable Peace* (Cambridge: Harvard University Press, 1948), p. 45.
18. Friedrich, *Inevitable Peace*, p. 33.
19. Friedrich, *Inevitable Peace*, p. 33.
20. Friedrich, *Inevitable Peace*, p. 46.
21. R.B. Mowat, *The European States System, A Study of International Relations*, 2nd edition (London: Oxford University Press, 1929; first published in 1923), p. 94.
22. Mowat, *The European States System*, p. 94.
23. Thomas Barclay, "Perpetual Peace, Official Schemes and Projects," *Contemporary Review*, 147 (January/June 1935), p. 679.
24. A.C.F. Beales, *The History of Peace: A Short Account of the Organized Movements for International Peace* (New York: The Dial Press, 1931), p. 36.
25. Beales, *The History of Peace*, p. 36.
26. Beales, *The History of Peace*, p. 36.
27. Beales, *The History of Peace*, p. 36.
28. Beales, *The History of Peace*, p. 36.
29. Beales, *The History of Peace*, p. 36.
30. Beales, *The History of Peace*, p. 36.
31. John Bourke, "Kant's Doctrine of 'Perpetual Peace,'" *Philosophy*, 17 (1942), p. 331.
32. Bourke, "Kant's Doctrine of 'Perpetual Peace,'" p. 331.
33. Beales, *The History of Peace*, p. 36.
34. Waldemar Gurian, "Perpetual Peace? Critical Remarks on Mortimer J. Adler's Book," *Review of Politics*, 6 (1944), pp. 228–38.
35. Gurian, "Perpetual Peace? Critical Remarks on Mortimer J. Adler's Book," p. 229.
36. Gurian, "Perpetual Peace? Critical Remarks on Mortimer J. Adler's Book," p. 229.
37. Bourke, "Kant's Doctrine of 'Perpetual Peace,'" p. 330.
38. Bourke, "Kant's Doctrine of 'Perpetual Peace,'" p. 325.
39. Bourke, "Kant's Doctrine of 'Perpetual Peace,'" p. 325.
40. Bourke, "Kant's Doctrine of 'Perpetual Peace,'" p. 325.
41. Bourke, "Kant's Doctrine of 'Perpetual Peace,'" p. 330.
42. Bourke, "Kant's Doctrine of 'Perpetual Peace,'" p. 330 (emphasis in original).
43. Bourke, "Kant's Doctrine of 'Perpetual Peace,'" pp. 330–31 (emphasis in original).
44. While it seems fairly clear that Bourke understands this ideal to be a federation, he is not completely clear on this point. While he states that Kant "rejects the notion of a world state," he sees fit to mention that it is "entertained" as an idea in another passage. Bourke, "Kant's Doctrine of 'Perpetual Peace,'" p. 332. Still, his discussion and analysis is devoted primarily to the idea of federation, and he suggests more than once that it is Kant's vision or ideal.
45. Bourke, "Kant's Doctrine of 'Perpetual Peace,'" p. 331.
46. Bourke, "Kant's Doctrine of 'Perpetual Peace,'" p. 331.

47. Bourke, "Kant's Doctrine of 'Perpetual Peace,'" p. 332.
48. Bourke, "Kant's Doctrine of 'Perpetual Peace,'" p. 332.
49. Immanuel Kant, *Perpetual Peace*, trans. Helen O'Brien, intro. Jessie Buckland, Grotius Society Publications: Texts for Students of International Relations, No. 7 (London: Sweet & Maxwell, 1927), p. 10.
50. Kant, *Perpetual Peace*, trans. O'Brien, intro. Buckland, p. 9.
51. Kant, *Perpetual Peace*, trans. O'Brien, intro. Buckland, p. 9.
52. J.F. Crawford, "Kant's Doctrines Concerning Perpetual Peace," *Monist*, 35 (1925), p. 312.
53. Crawford, "Kant's Doctrines Concerning Perpetual Peace," p. 313.
54. Crawford, "Kant's Doctrines Concerning Perpetual Peace," p. 313.
55. Crawford, "Kant's Doctrines Concerning Perpetual Peace," p. 310.
56. Crawford, "Kant's Doctrines Concerning Perpetual Peace," p. 310.
57. Crawford, "Kant's Doctrines Concerning Perpetual Peace," p. 310.
58. A.C. Armstrong, "Kant's Philosophy of Peace and War," *The Journal of Philosophy*, XXVIII, No. 8 (April 9, 1931), p. 198.
59. Armstrong, "Kant's Philosophy of Peace and War," p. 198.
60. Armstrong, "Kant's Philosophy of Peace and War," p. 202.
61. Armstrong, "Kant's Philosophy of Peace and War," p. 202.
62. Armstrong, "Kant's Philosophy of Peace and War," p. 203.
63. Armstrong, "Kant's Philosophy of Peace and War," p. 203.
64. Armstrong, "Kant's Philosophy of Peace and War," p. 203.
65. Armstrong, "Kant's Philosophy of Peace and War," p. 203.
66. Armstrong, "Kant's Philosophy of Peace and War," p. 203.

4 Pattern Two, Phase One: In Defense of State Sovereignty

1. F.H. Hinsley, *Power and the Pursuit of Peace* (Cambridge: Cambridge University Press, 1963), p. 62.
2. Hinsley, *Power and the Pursuit of Peace*, p. 67.
3. Hinsley, *Power and the Pursuit of Peace*, p. 62.
4. Hinsley, *Power and the Pursuit of Peace*, p. 62.
5. Hinsley, *Power and the Pursuit of Peace*, p. 62.
6. Hinsley, *Power and the Pursuit of Peace*, p. 62.
7. Immanuel Kant, *Perpetual Peace* in *Kant's Political Writings*, ed. Hans Reiss, trans. H.B. Nisbet (Cambridge: Cambridge University Press, 1970), p. 102.
8. Kant, *Perpetual Peace*, ed. Reiss, trans. Nisbet, pp. 102, 104, 105, respectively.
9. Hinsley, *Power and the Pursuit of Peace*, p. 63.
10. Hinsley, *Power and the Pursuit of Peace*, p. 63.
11. Hinsley, *Power and the Pursuit of Peace*, p. 64.
12. Hinsley, *Power and the Pursuit of Peace*, p. 69.
13. 1. No treaty of peace shall be held to be such, which is made with the secret reservation of the material for a future war. 2. No *state* having an independent

existence, whether it be small or great, may be acquired by another *state*, through inheritance, exchange, purchase or gift. 3. Standing armies shall gradually disappear. 4. No debts shall be contracted in connection with the foreign affairs of the *state*. 5. No *state* shall interfere by force in the constitution and government of another *state*. 6. No *state* at war with another shall permit such acts of warfare as must make mutual confidence impossible in time of future peace: such as the employment of assassins . . . the instigation of treason . . . etc. (Hinsley, *Power and the Pursuit of Peace*, p. 69 emphasis in original)

14. Hinsley, *Power and the Pursuit of Peace*, p. 69.
15. Hinsley, *Power and the Pursuit of Peace*, p. 69.
16. Hinsley, *Power and the Pursuit of Peace*, p. 69.
17. Hinsley, *Power and the Pursuit of Peace*, p. 69.
18. Hinsley, *Power and the Pursuit of Peace*, p. 69.
19. Hinsley, *Power and the Pursuit of Peace*, pp. 64–65.
20. Hinsley, *Power and the Pursuit of Peace*, p. 65.
21. Hinsley, *Power and the Pursuit of Peace*, p. 65.
22. Kant, *Perpetual Peace*, ed. Reiss, trans. Nisbet, p. 105.
23. Kant, *Perpetual Peace*, ed. Reiss, trans. Nisbet, p. 105.
24. Kant, *Perpetual Peace*, ed. Reiss, trans. Nisbet, pp. 105–06.
25. Hinsley, *Power and the Pursuit of Peace*, p. 65.
26. Hinsley, *Power and the Pursuit of Peace*, p. 65.
27. Hinsley, *Power and the Pursuit of Peace*, p. 65.
28. Hinsley, *Power and the Pursuit of Peace*, p. 66.
29. Hinsley, *Power and the Pursuit of Peace*, p. 66.
30. F.H. Hinsley, *Sovereignty* (London: C.A. Watts and Co., 1966), p. 216.
31. Hinsley, *Power and the Pursuit of Peace*, p. 66.
32. Hinsley, *Power and the Pursuit of Peace*, p. 66.
33. Hinsley, *Power and the Pursuit of Peace*, p. 66.
34. Hinsley, *Power and the Pursuit of Peace*, p. 66 (emphasis in original).
35. Hinsley, *Power and the Pursuit of Peace*, p. 66.
36. Hinsley, *Power and the Pursuit of Peace*, pp. 66–67
37. Hinsley, *Sovereignty*, p. 212.
38. F.H. Hinsley, *Nationalism and the International System*, Twentieth Century Studies, ed. Donald Tyerman (London: Hodder and Stoughton, 1973), p. 75.
39. Hinsley, *Nationalism and the International System*, p. 75.
40. Hinsley, *Power and the Pursuit of Peace*, p. 68.
41. Hinsley, *Power and the Pursuit of Peace*, p. 68.
42. Hinsley, *Power and the Pursuit of Peace*, p. 68.
43. Hinsley, *Power and the Pursuit of Peace*, p. 68.
44. Hinsley, *Nationalism and the International System*, p. 76.
45. Hinsley, *Power and the Pursuit of Peace*, pp. 71–72.
46. Kant, *Perpetual Peace*, ed. Reiss, trans. Nisbet, pp. 108–14.
47. Hinsley, *Power and the Pursuit of Peace*, p. 76.

48. Hinsley, *Power and the Pursuit of Peace*, p. 76.
49. Hinsley, *Power and the Pursuit of Peace*, p. 76.
50. Hinsley, *Power and the Pursuit of Peace*, p. 77.
51. Hinsley, *Power and the Pursuit of Peace*, p. 78.
52. Hinsley, *Power and the Pursuit of Peace*, p. 78.
53. Hinsley, *Power and the Pursuit of Peace*, p. 78.
54. Hinsley, *Power and the Pursuit of Peace*, p. 78.
55. Hinsley, *Power and the Pursuit of Peace*, p. 78.
56. Howard Williams and Ken Booth, "Kant: Theorist beyond Limits" in Ian Clark and Iver B. Neumann, eds., *Classical Theories of International Relations* (Houndmills, Basingstoke, Hampshire, and London: MacMillan Press, 1996), p. 72.
57. Frederick L. Schuman, *The Commonwealth of Man: An Inquiry into Power Politics and World Government* (London: Robert Hale, 1954), p. 349.
58. Schuman, *The Commonwealth of Man*, pp. 349–50.
59. Kenneth N. Waltz, "Kant, Liberalism, and War," *American Political Science Review*, 56 (1962), p. 331.
60. Waltz, "Kant, Liberalism, and War," pp. 331–37.
61. Waltz, "Kant, Liberalism, and War," pp. 336–37. Waltz makes the above comment in direct reference to the following quote from *Perpetual Peace* : "Every people, for the sake of its own security, thus may and ought to demand from any other that it shall enter along with it into a constitution, similar to the civil constitution, in which the right of each shall be secured." Immanuel Kant, *Eternal Peace and Other International Essays*, trans. W. Hastie (Boston, 1914), p. 81 in Waltz, "Kant, Liberalism, and War," p. 336.
62. Waltz, "Kant, Liberalism, and War," p. 337.
63. Waltz, "Kant, Liberalism, and War," p. 337.
64. Waltz, "Kant, Liberalism, and War," p. 337.
65. Waltz, "Kant, Liberalism, and War," p. 337.
66. Waltz, "Kant, Liberalism, and War," p. 337.
67. Waltz, "Kant, Liberalism, and War," p. 337.
68. Waltz, "Kant, Liberalism, and War," p. 337.
69. Waltz, "Kant, Liberalism, and War," p. 337.
70. Waltz, "Kant, Liberalism, and War," p. 337.
71. Wolfgang Schwarz, "Kant's Philosophy of Law and International Peace," *Philosophy and Phenomenological Research*, 23 (1962), pp. 71–80.
72. Schwarz, "Kant's Philosophy of Law and International Peace," p. 76.
73. Schwarz, "Kant's Philosophy of Law and International Peace," p. 76.
74. Schwarz, "Kant's Philosophy of Law and International Peace," p. 76.
75. Schwarz, "Kant's Philosophy of Law and International Peace," p. 80 quoting from Immanuel Kant's "Towards Eternal Peace," p. 47.
76. Schwarz, "Kant's Philosophy of Law and International Peace," p. 80 quoting from Immanuel Kant's "Towards Eternal Peace," p. 47.
77. Karl Jaspers, *Philosophy and the World*, trans. E.B. Ashton (Chicago: Henry Regnery, 1963), p. 88.

78. Kant, *Perpetual Peace*, ed. Reiss, trans. Nisbet, p. 97.
79. Jaspers, *Philosophy and the World*, p. 89.
80. Jaspers, *Philosophy and the World*, p. 90.
81. Jaspers, *Philosophy and the World*, p. 91 (emphasis in original).
82. Jaspers, *Philosophy and the World*, p. 91.
83. Jaspers, *Philosophy and the World*, p. 91.
84. Jaspers, *Philosophy and the World*, p. 91.
85. Jaspers, *Philosophy and the World*, pp. 91–92.
86. Jaspers, *Philosophy and the World*, p. 92.
87. Jaspers, *Philosophy and the World*, p. 96.
88. Jaspers, *Philosophy and the World*, p. 92.
89. Jaspers, *Philosophy and the World*, p. 92.
90. Jaspers, *Philosophy and the World*, p. 92.
91. Jaspers, *Philosophy and the World*, p. 96.
92. Jaspers, *Philosophy and the World*, pp. 96–97.
93. Jaspers, *Philosophy and the World*, p. 97.
94. F. Parkinson, *The Philosophy of International Relations*, Volume 52, Sage Library of Social Research (London, Beverly Hills: Sage Publication, 1977), p. 67.
95. Parkinson, *The Philosophy of International Relations*, p. 68.
96. Parkinson, *The Philosophy of International Relations*, p. 69.
97. Parkinson, *The Philosophy of International Relations*, p. 69.
98. Parkinson, *The Philosophy of International Relations*, p. 65.
99. Parkinson, *The Philosophy of International Relations*, p. 65.
100. Parkinson, *The Philosophy of International Relations*, p. 65.
101. Parkinson, *The Philosophy of International Relations*, p. 65.
102. Parkinson, *The Philosophy of International Relations*, p. 70.
103. Parkinson, *The Philosophy of International Relations*, p. 70.
104. W.B. Gallie, *Philosophers of Peace and War* (Cambridge: Cambridge University Press), pp. 8–36.
105. Gallie, *Philosophers of Peace and War*, p. 21.
106. Gallie, *Philosophers of Peace and War*, p. 20. Speaking of the similarity in interpretation between Gallie and Hinsley regarding the treaty or *foedus* they both believe Kant advocates, Gallie seems persuaded, even influenced by the whole of Hinsley's interpretation. He states that Kant's position in *Perpetual Peace* "was as original and unique as it is difficult to extract from the text of his pamphlet, and which indeed no one succeeded in extracting completely, until Professor F.H. Hinsley did so some fifteen years ago." Gallie, *Philosophers of Peace and War*, p. 11.
107. Gallie, *Philosophers of Peace and War*, p. 21.
108. Gallie, *Philosophers of Peace and War*, p. 20.
109. Gallie, *Philosophers of Peace and War*, p. 9.
110. Gallie, *Philosophers of Peace and War*, p. 9.
111. Gallie, *Philosophers of Peace and War*, p. 20.

112. Gallie, *Philosophers of Peace and War*, p. 23.
113. Gallie, *Philosophers of Peace and War*, p. 23.
114. Gallie, *Philosophers of Peace and War*, p. 24.
115. Gallie, *Philosophers of Peace and War*, p. 24.
116. Gallie, *Philosophers of Peace and War*, p. 24.
117. Gallie, *Philosophers of Peace and War*, p. 24.
118. Gallie, *Philosophers of Peace and War*, p. 24.
119. Gallie, *Philosophers of Peace and War*, p. 24.
120. Gallie, *Philosophers of Peace and War*, p. 25.
121. Gallie, *Philosophers of Peace and War*, p. 25 (emphasis in original).
122. Gallie, *Philosophers of Peace and War*, p. 10 (emphasis in original).
123. Gallie, *Philosophers of Peace and War*, p. 25 (emphasis in original).
124. Gallie, *Philosophers of Peace and War*, p. 25.
125. Gallie, *Philosophers of Peace and War*, p. 25.
126. Gallie, *Philosophers of Peace and War*, p. 27.
127. Gallie, *Philosophers of Peace and War*, p. 27.
128. Gallie, *Philosophers of Peace and War*, p. 27.
129. Gallie, *Philosophers of Peace and War*, p. 28.
130. Gallie, *Philosophers of Peace and War*, p. 28.
131. Gallie, *Philosophers of Peace and War*, p. 28.
132. Gallie, *Philosophers of Peace and War*, p. 28.
133. Gallie, *Philosophers of Peace and War*, p. 29.
134. Gallie, *Philosophers of Peace and War*, p. 29.
135. W.B. Gallie, "Wanted: A Philosophy of International Relations," *Political Studies*, 27 (1979), p. 485. In direct contrast to this statement by Gallie, it need not go unnoticed that interpreters such as Wheaton, Lorimer, and Mead whose textual analyses help to reveal the first phase of Pattern One, view the text as favoring "public legal coercion" as a solution to the problem of war at the international level.
136. Gallie, "Wanted: A Philosophy of International Relations," p. 485.
137. Gallie, "Wanted: A Philosophy of International Relations," p. 485.
138. Gallie, "Wanted: A Philosophy of International Relations," p. 485.
139. Susan Meld Shell, *The Rights of Reason: A Study of Kant's Philosophy and Politics* (Toronto: University of Toronto Press, 1980), p. 174.
140. Shell, *The Rights of Reason*, p. 174.
141. Shell, *The Rights of Reason*, p. 173.
142. Shell, *The Rights of Reason*, p. 173.
143. Shell, *The Rights of Reason*, p. 173.
144. Shell, *The Rights of Reason*, p. 173.
145. Shell, *The Rights of Reason*, p. 173.
146. Shell, *The Rights of Reason*, pp. 175–76.
147. Patrick Riley, *Kant's Political Philosophy* (Totowa, NJ: Rowman & Littlefield, 1983), p. 118.

148. Riley, *Kant's Political Philosophy*, p. 117.
149. Kant, *Perpetual Peace*, ed. Reiss, trans. Nisbet, p. 94.
150. Riley, *Kant's Political Philosophy*, p. 117.
151. Riley, *Kant's Political Philosophy*, p. 118.
152. Kant, *Perpetual Peace*, ed. Reiss, trans. Nisbet, p. 105.
153. Riley, *Kant's Political Philosophy*, p. 118.
154. Riley, *Kant's Political Philosophy*, p. 116.
155. Riley, *Kant's Political Philosophy*, p. 116.
156. Riley, *Kant's Political Philosophy*, p. 116.
157. Riley, *Kant's Political Philosophy*, p. 116 (emphasis in original).
158. Riley, *Kant's Political Philosophy*, p. 120.
159. Riley, *Kant's Political Philosophy*, p. 120.

5 Pattern Two, Phase Two: State Sovereignty Preserved I

1. Dean Babst, "A Force for Peace," *Industrial Research* (April 1972), pp. 55–58. Originally published as "Elective Governments—A Force for Peace," *The Wisconsin Sociologist*, 3, No. 1 (1964), pp. 9–14. Other early studies include: R.J. Rummell, *Understanding Conflict and War*, Volumes 1–5 (Los Angeles: Sage, 1975–1981); Bruce Russett and Harvey Starr, *World Politics: The Menu for Choice* (New York: W.H. Freeman, 1981); Peter Wallensteen, *Structure and War: On IR 1820–1968* (Stockholm: Raben and Sjogren, 1973).

2. Michael Doyle, "Kant, Liberal Legacies and Foreign Affairs, Parts 1 and 2," *Philosophy and Public Affairs*, 12, Nos. 3 and 4 (1983), pp. 205–35, 323–53. Howard Williams and Ken Booth note that this article, more than any other, "raised the profile of Kant's work [on international relations]." Howard Williams and Ken Booth, "Kant: Theorist Beyond Limits," in Ian Clark and Iver B. Neumann, eds., *Classical Theories of International Relations* (Houndmills, Basingstoke, Hampshire, and London: MacMillan Press, 1996), pp. 72–73.

3. Doyle, "Kant, Liberal Legacies, and Foreign Affairs, Part 1," p. 206.

4. To demonstrate the overflow of liberal peace scholarship over the recent past, included below is a pared down list of post-Doyle articles from the References section of Wade L. Huntley's, "Kant's Third Image: Systemic Sources of the Liberal Peace," *International Studies Quarterly*, 40 (1996), pp. 45–76; B. Bueno de Mesquita, R. Siverson, and G. Woller, "War and the Fate of Regimes: A Comparative Analysis," *American Political Science Review*, 86 (1992), pp. 638–46; S. Chan, "Mirror, Mirror on the Wall . . . Are the Freer Countries More Pacific?" *Journal of Conflict Resolution*, 28 (1984), pp. 617–48; N. Gleditsch, "Democracy and Peace," *Journal of Peace Research*, 29 (1992), pp. 369–76; J.D. Hagan, "Domestic Political Systems and War Proneness," *Mershon International Studies Review*, 38 (1994), pp. 183–207; D. Lake, "Powerful Pacifists: Democratic States and War," *American Political Science Review*, 86 (1992), pp. 24–37; C. Layne, "Kant or Cant: The Myth of the

184 • Notes

Democratic Peace," *International Security*, 19 (1994), pp. 5–49; J. Levy, "Domestic Politics and War," *Journal of Interdisciplinary History*, 18 (1988), pp. 653–73; Bruce Russett, *Grasping the Democratic Peace, Principles for a Post-Cold War Order* (Princeton: Princeton University Press, 1993); D. Spiro, "The Insignificance of the Liberal Peace," *International Security*, 19 (1994), pp. 50–86; H. Starr, "Why Don't Democracies Fight One Another?: Evaluating the Theory-Findings Feedback Loop," *Jerusalem Journal of International Relations*, 14 (1992), pp. 41–59. With the proliferation of these studies over the past several years, several scholars have reached the conclusion that the existence of a liberal peace is "as close as anything we have to an empirical law in international relations." Gleditsch, "Democracy and Peace," p. 372 and Levy, "Domestic Politics and War," pp. 661–62 in Huntley, "Kant's Third Image," p. 46.

5. See the Epilogue for evidence that Pattern Two, Phase Two is still predominant as the twenty-first century begins.

6. Doyle, "Kant, Liberal Legacies and Foreign Affairs, Part 1," Philosophy and public Affairs, 12 (1983), p 213 (emphasis in original).

7. Doyle, "Kant, Liberal Legacies and Foreign Affairs, Part 1," p. 225.

8. Doyle, "Kant, Liberal Legacies and Foreign Affairs, Part 1," p. 225.

9. Doyle, "Kant, Liberal Legacies and Foreign Affairs, Part 1," p. 225.

10. Doyle, "Kant, Liberal Legacies and Foreign Affairs, Part 1," p. 225.

11. Doyle, "Kant, Liberal Legacies and Foreign Affairs, Part 1," p. 225.

12. Doyle, "Kant, Liberal Legacies and Foreign Affairs, Part 1," pp. 225–26.

13. Immanuel Kant, *Perpetual Peace* in *Kant's Political Writings*, ed. Hans Reiss, trans. H.B. Nisbet (Cambridge: Cambridge University Press, 1970), p. 100.

14. Chris Brown, *International Relations Theory* (London: MacMillan Press, 1997), p. 36.

15. Kant, *Perpetual Peace*, ed. Reiss, trans. Nisbet, p. 100.

16. Doyle, "Kant, Liberal Legacies and Foreign Affairs, Part 1," p. 229.

17. Doyle, "Kant, Liberal Legacies and Foreign Affairs, Part 1," p. 229.

18. Doyle, "Kant, Liberal Legacies and Foreign Affairs, Part 1," p. 229. As noted in note 1 from the Introduction, for purposes of uniformity throughout the book, any text quoted from Kant's *Perpetual Peace*, excepting only that commentary by authors who may quote directly from other translations in their interpretation of the treatise, derives from the following translation: Immanuel Kant, *Perpetual Peace* in *Kant's Political Writings*, ed. Reiss, trans. Nisbet. Here, as opposed to the Nisbet translation, Doyle chooses to use a translation of *Perpetual Peace* from Immanuel Kant, *Perpetual Peace* in *The Enlightenment*, ed. Peter Gay (New York: Simon & Schuster, 1974), pp. 790–92 Considering how central this passage is to Pattern Two, Phase Two interpretation, I believe it is helpful to my argument to demonstrate how similar the two translations are. Compare the above translation to the following translation by Nisbet of exactly the same passage:

If, as is inevitably the case under this constitution, the consent of the citizens is required to decide whether or not war is to be declared, it is very natural that they will have great hesitation in embarking on so dangerous an enterprise. For this would mean calling down on themselves all the miseries of war, such as doing the fighting themselves, supplying the costs of the war from their own resources, painfully making good the ensuing devastation, and, as the crowning evil, having to takes upon themselves a burden of debt which will embitter peace itself and which can never be paid off on account of the constant threat of new wars. But under a constitution where the subject is not a citizen, and which is therefore not republican, it is the simplest thing in the world to go to war. For the head of state is not a fellow citizen, but the owner of the state, and a war will not force him to make the slightest sacrifice so far as his banquets, hunts, pleasure palaces and court festivals are concerned. He can thus decide on war, without any significant reason, as a kind of amusement, and unconcernedly leave it to the diplomatic corps (who are always ready for such purposes) to justify the war for the sake of propriety. (Kant, *Perpetual Peace*, ed. Reiss, trans. Nisbet, p. 100. A detailed comparison of both reveals little difference between the two)

19. Doyle, "Kant, Liberal Legacies and Foreign Affairs, Part 1," p. 226.
20. Doyle, "Kant, Liberal Legacies and Foreign Affairs, Part 1," p. 226.
21. Doyle, "Kant, Liberal Legacies and Foreign Affairs, Part 1," p. 226.
22. Doyle, "Kant, Liberal Legacies and Foreign Affairs, Part 1," p. 226 (emphasis in original). As Doyle says in a footnote below this comment, "I think Kant meant that the peace would be established among liberal regimes and would expand as new liberal regimes appeared. By a process of gradual extension the peace would become global and then perpetual; the occasion for wars with nonliberals would disappear as nonliberal regimes disappeared." Doyle, "Kant, Liberal Legacies and Foreign Affairs, Part 1," p. 226, Footnote 25.
23. Doyle, "Kant, Liberal Legacies and Foreign Affairs, Part 1," pp. 226–27.
24. Doyle, "Kant, Liberal Legacies and Foreign Affairs, Part 1," p. 227.
25. Doyle, "Kant, Liberal Legacies and Foreign Affairs, Part 1," p. 227.
26. Doyle, "Kant, Liberal Legacies and Foreign Affairs, Part 1," p. 227, Footnote 26.
27. Doyle, "Kant, Liberal Legacies and Foreign Affairs, Part 1," p. 227, Footnote 26.
28. Doyle, "Kant, Liberal Legacies and Foreign Affairs, Part 1," p. 227, Footnote 26.
29. Doyle, "Kant, Liberal Legacies and Foreign Affairs, Part 1," p. 228. Doyle breaks down Kant's positions into the following three categories (as Kant does himself): constitutional law, international law, and cosmopolitan law. The above discussion is obviously concerned with domestic constitutional law and is fundamental for Doyle in his interpretation of *Perpetual Peace*. As argued here, an established republic provides the "constitutional guarantee of caution" when it comes to potential war. Doyle, "Kant, Liberal Legacies and Foreign Affairs, Part 1," p. 230. But it should be noted that both international law ("a guarantee of respect") and cosmopolitan law ("the addition of material incentives" in the form of free trade and international commerce) are also discussed by Doyle as sources of long-term peace between states. Doyle, "Kant, Liberal Legacies and Foreign Affairs, Part 1," pp. 230–31.

30. Doyle, "Kant, Liberal Legacies and Foreign Affairs, Part 1," p. 232.
31. Doyle, "Kant, Liberal Legacies and Foreign Affairs, Part 1," p. 232.
32. Doyle, "Kant, Liberal Legacies and Foreign Affairs, Part 1," p. 232.
33. Doyle, "Kant, Liberal Legacies and Foreign Affairs, Part 1," p. 225.
34. Doyle, "Kant, Liberal Legacies and Foreign Affairs, Part 1," p. 225.
35. Doyle, "Kant, Liberal Legacies and Foreign Affairs, Part 1," p. 225.
36. Anthony Smith, "Kant's Political Philosophy: Rechsstaat or Council Democracy?" *Review of Politics*, 47 (April 1985), p. 258.
37. Smith, "Kant's Political Philosophy: Rechsstaat or Council Democracy?" p. 258.
38. Peter Calvocoresi, *A Time for Peace: Pacifism, Internationalism and Protest Forces in the Reduction of War* (London, Melbourne, Auckland, and Johannesburg: Hutchinson, 1987), p. 48.
39. Calvocoresi, *A Time for Peace*, p. 48.
40. Leslie A. Mulholland, "Kant on War and International Justice," *Kant-Studien*, 78 (1987), p. 33.
41. Mulholland, "Kant on War and International Justice," pp. 34 and 35, respectively.
42. Mulholland, "Kant on War and International Justice," p. 35.
43. Mulholland, "Kant on War and International Justice," p. 35.
44. Mulholland, "Kant on War and International Justice," p. 35.
45. Mulholland, "Kant on War and International Justice," p. 35.
46. Mulholland, "Kant on War and International Justice," p. 35.
47. Mulholland, "Kant on War and International Justice," p. 35.
48. Mulholland, "Kant on War and International Justice," p. 35.
49. Mulholland, "Kant on War and International Justice," p. 36.
50. Mulholland, "Kant on War and International Justice," p. 36.
51. Mulholland, "Kant on War and International Justice," p. 36.
52. Mulholland, "Kant on War and International Justice," p. 36.
53. Mulholland, "Kant on War and International Justice," p. 36.
54. Thomas L. Carson, "*Perpetual Peace*: What Kant Should Have Said," *Social Theory and Practice*, 14, No. 2 (Summer 1988), p. 184.
55. Carson, "*Perpetual Peace*: What Kant Should Have Said," p. 175.
56. Carson, "*Perpetual Peace*: What Kant Should Have Said," p. 175.
57. Carson, "*Perpetual Peace*: What Kant Should Have Said," p. 175.
58. Carson, "*Perpetual Peace*: What Kant Should Have Said," p. 180.
59. Carson, "*Perpetual Peace*: What Kant Should Have Said," p. 176.
60. Carson, "*Perpetual Peace*: What Kant Should Have Said," p. 176.
61. Carson, "*Perpetual Peace*: What Kant Should Have Said," p. 176.
62. Carson, "*Perpetual Peace*: What Kant Should Have Said," p. 177.
63. Carson, "*Perpetual Peace*: What Kant Should Have Said," p. 179.
64. Carson, "*Perpetual Peace*: What Kant Should Have Said," p. 179.
65. Carson, "*Perpetual Peace*: What Kant Should Have Said," p. 179.
66. Carson, "*Perpetual Peace*: What Kant Should Have Said," p. 179.

67. Ian Clark, *The Hierarchy of States: Reform and Resistance in the International Order* (Cambridge: Cambridge University Press, 1989), p. 55.
68. Clark, *The Hierarchy of States*, p. 49.
69. Clark, *The Hierarchy of States*, p. 55.
70. Clark, *The Hierarchy of States*, p. 55.
71. Clark, *The Hierarchy of States*, p. 55.
72. Clark, *The Hierarchy of States*, p. 55.
73. Clark, *The Hierarchy of States*, p. 55.
74. Clark, *The Hierarchy of States*, p. 55.
75. Sissela Bok, *A Strategy for Peace: Human Values and the Threat of War* (New York: Pantheon Books, 1989), p. 32.
76. Bok, *A Strategy for Peace*, p. 32.
77. Bok, *A Strategy for Peace*, p. 32.
78. Bok, *A Strategy for Peace*, p. 32.
79. Bok, *A Strategy for Peace*, pp. 32–33.
80. Bok, *A Strategy for Peace*, p. 33.

6 Pattern Two, Phase Two: State Sovereignty Preserved II

1. Howard Williams and Ken Booth claim that the perceived "liberal triumphalism" at the end of the 1980s and the notion that "World politics . . . seemed to be moving in a 'Kantian' direction elevated the status of the great Prussian philosopher within International Relations circles." Howard Williams and Ken Booth, "Kant: Theorist beyond Limits" in Ian Clark and Iver B. Neumann, eds., *Classical Theories of International Relations* (Houndmills, Basingstoke, Hampshire, and London: MacMillan Press, 1996), p. 73.
2. Andrew Hurrell, "Kant and the Kantian Paradigm in International Relations," *Review of International Studies*, 16 (1990), p. 183.
3. Hurrell, "Kant and the Kantian Paradigm," p. 183.
4. Hurrell, "Kant and the Kantian Paradigm," p. 183.
5. Hurrell, "Kant and the Kantian Paradigm," p. 185.
6. Hurrell, "Kant and the Kantian Paradigm," p. 185.
7. Hurrell, "Kant and the Kantian Paradigm," p. 194.
8. Hurrell, "Kant and the Kantian Paradigm," p. 189. Hurrell takes this quotation (along with all others in his article) from Immanuel Kant, *Perpetual Peace* in *Kant's Political Writings*, ed. Hans Reiss, trans. H.B. Nisbet (Cambridge: Cambridge University Press, 1970).
9. Hurrell, "Kant and the Kantian Paradigm," p. 190.
10. Hurrell, "Kant and the Kantian Paradigm," p. 190.
11. Hurrell, "Kant and the Kantian Paradigm," p. 190.
12. Hurrell, "Kant and the Kantian Paradigm," p. 192.
13. Hurrell, "Kant and the Kantian Paradigm," p. 192.
14. Hurrell, "Kant and the Kantian Paradigm," pp. 192–93 (emphasis in original).

15. Hurrell, "Kant and the Kantian Paradigm," p. 200.
16. Hurrell, "Kant and the Kantian Paradigm," p. 193.
17. Hurrell, "Kant and the Kantian Paradigm," p. 193.
18. Hurrell, "Kant and the Kantian Paradigm," p. 186.
19. Hurrell, "Kant and the Kantian Paradigm," p. 194.
20. Hurrell, "Kant and the Kantian Paradigm," p. 195.
21. Hurrell, "Kant and the Kantian Paradigm," p. 195.
22. Hurrell, "Kant and the Kantian Paradigm," p. 196.
23. Hurrell, "Kant and the Kantian Paradigm," p. 196.
24. Hurrell, "Kant and the Kantian Paradigm," p. 196.
25. Hurrell, "Kant and the Kantian Paradigm," p. 200.
26. Chris Brown, *International Relations Theory: New Normative Approaches* (Brighton: Harvester Press, 1992), p. 31 (emphasis in original).
27. Brown, *International Relations Theory*, p. 32.
28. Brown, *International Relations Theory*, p. 32.
29. Brown, *International Relations Theory*, p. 33.
30. Brown, *International Relations Theory*, p. 33.
31. Brown, *International Relations Theory*, p. 33.
32. Brown, *International Relations Theory*, p. 34.
33. Brown, *International Relations Theory*, p. 34.
34. Brown, *International Relations Theory*, p. 36. The restatement of the three different types of constitution is a direct quote from Kant, *Perpetual Peace*, ed. Reiss, trans. Nisbet, p. 98 (emphasis in original).
35. Brown, *International Relations Theory*, p. 36.
36. Brown, *International Relations Theory*, p. 36.
37. Brown, *International Relations Theory*, p. 36.
38. Brown, *International Relations Theory*, p. 36.
39. Brown, *International Relations Theory*, p. 36.
40. Brown, *International Relations Theory*, p. 41.
41. Brown, *International Relations Theory*, p. 41.
42. Brown, *International Relations Theory*, p. 37.
43. Brown, *International Relations Theory*, p. 37.
44. Brown, *International Relations Theory*, p. 37.
45. Fernando R. Tesòn, "The Kantian Theory of International Law," *Columbia Law Review*, 92 (January 1992), pp. 53–54. Tesón uses the following translation of *Perpetual Peace* throughout this article: Immanuel Kant, *Perpetual Peace and Other Essays on Politics, History and Morals*, intro. and trans. Ted Humphrey (Indianapolis: Hackett Publishing Co., 1983).
46. Tesòn, "The Kantian Theory of International Law," p. 54.
47. Tesòn, "The Kantian Theory of International Law," p. 54.
48. Tesòn, "The Kantian Theory of International Law," p. 54.
49. Tesòn, "The Kantian Theory of International Law," p. 54.
50. Tesòn, "The Kantian Theory of International Law," p. 55.
51. Tesòn, "The Kantian Theory of International Law," p. 56.

52. Tesòn, "The Kantian Theory of International Law," pp. 58–59.
53. Tesòn, "The Kantian Theory of International Law," p. 60.
54. Tesòn, "The Kantian Theory of International Law," p. 70.
55. Tesòn, "The Kantian Theory of International Law," p. 60. To avoid confusion, it should be noted that Tesón sees no difference between the terms "republican" and "liberal democracy." As other interpreters have done, he makes clear that Kant does not support a pure democracy, since it is necessarily despotism. He says "Kant's explanation of a republican constitution strongly suggests the idea of a constitutional democracy, conceived as a participatory political process constrained by respect for rights" and one that "allows people to govern themselves and to legislate by majority vote, provided that the rights of everyone [meaning minority rights or the rights of dissenters] are respected" as well. Tesòn, "The Kantian Theory of International Law," pp. 61–62.
56. Tesòn, "The Kantian Theory of International Law," p. 61.
57. Tesòn, "The Kantian Theory of International Law," p. 61.
58. Tesòn, "The Kantian Theory of International Law," p. 61.
59. Tesòn, "The Kantian Theory of International Law," p. 74.
60. Tesòn, "The Kantian Theory of International Law," p. 74.
61. Tesòn, "The Kantian Theory of International Law," p. 75.
62. Tesòn, "The Kantian Theory of International Law," p. 75.
63. Tesòn, "The Kantian Theory of International Law," p. 75.
64. Tesòn, "The Kantian Theory of International Law," p. 75.
65. Tesòn, "The Kantian Theory of International Law," p. 76.
66. Tesòn, "The Kantian Theory of International Law," p. 81.
67. Tesòn, "The Kantian Theory of International Law," p. 81 (emphasis in original).
68. Tesòn, "The Kantian Theory of International Law," p. 82.
69. Tesòn, "The Kantian Theory of International Law," p. 86.
70. Tesòn, "The Kantian Theory of International Law," p. 86 (emphasis in original).
71. Tesòn, "The Kantian Theory of International Law," pp. 86–87.
72. Tesòn, "The Kantian Theory of International Law," p. 87.
73. Tesòn, "The Kantian Theory of International Law," p. 87.
74. Tesòn, "The Kantian Theory of International Law," p. 87.
75. Tesòn, "The Kantian Theory of International Law," p. 87.
76. Tesòn, "The Kantian Theory of International Law," p. 87.
77. Tesòn, "The Kantian Theory of International Law," p. 88. Here, Tesòn quotes from the 1983 Humphrey translation.
78. Tesòn, "The Kantian Theory of International Law," p. 86.
79. Tesòn, "The Kantian Theory of International Law," p. 102.
80. Cecelia Lynch offers the following summary of Tesòn's thesis in a 1994 interpretation of *Perpetual Peace* to be discussed more thoroughly later: "Fernando Tesón, for example, has combined a liberal interpretation of Kant with the findings of the 'democratic peace' literature to argue in favor of founding international law on principles of respect for the sovereignty of liberal states only." Cecelia Lynch, "Kant, the Republican Peace, and

Moral Guidance in International Law," *Ethics and International Affairs*, 8 (1994), p. 46.

81. Gabriel L. Negretto, "Kant and the Illusion of Collective Security," *Journal of International Affairs*, 46 (Winter 1993), p. 506.
82. Negretto, "Kant and the Illusion of Collective Security," p. 507.
83. Negretto, "Kant and the Illusion of Collective Security," p. 507.
84. Negretto, "Kant and the Illusion of Collective Security," p. 507.
85. Negretto, "Kant and the Illusion of Collective Security," pp. 508–09.
86. Negretto, "Kant and the Illusion of Collective Security," p. 508.
87. Negretto, "Kant and the Illusion of Collective Security," p. 508 (emphasis in original).
88. Negretto, "Kant and the Illusion of Collective Security," p. 508.
89. Negretto, "Kant and the Illusion of Collective Security," pp. 508–09.
90. Negretto, "Kant and the Illusion of Collective Security," p. 508.
91. Negretto, "Kant and the Illusion of Collective Security," p. 509. Negretto notes in Footnote 4 that Kant's *Perpetual Peace* pamphlet is reprinted in Immanuel Kant, *On History*, ed. and trans. Lewis White Beck (New York: Bobbs-Merrill, 1963). Negretto, "Kant and the Illusion of Collective Security," p. 503.
92. Negretto, "Kant and the Illusion of Collective Security," p. 509.
93. Negretto, "Kant and the Illusion of Collective Security," p. 510.
94. Negretto, "Kant and the Illusion of Collective Security," p. 513.
95. Georg Cavallar, "Kant's Society of Nations: Free Federation or World Republic?" *Journal of the History of Philosophy*, 32 (July 1994), p. 476.
96. Cavallar, "Kant's Society of Nations," p. 476.
97. Cavallar, "Kant's Society of Nations," p. 476.
98. Cavallar, "Kant's Society of Nations," p. 476.
99. Cavallar, "Kant's Society of Nations," p. 476.
100. Cavallar, "Kant's Society of Nations," p. 477.
101. Cavallar, "Kant's Society of Nations," p. 477.
102. Cavallar, "Kant's Society of Nations," p. 477.
103. Cavallar, "Kant's Society of Nations," pp. 461–62.
104. Cavallar, "Kant's Society of Nations," p. 466.
105. Cavallar, "Kant's Society of Nations," pp. 466–70.
106. Cavallar, "Kant's Society of Nations," p. 466.
107. Cavallar, "Kant's Society of Nations," p. 467.
108. Cavallar, "Kant's Society of Nations," p. 467.
109. Cavallar, "Kant's Society of Nations," p. 467.
110. Cavallar, "Kant's Society of Nations," p. 467.
111. Cavallar, "Kant's Society of Nations," pp. 468–69.
112. Cavallar, "Kant's Society of Nations," p. 468.
113. Cavallar, "Kant's Society of Nations," p. 471.
114. Cavallar, "Kant's Society of Nations," p. 471.
115. Cavallar, "Kant's Society of Nations," p. 469.

116. Cavallar, "Kant's Society of Nations," p. 470.
117. Cavallar, "Kant's Society of Nations," p. 472.
118. Cavallar, "Kant's Society of Nations," p. 472 (emphasis in original).
119. Cavallar, "Kant's Society of Nations," p. 473.
120. Cavallar, "Kant's Society of Nations," p. 472 (emphasis in original).
121. Cavallar, "Kant's Society of Nations," p. 474.
122. Cavallar, "Kant's Society of Nations," p. 474.
123. Cavallar, "Kant's Society of Nations," p. 480.
124. Jürg Martin Gabriel, *Worldviews and Theories of International Relations* (New York: St. Martin's Press, 1994), p. 51.
125. Gabriel, *Worldviews and Theories*, p. 52.
126. Gabriel, *Worldviews and Theories*, p. 52.
127. Gabriel, *Worldviews and Theories*, p. 52.
128. Gabriel, *Worldviews and Theories*, p. 52.
129. Gabriel, *Worldviews and Theories*, p. 53.
130. Gabriel, *Worldviews and Theories*, p. 53.
131. Gabriel, *Worldviews and Theories*, p. 53.
132. Gabriel, *Worldviews and Theories*, p. 53.
133. Gabriel, *Worldviews and Theories*, pp. 54–55.
134. Gabriel, *Worldviews and Theories*, p. 55.
135. Gabriel, *Worldviews and Theories*, p. 55.
136. Gabriel, *Worldviews and Theories*, p. 56. While Gabriel calls it "crucial" here, James Lee Ray, in a book about the liberal peace written during this same period, refers to the "consent of the citizens" selection from *Perpetual Peace* as "The essence of Kant's argument that democracy is an important force for peace." James Lee Ray, *Democracy and International Conflict: An Evaluation of the Democratic Peace Proposition* (Columbia, S.C.: University of South Carolina Press, 1995), p. 1.
137. Gabriel, *Worldviews and Theories*, p. 56.
138. Gabriel, *Worldviews and Theories*, p. 56.
139. Gabriel, *Worldviews and Theories*, p. 56.
140. Gabriel, *Worldviews and Theories*, p. 56.
141. Gabriel, *Worldviews and Theories*, p. 56.
142. Gabriel, *Worldviews and Theories*, p. 56.
143. Gabriel, *Worldviews and Theories*, p. 58.
144. Gabriel, *Worldviews and Theories*, pp. 57–58.
145. Gabriel, *Worldviews and Theories*, p. 58.
146. Charles Covell, *Kant, Liberalism and the Pursuit of Justice in the International Order*, Studies in the History of International Relations, Band 1 (Munster, Hamburg: Lit, 1994), p. 23.
147. Covell, *Kant, Liberalism and the Pursuit of Justice*, p. 25.
148. Covell, *Kant, Liberalism and the Pursuit of Justice*, p. 27.
149. Covell, *Kant, Liberalism and the Pursuit of Justice*, p. 27.
150. Covell, *Kant, Liberalism and the Pursuit of Justice*, p. 27.

151. Covell, *Kant, Liberalism and the Pursuit of Justice*, p. 27.
152. Covell, *Kant, Liberalism and the Pursuit of Justice*, pp. 27–28.
153. Covell, *Kant, Liberalism and the Pursuit of Justice*, p. 28.
154. Covell, *Kant, Liberalism and the Pursuit of Justice*, p. 29.
155. Covell, *Kant, Liberalism and the Pursuit of Justice*, p. 29.
156. Covell, *Kant, Liberalism and the Pursuit of Justice*, p. 29.
157. Covell, *Kant, Liberalism and the Pursuit of Justice*, p. 30.
158. Covell, *Kant, Liberalism and the Pursuit of Justice*, p. 30.
159. Covell, *Kant, Liberalism and the Pursuit of Justice*, p. 30. Covell also reaffirms this in another similar passage in Chapter Three of his book:

> For Kant, no international order could promote a lasting peace between states which required the separate states to surrender their sovereign independence to an international state, or to a world government. Hence, he insisted that international peace could come about only through the *voluntary* acceptance by states of an international rule of law, where this rule of law presupposed, as the condition of its own legitimacy, the retention by the states that accepted its authority of the rights that were essential to their sovereignty and independence. Covell, *Kant, Liberalism and the Pursuit of Justice*, p. 71 (emphasis in original).

160. Daniele Archibugi, "Models of International Organization in Perpetual Peace Projects," *Review of International Studies*, 18 (1992), p. 311.
161. Archibugi, "Models of International Organization," p. 311.
162. Archibugi, "Models of International Organization," p. 312.
163. Archibugi, "Models of International Organization," p. 312.
164. Michael C. Williams, "Reason and Realpolitik: Kant's Critique of International Politics," *Canadian Journal of Political Science*, 25 (March 1992), p. 110.
165. Williams, "Reason and Realpolitik," pp. 110–11.
166. Williams, "Reason and Realpolitik," p. 111. Williams references Doyle's 1983 article after making this comment.
167. Otfried Hoffe, *Immanuel Kant*, translated by Marshall Farrier (originally published in German by G.H. Beck' sche Verlagsbuchhandlung, 1992; Albany: State University of New York Press, 1994), p. 187.
168. Hoffe, *Immanuel Kant*, p. 187.
169. Hoffe, *Immanuel Kant*, p. 187.
170. Hoffe, *Immanuel Kant*, p. 187.
171. Jens Bartleson, "The Trial of Judgment: A Note on Kant and the Paradoxes of Internationalism," *International Studies Quarterly*, 39 (1995), p. 266.
172. Bartleson, "The Trial of Judgment," p. 266.
173. Bartleson, "The Trial of Judgment," p. 266.
174. Bartleson, "The Trial of Judgment," p. 266.
175. Bartleson, "The Trial of Judgment," p. 267.
176. Allen Wood, "Kant's Project for Perpetual Peace" in *Proceedings of the Eighth International Kant Congress*, Memphis 1995, Volume One (Milwaukee: Marquette University Press, 1995), p. 3.

177. In addition to the more relevant Eighth International Kant Congress, the following Kant congresses were considered in my research: L.W. Beck, ed., *Proceedings of the Third International Kant Congress*, Two Volumes (Dordrecht, Holland: D. Reidel Publishing Company, 1972); Gerhard Funke and Thomas M. Seebohm, eds., *Proceedings of the Sixth International Kant Congress*, Two Volumes (Washington, D.C.: University Press of America, 1989).

178. The following papers from the Eighth International Kant Congress that generally discuss *Perpetual Peace* can be found in Hoke Robinson, ed., *Proceedings of the Eighth International Kant Congress*, Two Volumes (Milwaukee: Marquette University Press, 1995): Sharon Byrd, "Perpetual Peace: A 20th Century Project," pp. 343–57; Sharon Byrd, "The State as a 'Moral Person,'" pp. 171–89; Georg Geismann, "On the Philosophically Unique Realism of Kant's Doctrine of Eternal Peace," pp. 273–89; Paul Guyer, "Nature, Morality and the Possibility of Peace," pp. 51–69; Ludwig Siep, "Kant and Hegel on Peace and International Law," pp. 259–72; Harry Van der Linden, "Kant: the Duty to Promote International Peace and Political Intervention," pp. 71–79; Allen Wood, "Kant's Project for Perpetual Peace," pp. 3–18.

179. Kenneth W. Thompson, *Fathers of International Thought, The Legacy of Political Theory* (Baton Rouge and London: Louisiana State University Press, 1994), p. 108.

180. Thompson, *Fathers of International Thought*, p. 108.

181. Thompson, *Fathers of International Thought*, p. 108.

182. Thompson, *Fathers of International Thought*, p. 108.

183. Thompson, *Fathers of International Thought*, pp. 108–09.

184. Thompson, *Fathers of International Thought*, p. 110.

185. Thompson, *Fathers of International Thought*, p. 110.

186. Thompson, *Fathers of International Thought*, pp. 110–11.

187. Lynch, "Kant, the Republican Peace, and Moral Guidance in International Law," p. 39.

188. Lynch, "Kant, the Republican Peace, and Moral Guidance in International Law," pp. 40–41.

189. Lynch, "Kant, the Republican Peace, and Moral Guidance in International Law," p. 41.

190. Lynch, "Kant, the Republican Peace, and Moral Guidance in International Law," pp. 45–46.

191. Lynch, "Kant, the Republican Peace, and Moral Guidance in International Law," p. 54.

7 Pattern Two, Phase Two: State Sovereignty Preserved III

1. Howard Williams, *Kant's Political Philosophy* (New York: St. Martin's Press, 1983), p. 244.

2. Williams, *Kant's Political Philosophy*, p. 246.

3. Williams, *Kant's Political Philosophy*, p. 250.

4. Williams, *Kant's Political Philosophy*, p. 250.

5. Williams, *Kant's Political Philosophy*, p. 250.

6. Williams, *Kant's Political Philosophy*, p. 250.
7. Williams, *Kant's Political Philosophy*, p. 254.
8. Williams, *Kant's Political Philosophy*, p. 254.
9. Williams, *Kant's Political Philosophy*, p. 254.
10. Williams, *Kant's Political Philosophy*, p. 254.
11. Williams, *Kant's Political Philosophy*, p. 254.
12. Williams, *Kant's Political Philosophy*, p. 254.
13. Williams, *Kant's Political Philosophy*, p. 255.
14. Williams, *Kant's Political Philosophy*, p. 258.
15. Williams, *Kant's Political Philosophy*, pp. 255–56.
16. Williams, *Kant's Political Philosophy*, p. 256.
17. Williams, *Kant's Political Philosophy*, p. 256.
18. Williams, *Kant's Political Philosophy*, p. 259.
19. Williams, *Kant's Political Philosophy*, p. 269.
20. Williams, *Kant's Political Philosophy*, p. 256.
21. Howard Williams, *International Relations in Political Theory* (Milton Keynes: Open University Press, 1992), p. 80.
22. Williams, *International Relations in Political Theory*, p. 87.
23. Williams, *International Relations in Political Theory*, p. 88.
24. Williams, *International Relations in Political Theory*, p. 88.
25. Williams, *International Relations in Political Theory*, p. 88.
26. Williams, *International Relations in Political Theory*, p. 89.
27. Williams, *International Relations in Political Theory*, p. 88.
28. Howard Williams and Ken Booth, "Kant: Theorist beyond Limits" in Ian Clark and Iver B. Neuman, eds., *Classical Theories of International Relations* (Houndsmills, Basingstoke, and London: MacMillan Press, 1996), p. 81.
29. Williams and Booth, "Kant: Theorist beyond Limits," p. 89.
30. Williams and Booth, "Kant: Theorist beyond Limits," p. 89.
31. Williams and Booth, "Kant: Theorist beyond Limits," p. 90.
32. Williams and Booth, "Kant: Theorist beyond Limits," p. 90.
33. Williams and Booth, "Kant: Theorist beyond Limits," p. 90.
34. Williams and Booth, "Kant: Theorist beyond Limits," p. 90.
35. Williams and Booth, "Kant: Theorist beyond Limits," p. 90.
36. Wade L. Huntley, "Kant's Third Image: Systemic Sources of the Liberal Peace," *International Studies Quarterly*, 40 (1996), p. 45.
37. Huntley, "Kant's Third Image," p. 45.
38. Huntley, "Kant's Third Image," p. 49.
39. Huntley, "Kant's Third Image," p. 50.
40. Huntley, "Kant's Third Image," p. 50.
41. Huntley, "Kant's Third Image," p. 50.
42. Huntley, "Kant's Third Image," p. 50.
43. Huntley, "Kant's Third Image," p. 50.
44. Huntley, "Kant's Third Image," p. 51.

45. Huntley, "Kant's Third Image," p. 51 (emphasis in original).
46. Huntley, "Kant's Third Image," p. 60.
47. Huntley, "Kant's Third Image," p. 60.
48. Huntley, "Kant's Third Image," p. 60.
49. Howard Williams, David Sullivan, and Gwynn Matthews, *Francis Fukuyama and the End of History, Political Philosophy Now* (Cardiff: University of Wales Press, 1997), p. 12.
50. Williams et al., *Francis Fukuyama and the End of History*, p. 12.
51. Williams et al., *Francis Fukuyama and the End of History*, p. 13.
52. Williams et al., *Francis Fukuyama and the End of History*, pp. 12–13.
53. Williams et al., *Francis Fukuyama and the End of History*, p. 13.
54. Fareed Zakaria, "The Rise of Illiberal Democracy," *Foreign Affairs* (November/December 1997), p. 36.
55. Zakaria, "The Rise of Illiberal Democracy," p. 37.
56. Michael Doyle, *Ways of War and Peace: Realism, Liberalism, and Socialism* (New York and London: W.W. Norton & Company, 1997), p. 254.
57. Doyle, *Ways of War and Peace*, p. 258.
58. Doyle, *Ways of War and Peace*, p. 258.
59. Charles Covell, *Kant & the Law of Peace: A Study in the Philosophy of International Law and International Relations* (London: MacMillan Press, 1998), p. 104.
60. Covell, *Kant & the Law of Peace*, p. 104.
61. Covell, *Kant & the Law of Peace*, p. 106.
62. Covell, *Kant & the Law of Peace*, p. 67.
63. Covell, *Kant & the Law of Peace*, p. 67.
64. Covell, *Kant & the Law of Peace*, p. 121.
65. Covell, *Kant & the Law of Peace*, p. 122.
66. Covell, *Kant & the Law of Peace*, p. 124.
67. Covell, *Kant & the Law of Peace*, p. 125. As do several of the interpreters writing from the mid-twentieth century onward, Covell contrasts Kant's proposal in *Perpetual Peace* with the Abbè de St. Pierre's. He states quite clearly that "Kant's rejection of international government within the framework of an international state or world state, as the basis for a lasting peace between states, underlines the fundamental contrast between the argument of *Perpetual Peace* and the argument contained in a notable plan for perpetual peace which had been set out in the early decades of the eighteenth century." Covell, *Kant & the Law of Peace*, p. 125.
68. Covell, *Kant & the Law of Peace*, p. 97.
69. Covell, *Kant & the Law of Peace*, p. 97.
70. Covell, *Kant & the Law of Peace*, p. 183.
71. Covell, *Kant & the Law of Peace*, p. 183.
72. John Rawls, *The Law of Peoples* (Cambridge and London: Harvard University Press, 1999), p. 36. In coming to this conclusion, Rawls quotes the following passage:

> The idea of international law presupposes the separate existence of independent neighboring states. Although this condition is itself a state of war (unless

federative union prevents the outbreak of hostilities), this is rationally preferable to the amalgamation of states under one superior power, as this would end
in universal monarchy, and laws always lose in vigor what government gains in
extent; hence a condition of soulless despotism falls into anarchy after stifling
seeds of good. (Rawls, *The Law of Peoples*, Footnote 40, p. 36)

73. Rawls, *The Law of Peoples*, p. 54.
74. Rawls, *The Law of Peoples*, p. 54.
75. Rawls, *The Law of Peoples*, p. 54.
76. Harold Kleinschmidt, *The Nemesis of Power: A History of International Relations Theories* (London: Reakton Books, 2000), p. 138.
77. Kleinschmidt, *The Nemesis of Power*, p. 138.
78. Kleinschmidt, *The Nemesis of Power*, p. 138.
79. Kleinschmidt, *The Nemesis of Power*, p. 138.
80. Kleinschmidt, *The Nemesis of Power*, p. 138.
81. Kleinschmidt, *The Nemesis of Power*, p. 138.
82. Kleinschmidt, *The Nemesis of Power*, p. 138.
83. Kleinschmidt, *The Nemesis of Power*, pp. 138–39.
84. Kleinschmidt, *The Nemesis of Power*, p. 139.
85. Kleinschmidt, *The Nemesis of Power*, p. 152.
86. Kleinschmidt, *The Nemesis of Power*, p. 139.
87. Kleinschmidt, *The Nemesis of Power*, p. 139.
88. Kleinschmidt, *The Nemesis of Power*, p. 139.

8 Pattern Formation as a Function of the Rise and Decline of Hopes for Peace Through International Organization

1. Inis Claude, Jr., *Swords into Plowshares: The Problems and Progress of International Organization* (New York: Random House, 1959), p. 26. Claude comically quotes Rousseau who once described international conferences of the eighteenth century as places "where we deliberate in common council whether the table will be round or square, whether the hall will have more doors or less, whether such and such a plenipotentiary will have his face or back turned toward the window." Claude, *Swords into Plowshares*, pp. 26–27.
2. Claude, *Swords into Plowshares*, p. 27.
3. Claude, *Swords into Plowshares*, p. 23 (emphasis in original).
4. Claude, *Swords into Plowshares*, p. 27.
5. Claude, *Swords into Plowshares*, p. 28.
6. Claude, *Swords into Plowshares*, p. 32.
7. Claude, *Swords into Plowshares*, p. 30.
8. Claude, *Swords into Plowshares*, p. 30.
9. Claude, *Swords into Plowshares*, pp. 32–33.

10. Claude, *Swords into Plowshares*, p. 31.
11. Clive Archer, *International Organizations* (2nd. ed.) (London: Routledge Press, 1992), p. 10.
12. Claude, *Swords into Plowshares*, p. 32.
13. Claude, *Swords into Plowshares*, pp. 19–42.
14. John Pinder, "The Federal Idea and the British Liberal Tradition" in Andrea Bosco, ed., *The Federal Idea: The History of Federalism from Enlightenment to 1945*, Volume I (London: Lothian Foundation Press, 1991), p. 107. Here, he offers the examples of Canada, Australia, and South Africa as places where both British Liberals and Conservatives promoted federal proposals during the nineteenth century.
15. Pinder, "The Federal Idea and the British Liberal Tradition," p. 107.
16. Pinder, "The Federal Idea and the British Liberal Tradition," p. 108.
17. Pinder, "The Federal Idea and the British Liberal Tradition," p. 108.
18. Hidemi Suganami, *Domestic Analogy in Proposals for World Order, 1814–1945: The Transfer of Legal and Political Principles from the Domestic to the International Sphere in Thought on International Law and Relations* (University of London, Ph.D. Thesis, 1985), p. 29.
19. Suganami, *Domestic Analogy in Proposals for World Order*, p. 28.
20. Suganami, *Domestic Analogy in Proposals for World Order*, p. 2.
21. Suganami, *Domestic Analogy in Proposals for World Order*, pp. 66–90. Regarding nineteenth-century thinkers like Lorimer and Ladd who apply the domestic analogy, Suganami states the following:

> It is little wonder then that these nineteenth century writers believed that there was something to be learned from their domestic experience. Whether they were right in applying it to the international sphere in the way they did is open to question. But it is clear that they were all favourably impressed by the advances made in the domestic sphere of some states, saw this as a mark of human progress, and thus thought it right to apply the relevant principles of domestic organisation to the hitherto comparatively underdeveloped area of international relations . . . It is important to note that the international system of the period, in which these writers produced their plans, was largely lacking in formal international organisation. The relative lack of formal organisation at the international level may explain why these writers relied rather conspicuously on concrete domestic models. (Suganami, *Domestic Analogy in Proposals for World Order*, p. 92)

22. This point is made with more detail and analysis in chapter 2.
23. Pinder, "The Federal Idea and the British Liberal Tradition," p. 113.
24. David Long, *J.A. Hobson's Approach to International Relations: An Exposition and Critique* (University of London, Ph.D. Thesis, 1991), p. 177.
25. Long, *J.A. Hobson's Approach to International Relations*, p. 178.
26. Long, *J.A. Hobson's Approach to International Relations*, p. 177.

27. Long, *J.A. Hobson's Approach to International Relations*, p. 188.
28. H.G. Wells quoted in John H. Latane, ed., *Development of the League of Nations Idea: Documents and Correspondence of Theodore Marburg*, Volume II (New York: MacMillan, 1932), p. 784.
29. Latane, *Development of the League of Nations Idea*, Volume II, p. 784. Latane notes the following in his Introduction to this work: "The steady progress of the movement for a League of Nations, which resulted in the incorporation of the Covenant of the League of Nations in the Treaty of Versailles in 1919, was due to the efforts of groups of public-spirited men in this country [America] and in England, reinforced later by smaller groups in other countries, both belligerent and neutral." Latane, *Development of the League of Nations Idea*, Volume II, p. VI.
30. Martin Ceadel, "Supranationalism in the British Peace Movement during the Early Twentieth Century" in Andrea Bosco, ed., *The Federal Idea: The History of Federalism from Enlightenment to 1945*, Volume I (London: Lothian Foundation Press, 1991), p. 169.
31. Ceadel, "Supranationalism in the British Peace Movement," pp. 176–89.
32. Latane, *Development of the League of Nations Idea*, Volume II, pp. 763–828.
33. Ceadel, "Supranationalism in the British Peace Movement," p. 175 citing M. Campbell Smith's introductory essay in Immanuel Kant, *Perpetual Peace: A Philosophical Essay*, intro. and trans. M. Campbell Smith, pref. Professor R. Latta (London: Swan Sonnenschein & Co., 1903).
34. Immanuel Kant, *Perpetual Peace: A Philosophical Essay*, intro. and trans. Smith, pref. Latta, pp. 1–2.
35. Kant, *Perpetual Peace: A Philosophical Essay*, intro. and trans. Smith, pref. Latta, p. 2.
36. Leonard Woolf, "Review of Kant's 'Perpetual Peace,' " *New Statesman* (July 31, 1915), p. 399.
37. Woolf, "Review of Kant's 'Perpetual Peace,' " p. 399.
38. Peter Wilson, *The International Theory of Leonard Woolf: An Exposition, Analysis, and Assessment in the Light of His Reputation as a Utopian* (University of London, Ph.D. Thesis, 1997), p. 153.
39. Wilson, *The International Theory of Leonard Woolf*, pp. 153 and 154, respectively. Wilson demonstrates that the similarities between the Woolf-Webb plan and the League Covenant were very evident, especially with regard to the following:

> The outlawing of aggression; the notion of making "common cause" against any state in breach of its fundamental obligations; the emphasis placed on economic and social sanctions; the distinction between justiciable and non-justiciable disputes (and the definition of justiciable disputes); the obligation to refer all other unresolved disputes to an International Council; the idea of a "cooling-off period" (twelve months in the Woolf-Webb plan, three months in the Covenant); the obligation to submit all treaties to a League Secretariat for registration and publication; and the obligation to promote cooperation in the economic and social spheres. (Wilson, *The International Theory of Leonard Woolf*, pp. 153–54)

Wilson also demonstrates the practical impact of Woolf's *International Government* on the League Covenant. He remarks:

Late in 1918, Sydney Waterlow, a member of the newly formed League of Nations Section of the Foreign Office, was asked to write a paper on "International Government under the League of Nations." Waterlow had recently read Woolf's book on the subject and was greatly impressed. He drew extensively from it when writing his paper and, indeed, "lifted almost verbatim" the sections dealing with the international cooperation on labour conditions, public health, transport, and economic and social policy. The paper was well received by Lord Cecil, the head of the section, and the bulk of it was subsequently incorporated into the British Draft Covenant. This later formed the basis of discussions between the British and US delegations at Versailles. (Wilson, *The International Theory of Leonard Woolf*, pp. 154–55)

40. Claude, *Swords into Plowshares*, p. 43 (emphasis in original).
41. Claude, *Swords into Plowshares*, p. 43 (emphasis in original).
42. Gerard J. Mangone, *A Short History of International Organization* (New York: McGraw-Hill Book Company, 1954), pp. 120–21.
43. Claude, *Swords into Plowshares*, p. 47.
44. Claude, *Swords into Plowshares*, p. 45. Claude is emphatic that the formation of the League was influenced by these two primary factors. Besides the obvious point that the League was a "product" of World War I, he is careful to give credit to the aspirations for international organization that flowed from the nineteenth century. He notes that "The League was also the product of nineteenth-century beginnings in the sense that it picked up ideas, adopted the assumptions, and reacted to the awareness which had been emergent in that earlier period." Claude, *Swords into Plowshares*, p. 46.
45. Mangone, *A Short History of International Organization*, p. 132.
46. Archer, *International Organizations*, p. 23.
47. Claude, *Swords into Plowshares*, p. 46.
48. Claude, *Swords into Plowshares*, p. 60.
49. Sir Alfred Zimmern, *The League of Nations and the Rule of Law, 1918–1935* (London: MacMillan & Co., 1939), pp. 287–88.
50. Zimmern, *The League of Nations and the Rule of Law, 1918–1935*, p. 288.
51. Zimmern, *The League of Nations and the Rule of Law, 1918–1935*, p. 290.
52. R.B. Mowat, *The European States System: A Study of International Relations* (2nd. ed.) (London: Oxford University Press, 1929; first published in 1923), p. 94.
53. Ceadel, "Supranationalism in the British Peace Movement," p. 171.
54. Mangone, *A Short History of International Organization*, p. 172.
55. Mangone, *A Short History of International Organization*, pp. 144–46.
56. Mangone, *A Short History of International Organization*, p. 145.
57. Mangone, *A Short History of International Organization*, p. 145.
58. A. Leroy Bennett, *International Organizations: Principles and Issues* (6th ed.) (London: Prentice-Hall International, 1995), p. 35.

59. Mangone, *A Short History of International Organization*, p. 153.
60. Bruce Collins, "American Federalism and the Sectional Crisis, 1844–1860" in Andrea Bosco, ed., *The Federal Idea: The History of Federalism from Enlightenment to 1945*, Volume I (London: Lothian Foundation Press, 1991), p. 51.
61. Peter Wilson, "The New Europe Debate in Wartime Britain" in Philomena Murray and Paul Rich, eds., *Visions of European Unity* (Boulder, CO: Westview, 1996), p. 50.
62. Wilson, "The New Europe Debate in Wartime Britain," p. 50.
63. Wilson, "The New Europe Debate in Wartime Britain," p. 50.
64. Pinder, "The Federal Idea and the British Liberal Tradition," p. 114.
65. Pinder, "The Federal Idea and the British Liberal Tradition," p. 114.
66. Wilson, "The New Europe Debate in Wartime Britain," p. 47.
67. Wilson, "The New Europe Debate in Wartime Britain," p. 46.
68. Wilson, "The New Europe Debate in Wartime Britain," p. 46. Wilson draws from Woolf's *The War for Peace* (London: George Routledge, 1940); *The Future of International Government* (The Labour Party: Transport House, 1940); and *The International Postwar Settlement* (London: Fabian Publications, 1944) in making the above points.
69. Woolf, *The International Postwar Settlement*, p. 6 quoted in Wilson, "The New Europe Debate in Wartime Britain," p. 47.
70. Wilson, "The New Europe Debate in Wartime Britain," p. 46.
71. Wilson, "The New Europe Debate in Wartime Britain," p. 46.
72. Wilson, "The New Europe Debate in Wartime Britain," p. 47.
73. Lionel Robbins, *Economic Planning and International Order* (London: MacMillan, 1937), p. 240 quoted in Wilson, "The New Europe Debate in Wartime Britain," p. 47.
74. Wilson, "The New Europe Debate in Wartime Britain," p. 48. Wilson draws from Mitrany's *A Working Peace System* (Chicago: Quadrangle Books, 1966; first published 1943) in making the following points.
75. Wilson, "The New Europe Debate in Wartime Britain," p. 49.
76. F.A. Hayek, *The Road to Serfdom* (London: George Routledge & Sons, 1944), p. 172 quoted in Wilson, "The New Europe Debate in Wartime Britain," p. 47.
77. Wilson, "The New Europe Debate in Wartime Britain," p. 47.
78. Andrea Bosco, "Introduction" in Andrea Bosco, ed., *The Federal Idea: The History of Federalism from Enlightenment to 1945*, Volume I (London: Lothian Foundation Press, 1991), p. 11.
79. Bosco, "Introduction," pp. 11–12.
80. Bosco, "Introduction," p. 12.
81. Bosco, "Introduction," p. 12.
82. Michael Howard, "The Historical Development of the UN's Role in International Security" in Adam Roberts and Benedict Kingsbury, eds., *United Nations, Divided World: The UN's Roles in International Relations* (2nd ed.) (Oxford: Clarendon Press, 1993), p. 63.
83. Claude, *Swords into Plowshares*, p. 63.

84. Claude, *Swords into Plowshares*, p. 63.
85. Claude, *Swords into Plowshares*, p. 63.
86. Claude, *Swords into Plowshares*, p. 63.
87. Claude, *Swords into Plowshares*, p. 65.
88. Mangone, *A Short History of International Organization*, p. 199.
89. Claude, *Swords into Plowshares*, p. 65.
90. Claude, *Swords into Plowshares*, p. 76 (emphasis in original).
91. Leland M. Goodrich, "From League of Nations to United Nations," *International Organization*, 1, 1 (February 1947), p. 3.
92. Joseph Preston Baratta, "Grenville Clark, World Federalist" in Andrea Bosco, ed., *Annals of the Lothian Foundation*, Volume I (London: Lothian Foundation Press, 1992), p. 200. Wilson traces the evolution of Leonard Woolf's views on international government from the more modest proposals of the Fabian Society Study "Suggestions for the Prevention of War" published in 1915 through his more radical proposals of the 1940s. Wilson, *The International Theory of Leonard Woolf*, pp. 86–149. Wilson notes that, like the Americans, Woolf advocated a "world authority" to bring atomic energy under control during the 1940s. Wilson, *The International Theory of Leonard Woolf*, p. 146.
93. Baratta, "Grenville Clark, World Federalist," p. 201.
94. Baratta, "Grenville Clark, World Federalist," p. 201 (emphasis in original).
95. Baratta, "Grenville Clark, World Federalist," p. 187 and p. 201, respectively.
96. Baratta, "Grenville Clark, World Federalist," p. 201.
97. Baratta, "Grenville Clark, World Federalist," p. 201.
98. Baratta, "Grenville Clark, World Federalist," p. 201.
99. Baratta, "Grenville Clark, World Federalist," p. 201.
100. Cord Meyer, *Facing Reality: From World Federalism to the CIA* (New York: Harper & Row Publishers, 1980), p. 45.
101. Meyer, *Facing Reality*, p. 45.
102. Mangone states that the "Hague Peace Conferences of the early twentieth century tried to regulate practices of international war; the League of Nations from 1920 on sought to regulate war itself. During the Second World War the United Nations, under the benign guardianship of the five great powers, was designed to eliminate all aggressive wars . . . all three endeavours to block the arbitrary practice of violence by nations against each other." Mangone, *A Short History of International Organization*, p. 7.
103. Ceadel, "Supranationalism in the British Peace Movement," p. 173.
104. Ceadel, "Supranationalism in the British Peace Movement," p. 189.
105. Pinder, "The Federal Idea and the British Liberal Tradition," p. 115.
106. Pinder, "The Federal Idea and the British Liberal Tradition," p. 115.
107. Long, *J.A. Hobson's Approach to International Relations*, p. 209.
108. Suganami, *Domestic Analogy in Proposals for World Order*, p. 20.
109. Wilson, "The New Europe Debate in Wartime Britain," p. 56.
110. Wilson, "The New Europe Debate in Wartime Britain," p. 57.

111. Wilson, "The New Europe Debate in Wartime Britain," p. 57.
112. Wilson, "The New Europe Debate in Wartime Britain," p. 57.
113. Wilson, "The New Europe Debate in Wartime Britain," p. 57.
114. Wilson, "The New Europe Debate in Wartime Britain," p. 57.
115. Mangone, *A Short History of International Organization*, p. 199.
116. Baratta, "Grenville Clark, World Federalist," pp. 208–09.
117. Baratta, "Grenville Clark, World Federalist," p. 209.
118. Baratta, "Grenville Clark, World Federalist," p. 209.
119. Baratta, "Grenville Clark, World Federalist," p. 209.
120. Baratta, "Grenville Clark, World Federalist," p. 209.
121. Baratta, "Grenville Clark, World Federalist," p. 209.
122. Meyer, *Facing Reality*, pp. 44–65.
123. Baratta, "Grenville Clark, World Federalist," p. 209.
124. Baratta, "Grenville Clark, World Federalist," p. 209.
125. Mangone, *A Short History of International Organization*, p. 175.
126. Adam Roberts and Benedict Kingsbury, "Introduction: The UN's Roles in International Society since 1945" in Adam Roberts and Benedict Kingsbury, eds., *United Nations, Divided World: The UN's Roles in International Relations* (2nd ed.) (Oxford: Clarendon Press, 1993), p. 8.
127. Roberts and Kingsbury, "Introduction: The UN's Roles in International Society since 1945," p. 41.
128. Claude, *Swords into Plowshares*, p. 81.
129. Meyer, *Facing Reality*, p. 36.
130. Meyer, *Facing Reality*, p. 36.
131. Roberts and Kingsbury, "Introduction: The UN's Roles in International Society since 1945," p. 11.
132. Michael Howard, "The Historical Development of the UN's Role in International Security" in Adam Roberts and Benedict Kingsbury, eds., *United Nations, Divided World: The UN's Roles in International Relations* (2nd ed.) (Oxford: Clarendon Press, 1993), p. 67.
133. Howard, "The Historical Development of the UN's Role in International Security," p. 67.
134. Howard, "The Historical Development of the UN's Role in International Security," p. 67.
135. Howard, "The Historical Development of the UN's Role in International Security," p. 67.
136. Howard, "The Historical Development of the UN's Role in International Security," pp. 67–68.
137. Howard, "The Historical Development of the UN's Role in International Security," p. 77.
138. Paul F. Diehl, "Introduction" in Paul F. Diehl, ed., *The Politics of Global Governance: International Organizations in an Interdependent World* (Boulder: Lynne Rienner Publishers, 1997), p. 3.

139. Howard, "The Historical Development of the UN's Role in International Security," p. 77.
140. Diehl, "Introduction," p. 3.
141. Diehl, "Introduction," p. 3.
142. Diehl, "Introduction," p. 3.
143. Brian Urquhart, "The UN and International Security after the Cold War" in Adam Roberts and Benedict Kingsbury, eds., *United Nations, Divided World: The UN's Role in International Relations* (2nd ed.) (Oxford: Clarendon Press, 1993), p. 82.
144. Urquhart, "The UN and International Security after the Cold War," p. 82.
145. Urquhart, "The UN and International Security after the Cold War," p. 82.
146. Howard notes that "The UN has achieved much . . . It preserved those elements of international cooperation—the World Health Organization, the International Labour Organization, and the International Court of Justice—which already existed . . . It eased the transformation of the world from a Eurocentric to a truly global system . . . It . . . enables the smallest and least considerable of its members to feel themselves part of a world community." Howard, "The Historical Development of the UN's Role in International Security," pp. 79–80. Roberts and Kingsbury explain that the "UN's contribution came to be seen by many as being less in the field of peace between major powers than in other areas: defusing certain regional conflicts, advocating self-determination, assisting decolonization, codifying international law, protecting human rights, and providing a possible framework for social and economic improvement, even for redistribution of wealth on a global scale." Roberts and Kingsbury, "Introduction: The UN's Roles in International Society since 1945," p. 19. Mangone explains, "In number and in function, international organizations have multiplied rapidly during the last century." Mangone, *A Short History of International Organization*, p. 10.
147. Howard, "The Historical Development of the UN's Role in International Security," pp. 79–80.
148. Peter Wilenski, "The Structure of the UN in the Post-Cold War Period" in Adam Roberts and Benedict Kingsbury, eds., *United Nations, Divided World: The UN's Roles in International Relations* (2nd ed.) (Oxford: Clarendon Press, 1993), p. 437.
149. Wilenski, "The Structure of the UN in the Post-Cold War Period," p. 437.
150. F.S. Northedge, *The League of Nations: Its Life and Times, 1920–1946* (Leicester: Leicester University Press, 1986), p. 282.
151. Chris Brown, *Understanding International Relations* (London: MacMillan Press, 1997), p. 31.
152. Brown, *Understanding International Relations*, p. 31.

9   From the Turmoil of International Anarchy to the Calm of the Liberal Peace

1. Note 4 in chapter 5 offers a lengthy list of articles that present arguments both for and against the liberal peace claim.

2. Bruce Russett, *Controlling the Sword: The Democratic Governance of National Security* (Cambridge, MA: Harvard University Press, 1990), pp. 119–23 cited in Wade L. Huntley, "Kant's Third Image: Systemic Sources of the Liberal Peace," *International Studies Quarterly*, 40 (1996), p. 45.

3. J. Levy, "Domestic Politics and War," *Journal of Interdisciplinary History*, 18 (1988), pp. 661–62 and N. Gleditsch, "Democracy and Peace," *Journal of Peace Research*, 29 (1992), p. 372 cited in Huntley, "Kant's Third Image," p. 46.

4. Chris Brown, *International Relations Theory* (Brighton: Harvester Press, 1992), p. 40.

5. Kenneth Waltz, *Man, the State and War* (New York: Columbia University Press, 1959), pp. 80–123. Kenneth Waltz, *Theory of International Politics* (Reading, MA: Addison-Wesley, 1979), pp. 18–37.

6. J.D. Singer and Associates, *Explaining War: Selected Papers from the Correlates of War Project* (London: Sage Publications, 1979) cited in Brown, *International Relations Theory*, p. 41.

7. Howard Williams and Ken Booth, "Kant: Theorist beyond Limits" in Ian Clark and Iver B. Neumann, eds., *Classical Theories of International Relations* (Houndmills, Basingstoke, Hampshire, and London: MacMillan Press, 1996), pp. 89–90.

8. Michael Doyle, "Kant, Liberal Legacies and Foreign Affairs, Part 1," *Philosophy and Public Affairs*, 12 (1983), pp. 209–12.

9. Doyle, "Kant, Liberal Legacies and Foreign Affairs, Part 1," p. 212. Importantly, I use the terms "liberal" or "illiberal" and Doyle's terms "liberal regime(s)/state(s)/republic(s)" or "non-liberal regime(s)/state(s)" throughout this chapter. The terms " 'republican,' representative government(s)" or "non-republican, unrepresentative government(s)" are also used and are a subcategory of Doyle's terms "liberal regime(s)/state(s)/republic(s)" or "non-liberal regime(s)/state(s)," respectively. According to Doyle's adopted terminology and definition here, a "liberal regime [or state]" necessarily has "republican, representative government." The key is to avoid use of the terms "democratic" or "democracy" (unless it is understood to be "representative democracy" as in the Freedom House survey later) in discussion of *Perpetual Peace*. Kant was clearly against the establishment of pure "democracy" since it was not "representative." In *Perpetual Peace*, he states, "Of the three forms of sovereignty [autocracy, aristocracy and democracy], *democracy*, in the truest sense of the word, is necessarily a *despotism*, because it establishes an executive power through which all the citizens may make decisions about (and indeed against) the single individual without his consent, so that decisions are made by all the people and yet not by all the people; and this means that the general will is in contradiction with itself, and thus also with freedom." Immanuel Kant, *Perpetual Peace*, ed. Hans Reiss, trans. H.B. Nisbet (Cambridge: Cambridge University Press, 1970), p. 101 (emphasis in original). This is a further reason why I choose the phrase "liberal peace" over the more widely used phrase "democratic peace" throughout this

chapter and the book as a whole. Many scholars do, however, use the latter phrase throughout their studies and articles on the subject.

10. Doyle, "Kant, Liberal Legacies and Foreign Affairs Part 1," p. 209.
11. Doyle, "Kant, Liberal Legacies and Foreign Affairs, Part 1," p. 209.
12. Doyle, "Kant, Liberal Legacies and Foreign Affairs, Part 1," p. 210.
13. Doyle, "Kant, Liberal Legacies and Foreign Affairs, Part 1," pp. 210–11.
14. Doyle, "Kant, Liberal Legacies and Foreign Affairs, Part 1," pp. 211–12.
15. Adrian Karatnycky, ed., Freedom House, *Freedom in the World: The Annual Survey of Political Rights & Civil Liberties 1999–2000* (New York: Freedom House, 2000).
16. Karatnycky, ed., Freedom House, The Map of Freedom 2000, http://www.freedomhouse.org/survey/2000/karat.html (accessed October 6, 2000).
17. Karatnycky, Freedom House, *Freedom in the World*, p. 590.
18. Karatnycky, Freedom House, *Freedom in the World*, pp. 583–84. Freedom House expands on Doyle's criteria to include the following more detailed version:

1. Is the head of state and/or head of government or other chief authority elected through free and fair elections? 2. Are the legislative representatives elected through free and fair elections? 3. Are their fair electoral laws, equal campaigning opportunities, fair polling, and honest tabulation of ballots? 4. Are the voters able to endow their freely elected representatives with real power? 5. Do the people have the right to organize in different political parties or other political groupings of their choice, and is the system open to the rise and fall of these competing parties or groupings? 6. Is there a significant opposition vote, de facto opposition power, and a realistic possibility for the opposition to increase its support or gain power through elections? 7. Are the people free from domination by military, foreign powers, totalitarian parties, religious hierarchies, economic oligarchies, or any other powerful group? 8. Do cultural, ethnic, religious, and other minority groups have reasonable self-determination, self-government, autonomy, or participation through informal consensus in the decision-making process? And finally, for what Freedom House calls "discretionary political rights" questions, they ask first for traditional monarchies that have no parties or electoral process, whether the system provides for consultation with the people, encourage discussion of policy, and allow the right to petition the ruler, and second whether the government or occupying power is deliberately changing the ethnic composition of a country or territory so as to destroy a culture or tip the political balance in favor of another group?

The Freedom House survey also includes an extensive "Civil Liberties Checklist" used in tandem with the "Political Liberties Checklist" to rate countries as "free," "partly free," or "not free." Karatnycky, Freedom House, *Freedom in the World*, pp. 584–85. Within that checklist, there is a section on "Personal Autonomy and Economic Rights," which basically embraces Doyle's criterion for inclusion in the "liberal regime" category of a "market and private property economy."

19. Doyle, "Kant, Liberal Legacies and Foreign Affairs, Part 1," p. 209. In note "b" to his table of liberal regimes, Doyle explains, "There are domestic variations within these liberal regimes. For example, Switzerland was liberal only in certain cantons; the United States was liberal only north of the Mason-Dixon line until 1865, when it became liberal throughout. These lists also exclude ancient 'republics,' since none appear to fit Kant's criteria." Doyle, "Kant, Liberal Legacies and Foreign Affairs, Part 1," p. 212.

20. Kant, *Perpetual Peace*, ed. Reiss, trans. Nisbet, p. 104.

21. Kant, *Perpetual Peace*, ed. Reiss, trans. Nisbet, p. 104.

22. Doyle, "Kant, Liberal Legacies and Foreign Affairs, Part 1," p. 213 (emphasis in original).

23. Doyle, "Kant, Liberal Legacies and Foreign Affairs, Part 1," p. 213.

24. Doyle, "Kant, Liberal Legacies and Foreign Affairs, Part 1," pp. 214–15.

25. In Footnote 7 to his "well-known statement" already excerpted, Doyle does make the admission that "There appear to be some exceptions to the tendency for liberal states not to engage in a war with each other." Doyle, "Kant, Liberal Legacies and Foreign Affairs, Part 1," Footnote 7, p. 213. His first example is Peru and Ecuador. His explanation is that "for each, the war came within one to three years after the establishment of a liberal regime [and] before the pacifying effects of liberalism could become deeply engrained." Doyle, "Kant, Liberal Legacies and Foreign Affairs, Part 1," Footnote 7, p. 213. He also considers the clashes between Israelis and Palestinians along the border in Lebanon as a possible exception.

26. Doyle, "Kant, Liberal Legacies and Foreign Affairs, Part 1," pp. 213–15.

27. Doyle, "Kant, Liberal Legacies and Foreign Affairs, Part 1," pp. 215–16.

28. Doyle, "Kant, Liberal Legacies and Foreign Affairs, Part 1," p. 216.

29. Doyle, "Kant, Liberal Legacies and Foreign Affairs, Part 1," p. 216.

30. Doyle, "Kant, Liberal Legacies and Foreign Affairs, Part 1," p. 216.

31. Doyle, "Kant, Liberal Legacies and Foreign Affairs, Part 1," p. 216.

32. Doyle, "Kant, Liberal Legacies and Foreign Affairs, Part 1," p. 217.

33. Doyle, "Kant, Liberal Legacies and Foreign Affairs, Part 1," p. 217.

34. Doyle, "Kant, Liberal Legacies and Foreign Affairs, Part 1," p. 217.

35. Doyle, "Kant, Liberal Legacies and Foreign Affairs, Part 1," p. 217.

36. Doyle, "Kant, Liberal Legacies and Foreign Affairs, Part 1," p. 217.

37. John Rawls, *The Law of Peoples* (Cambridge, MA: Harvard University Press, 1999), p. 51.

38. Rawls, *The Law of Peoples*, p. 51.

39. Rawls, *The Law of Peoples*, p. 52. Rawls's list includes the Peloponnesian war, the Second Punic war, the religious wars of the sixteenth and seventeenth centuries, and the great wars of the nineteenth century such as the Napoleonic wars, Bismarck's war, and the American Civil War. Rawls, *The Law of Peoples*, p. 52.

40. Rawls, *The Law of Peoples*, pp. 52–53.

41. Rawls, *The Law of Peoples*, p. 53.

42. Rawls, *The Law of Peoples*, p. 53.
43. Rawls, *The Law of Peoples*, p. 54.
44. Rawls, *The Law of Peoples*, p. 54.
45. Doyle notes the following important point from Melvin Small and J. David Singer's influential work *Resort to Arms*: "Significantly, the most war-affected states have not been liberal republics." Melvin Small and J. David Singer, *Resort to Arms* (Beverly Hills, CA: Sage Publications, 1982), pp. 176–79 cited in Doyle, "Kant, Liberal Legacies and Foreign Affairs, Part 1," p. 228.
46. Kant, *Perpetual Peace*, ed. Reiss, trans. Nisbet, p. 105.
47. Kant, *Perpetual Peace*, ed. Reiss, trans. Nisbet, p. 105.
48. A.C.F. Beales, *The History of Peace: A Short History of the Organized Movements for International Peace* (New York: The Dial Press, 1931), p. 36.
49. R.B. Mowat, *The European States System: A Study of International Relations* (2nd ed.) (London: Oxford University Press, 1929; first published in 1923), p. 94.
50. Doyle, "Kant, Liberal Legacies and Foreign Affairs, Part 1," p. 210.
51. Doyle, "Kant, Liberal Legacies and Foreign Affairs, Part 1," p. 210.
52. Kant, *Perpetual Peace*, ed. Reiss, trans. Nisbet, p. 104 (emphasis in original).
53. Kant, *Perpetual Peace*, ed. Reiss, trans. Nisbet, p. 104 (emphasis in original).
54. Kant, *Perpetual Peace*, ed. Reiss, trans. Nisbet, p. 104.
55. Williams and Booth, "Kant: Theorist beyond Limits," p. 73.
56. Williams and Booth, "Kant: Theorist beyond Limits," p. 73.
57. Francis Fukuyama, *The End of History and the Last Man* (London: Hamish Hamilton, 1992).

Epilogue

1. Kofi Annan, "Why Democracy Is an International Issue," Cyril Foster Lecture at Oxford University, June 19, 2001 (University of Oxford: Press Office), p. 1; http://www.admin.ox.ac.uk/po/annan.html (accessed June 23, 2001).
2. Annan, "Why Democracy Is an International Issue," p. 1.
3. Annan, "Why Democracy Is an International Issue," p. 2.
4. Annan, "Why Democracy Is an International Issue," p. 2.
5. Howard Williams, *Kant's Critique of Hobbes: Sovereignty & Cosmopolitanism*, Political Philosophy Now (Cardiff: University of Wales Press, 2003), p. 197.
6. Williams, *Kant's Critique of Hobbes*, p. 197.
7. Williams, *Kant's Critique of Hobbes*, pp. 231–32.
8. Williams, *Kant's Critique of Hobbes*, p. 199.
9. Please see chapter seven, pp. 279–82 for a complete discussion of Howard Williams and Ken Booth, "Kant: Theorist beyond Limits" in Ian Clark and Iver B. Neuman, eds., *Classical Theories of International Relations* (Houndsmills, Basingstoke, and London: MacMillan Press, 1996).
10. Antonio Franceschet, *Kant and Liberal Internationalism: Sovereignty, Justice & Global Reform* (New York: Palgrave MacMillan, 2002), p. 58.

11. Franceschet, *Kant and Liberal Internationalism*, p. 59.
12. Franceschet, *Kant and Liberal Internationalism*, p. 59 (emphasis in original).
13. Franceschet, *Kant and Liberal Internationalism*, p. 60.
14. Franceschet, *Kant and Liberal Internationalism*, p. 60 (emphasis in original).
15. Franceschet, *Kant and Liberal Internationalism*, pp. 60–61.
16. Jürg Martin Gabriel, *Worldviews and Theories of International Relations* (New York: St. Martin's Press, 1994), p. 51.
17. Franceschet, *Kant and Liberal Internationalism*, p. 61.
18. Franceschet, *Kant and Liberal Internationalism*, p. 61 (emphasis in original).
19. Franceschet, *Kant and Liberal Internationalism*, p. 60.
20. Donald J. Puchala, *Theory and History in International Relations* (New York: Routledge, 2003), p. 193.
21. Puchala, *Theory and History in International Relations*, p. 193.
22. Puchala, *Theory and History in International Relations*, p. 195.
23. George W. Bush, "In Bush's Words 'Iraq's Democracy Will Succeed,'" Speech given on the occasion of the Twentieth Anniversary of the National Endowment for Democracy, November 6, 2003, Transcription by FDCH e-Media, pp. 1–5; http:www.nytimes.com/2003/11/06/politics/06TEXT-BUSH.html (accessed February 4, 2004).
24. George W. Bush, State of the Union Address, United States Capitol, Washington, DC, January 20, 2004 (White House Press Office); http://www.whitehouse.gov/news/releases/2004/01/20041020-7.html (accessed February 4, 2004).

Bibliography

Annan, Kofi. "Why Democracy Is an International Issue." Cyril Foster Lecture at Oxford University, June 19, 2001. Press Office of the University of Oxford: 1–6. Http://www.admin.ox.ac.uk/po/annan.html (accessed June 23, 2001).

Archer, Clive. *International Organizations*. Second Edition. London: Routledge Press, 1992.

Archibugi, Daniele. "Models of International Organization in Perpetual Peace Projects." *Review of International Studies* 18 (1992): 295–317.

Arendt, H. and Beiner, R., eds. *Lectures on Kant's Political Philosophy*. Chicago: Chicago University Press, 1982.

Armstrong, A.C. "Kant's Philosophy of Peace and War." *The Journal of Philosophy* XXVIII (8) (April 9, 1931): 197–204.

Axinn, Sidney. "Kant on World Government" in Funke, Gerhard, and Seebohm, Thomas M., eds., *Proceedings of the Sixth International Kant Congress*. Two Volumes. Washington, D.C.: University Press of America, 1989: 243–51.

Babst, Dean. "A Force for Peace." *Industrial Research* (April 1972): 55–58. Originally published as "Elective Governments—A Force for Peace." *The Wisconsin Sociologist* 3 (1)(1964): 9–14.

Baratta, Joseph Preston. "Grenville Clark, World Federalist" in Bosco, Andrea, ed., *Annals of the Lothian Foundation*. Volume I. London: Lothian Foundation Press, 1992: 187–219.

Barclay, Thomas. "Perpetual Peace, Official Schemes and Projects." *Contemporary Review* 147 (January/June, 1935): 678–83.

Bartleson, Jens. "The Trial of Judgment: A Note on Kant and the Paradoxes of Internationalism." *International Studies Quarterly* 39 (June 1995): 255–80.

Beales, A.C.F. *The History of Peace: A Short Account of the Organized Movements for International Peace*. New York: The Dial Press, 1931.

Beck, L.W. *Studies in the Philosophy of Kant*. Indianapolis: Bobbs-Merrill, 1965.

Beck, L.W., ed. *Proceedings of the Third International Kant Congress*. Two Volumes. Dordrecht, Holland: D. Reidel Publishing Company, 1972.

Bennett, A. Leroy. *International Organizations: Principles and Issues*. Sixth Edition. London: Prentice-Hall International, 1995.

Bohman, James and Lutz-Bachmann, Matthias, eds. *Perpetual Peace: Essays on Kant's Cosmopolitan Ideal*. Boston: MIT Press, 1997.

Bok, Sissela. *A Strategy for Peace: Human Values and the Threat of War.* New York: Pantheon Books, 1989.

Booth, James William. *Interpreting the World: Kant's Philosophy of History and Politics.* Toronto: University of Toronto Press, 1986.

Bosco, Andrea. "Introduction" in Bosco, Andrea, ed., *The Federal Idea: The History of Federalism from Enlightenment to 1945.* Volume I. London: Lothian Foundation Press, 1991: 3–17.

Bosco, Andrea, ed. *The Federal Idea: The History of Federalism from Enlightenment to 1945.* Volume I. London: Lothian Foundation Press, 1991.

Bosco, Andrea, ed. *Annals of the Lothian Foundation.* Volume I. London: Lothian Foundation Press, 1992.

Boucher, David. *Political Theories of International Relations.* Oxford: Oxford University Press, 1998.

Bourke, John. "Kant's Doctrine of 'Perpetual Peace.'" *Philosophy* 17 (1942): 324–33.

Brown, Chris. *International Relations Theory: New Normative Approaches.* Brighton: Harvester Press, 1992.

Brown, Chris. *Understanding International Relations.* London: MacMillan Press, 1997.

Bueno de Mesquita, B., Siverson, R., and Woller, G. "War and The Fate of Regimes: A Comparative Analysis." *American Political Science Review* 86 (1992): 638–46.

Bull, Hedley. *The Anarchical Society: A Study of Order in World Politics.* New York: Columbia University Press, 1977.

Bush, George W. "In Bush's Words 'Iraq's Democracy Will Succeed.'" Speech given on the occasion of the Twentieth Anniversary of the National Endowment for Democracy, November 6, 2003. Transcription by FDCH e -Media, 1–5. Http:www.nytimes.com/2003/11/06/politics/06TEXT-BUSH.html (accessed February 4, 2004).

Bush, George W. State of the Union Address, United States Capitol, Washington, DC, January 20, 2004. White House Press Office. Http://www.whitehouse.gov/news/releases/2004/01 /20041020-7.html (accessed February 4, 2004).

Butler, Nicholas Murray. *The Path to Peace: Essays and Addresses on Peace and Its Making.* New York and London: Charles Scribner's Sons, 1930.

Butterfield, Henry and Wight, Martin, eds. *Diplomatic Investigations.* Cambridge, MA: Harvard University Press, 1966.

Byrd, Sharon. "Perpetual Peace: A 20th Century Project" in Robinson, Hoke, ed., *Proceedings of the Eighth International Kant Congress.* Two Volumes. Milwaukee: Marquette University Press, 1995: 343–57.

Byrd, Sharon. "The State as a 'Moral Person'" in Robinson, Hoke, ed., *Proceedings of the Eighth International Kant Congress.* Two Volumes. Milwaukee: Marquette University Press, 1995: 171–89.

Calvocoresi, Peter. *A Time for Peace: Pacifism, Internationalism and Protest Forces in the Reduction of War.* London, Melbourne, Auckland, and Johannesburg: Hutchinson Press, 1987.

Carr, E.H. *The Twenty Years' Crisis, 1919–1939: An Introduction to the Study of International Relations.* London: MacMillan and Co., 1939.

Carr, E.H. *From Napoleon to Stalin and Other Essays.* London: MacMillan Press, 1980.

Carson, Thomas L. " 'Perpetual Peace': What Kant Should Have Said." *Social Theory and Practice* 14 (Summer 1988): 173–211.

Cavallar, Georg. "Kant's Society of Nations: Free Federation or World Republic?" *Journal of the History of Philosophy* 32 (July 1994): 461–82.

Ceadel, Martin. "Supranationalism in the British Peace Movement during the Early Twentieth Century" in Bosco, Andrea, ed., *The Federal Idea: The History of Federalism from Enlightenment to 1945.* Volume I. London: Lothian Foundation Press, 1991: 169–91.

Chan, S. "Mirror, Mirror on the Wall . . . Are the Freer Countries More Pacific?" *Journal of Conflict Resolution* 28 (1984): 617–48.

Choate, J.H. *The Two Hague Conferences.* Princeton: Princeton University Press, 1913.

Clark, Ian. *The Hierarchy of States: Reform and Resistance in the International Order.* Cambridge: Cambridge University Press, 1989.

Clark, Ian. *Globalization and Fragmentation: International Relations in the Twentieth Century.* Oxford: Oxford University Press, 1997.

Clark, Ian and Neumann, Iver B., eds. *Classical Theories of International Relations.* Houndmills, Basingstoke, Hampshire, and London: MacMillan Press, 1996.

Claude, Jr., Inis L. *Swords into Plowshares: The Problems and Progress of International Organization.* New York: Random House, 1959.

Collins, Bruce. "American Federalism and the Sectional Crisis, 1844–1860" in Bosco, Andrea, ed., *The Federal Idea: The History of Federalism from Enlightenment to 1945.* Volume I. London: Lothian Foundation Press, 1991: 51–66.

Covell, Charles. *Kant, Liberalism and the Pursuit of Justice in the International Order.* Studies in the History of International Relations. Band 1. Munster: Lit, 1994.

Covell, Charles. *Kant and the Law of Peace: A Study in the Philosophy of International Law and International Relations.* Houndmills, Basingstoke, Hampshire, and London: MacMillan Press, 1998.

Crawford, J.F. "Kant's Doctrines Concerning Perpetual Peace." *Monist* 35 (1925): 296–314.

Davis, John William, ed. *Value and Valuation: Axiological Studies in Honor of Robert S. Hartman.* Knoxville: The University of Tennessee Press, 1972.

Deutsch, Karl et al. *Political Community in the North Atlantic Area.* Princeton: Princeton University Press, 1957.

Diehl, Paul F. "Introduction" in Diehl, Paul F. ed., *The Politics of Global Governance: International Organizations in an Interdependent World.* Boulder: Lynne Rienner Publishers, 1997: 1–6.

Diehl, Paul F., ed. *The Politics of Global Governance: International Organizations in an Interdependent World.* Boulder: Lynne Rienner Publishers, 1997.

Donelan, Michael. *The Reason of States: A Study in International Political Theory.* London: George Allen & Unwin, 1978.

Donelan, Michael. *Elements of International Political Theory.* Oxford: Clarendon Press, 1990.

Doyle, Michael. "Kant, Liberal Legacies, and Foreign Affairs, Part 1." *Philosophy and Public Affairs* 12 (1983): 205–35.

Doyle, Michael. "Kant, Liberal Legacies, and Foreign Affairs, Part 2." *Philosophy and Public Affairs* 12 (1983): 323–53.

Doyle, Michael. *Ways of War and Peace: Realism, Liberalism, and Socialism.* New York & London: W.W. Norton & Company, 1997.

Doyle, Michael and Ikenberry, G. John, eds. *New Thinking in International Relations Theory.* Boulder: Westview Press, 1997.

Erzberger, Mathias. *The League of Nations: The Way to the World's Peace.* Translated by Bernard Miall. London: Hodder & Stoughton, 1919.

Forsythe, David. *Human Rights and Peace: International and National Dimensions.* Lincoln: University of Nebraska Press, 1993.

Franceschet, Antonio. *Kant and Liberal Internationalism: Sovereignty, Justice & Global Reform.* New York: Palgrave Macmillan, 2002.

Friedrich, Carl Joachim. *Inevitable Peace.* Cambridge, MA: Harvard University Press, 1948.

Friedrich, Carl Joachim. *The Philosophy of Kant.* New York: Random House, 1949.

Funke, Gerhard and Seebohm, Thomas M., eds. *Proceedings of the Sixth International Kant Congress.* Two Volumes. Washington, D.C.: University Press of America, 1989.

Fukuyama, Francis. *The End of History and the Last Man.* London: Hamish Hamilton, 1992.

Gabriel, Jürg Martin. *Worldviews and Theories of International Relations.* New York: St. Martin's Press, 1994.

Gallie, W.B. *Philosophers of Peace and War.* Cambridge: Cambridge University Press, 1978.

Gallie, W.B. "Wanted: A Philosophy of International Relations." *Political Studies* 27 (1979): 484–92.

Galston, W.A. *Kant and the Problem of History.* Chicago: Chicago University Press, 1975.

Gargaz, Pierre Andre. *A Project of Universal and Perpetual Peace.* New York: Garland Publishing, 1973.

Geismann, Georg. "On the Philosophically Unique Realism of Kant's Doctrine of Eternal Peace" in Robinson, Hoke, ed., *Proceedings of the Eighth International Kant Congress.* Two Volumes. Milwaukee: Marquette University Press, 1995: 273–89.

Gleditsch, N. "Democracy and Peace." *Journal of Peace Research* 29 (1992): 369–76.

Glossop, Ronald J. *World Federation: A Critical Analysis of World Government.* Jefferson, North Carolina and London: McFarland & Company, 1993.

Goodrich, Leland M. "From League of Nations to United Nations." *International Organization* 1 (1) (February 1947): 3–21.

Griffiths, Martin. *Realism, Idealism, & International Politics: A Reinterpretation.* London: Routledge, 1992.

Gunnell, John G. *Political Theory: Tradition and Interpretation.* Cambridge, MA: Wintrop Publishers, 1979.

Gurian, Waldemar. "Perpetual Peace? Critical Remarks on Mortimer J. Adler's Book." *Review of Politics* 6 (1944): 228–38.

Guyer, Paul. "Nature, Morality and the Possibility of Peace" in Robinson, Hoke, ed., *Proceedings of the Eighth International Kant Congress.* Two Volumes. Milwaukee: Marquette University Press, 1995: 51–69.

Hagan, J.D. "Domestic Political Systems and War Proneness." *Mershon International Studies Review* 38 (1994): 183–207.

Harrison, Austin. "Kant on the League of Nations." *English Review* XXIX (November 1919): 454–62.

Hayek, F.A. *The Road to Serfdom.* London: George Routledge & Sons, 1944.

Hazzard, Shirley. *Defeat of an Ideal: A Study of the Self- Destruction of the UN.* London: MacMillan, 1973.

Heatley, D.P. *Diplomacy and the Study of International Relations.* Oxford: Clarendon Press, 1919.

Hemleben, S.J. *Plans for Peace through Six Centuries.* Chicago: Chicago University Press, 1943.

Hicks, Frederick Charles. *The New World Order.* New York: Doubleday Page, 1920.

Hill, David Jayne. *The Rebuilding of Europe: A Survey of Forces and Conditions.* New York: The Century Co., 1917.

Hinsley, F.H. *Power and the Pursuit of Peace.* Cambridge: Cambridge University Press, 1963.

Hinsley, F.H. *Sovereignty.* London: C.A. Watts and Co., 1966.

Hinsley, F.H. *Nationalism and the International System.* Twentieth Century Studies. Edited by Donald Tyerman. London: Hodder and Stoughton, 1973.

Hobbes, Thomas. *Leviathin.* New York: Collier Books, 1962.

Hobsbawn, E.J. *The Age of Revolution: Europe 1789 1848.* London: Weidenfeld and Nicolson, 1962.

Hoffe, Otfried. *Immanuel Kant.* Translated by Marshall Farrier. Albany: State University of New York Press, 1994. Originally published in German by C.H. Beck'sche, Verlagsbuchhandlung (Oscar Beck), 1992.

Howard, Michael. *War and the Liberal Conscience.* Oxford: Oxford University Press, 1981.

Howard, Michael. "The Historical Development of the UN's Role in International Security" in Roberts, Adam and Kingsbury, Benedict, eds., *United Nations, Divided World: The UN's Roles in International Relations.* Second Edition. Oxford: Clarendon Press, 1993: 63–80.

Hughan, Jessie Wallace. *A Study of International Government.* New York: Thomas Y. Crowell, 1923.

Huntley, Wade L. "Kant's Third Image: Systemic Sources of the Liberal Peace." *International Studies Quarterly* 40 (1996): 45–76.

Hurrell, Andrew. "Kant and the Kantian Paradigm in International Relations." *Review of International Studies* 16 (1990): 183–205.

Hutchings, Kimberly. *Kant, Critique, and Politics.* New York: Routledge, 1996.

Jaspers, Karl. *Philosophy and the World.* Translated by E.B. Ashton. Chicago: Regnery, 1963.

Kant, Immanuel. *Eternal Peace.* Translated by J.D. Morell. London: Hodder & Stoughton, 1884.

Kant, Immanuel. *Perpetual Peace* in Kant's *Principle of Politics.* Edited and Translated by W. Hastie. Edinburgh: T. & T. Clark, 1891.

Kant, Immanuel. *Perpetual Peace.* Translated by Benjamin F. Trueblood. Boston: The American Peace Society, 1897.

Kant, Immanuel. *Perpetual Peace: A Philosophical Essay.* Introduction and Translation by M. Campbell Smith. Preface by Professor R. Latta. London: Swan Sonnenschein and Co., 1903.

Kant, Immanuel. *Eternal Peace and Other International Essays.* Translated by W. Hastie. Boston: 1914.

Kant, Immanuel. *Perpetual Peace.* Translated by Helen O'Brien. Introduction by Jessie Buckland. Grotius Society Publications: Texts for Students of International Relations, No. 7. London: Sweet & Maxwell, 1927.

Kant, Immanuel. *Perpetual Peace.* Introduction by Nicholas Murray Butler. New York: Columbia University Press, 1939.

Kant, Immanuel. *Perpetual Peace* in *On History.* Edited and Translated by Lewis White Beck. New York: Bobbs-Merrill, 1963.

Kant, Immanuel. *Perpetual Peace* in *Kant's Political Writings.* Edited by Hans Reiss. Translated by H.B. Nisbet. Cambridge: Cambridge University Press, 1970.

Kant, Immanuel. *Perpetual Peace* in *The Enlightenment.* Edited by Peter Gay. New York: Simon & Schuster, 1974.

Kant, Immanuel. *Perpetual Peace and Other Essays on Politics, History and Morals.* Introduction and Translation by Ted Humphrey. Indianapolis: Hackett Publishing Co., 1983.

Kant, Immanuel. *Perpetual Peace* in *Kant Selections.* Edited by Lewis White Beck. New York, London: MacMillan Press, 1988.

Karatnycky, Adrian, ed. Freedom House. *Freedom in the World: The Annual Survey of Political Rights & Civil Liberties 1999–2000.* New York: Freedom House, 2000.

Karatnycky, Adrian, ed. Freedom House. *The Map of Freedom 2000.* Http://www. freedomhouse.org/survey/2000/karat.html (accessed October 6, 2000).

Kleinschmidt, Harold. *The Nemesis of Power: A History of International Relations Theories.* London: Reakton Books, 2000.

Knutsen, Torbjorn L. *The History of International Relations Theory: An Introduction.* Manchester: Manchester University Press, 1992.

Lake, D. "Powerful Pacifists: Democratic States and War." *American Political Science Review* 86 (1992): 24–37.

Latane, John H., ed. *Development of the League of Nations Idea: Documents and Correspondence of Theodore Marburg.* Two Volumes. New York: MacMillan, 1932.

Layne, C. "Kant or Cant: The Myth of the Democratic Peace." *International Security* 19 (1994): 5–49.

Levy, J. "Domestic Politics and War." *Journal of Interdisciplinary History* 18 (1988): 653–73.

Lloyd, Lorna. "Philip Noel-Baker and Peace Through Law" in Long, David and Wilson, Peter, eds. *Thinkers of the Twenty Years' Crisis: Inter-War Idealism Reassessed*. Oxford: Clarendon Press, 1995: 25–57.

Long, David. *J.A. Hobson's Approach to International Relations: An Exposition and Critique*. University of London, Ph.D. Thesis, 1991.

Long, David and Wilson, Peter, eds. *Thinkers of the Twenty Years' Crisis: Inter-War Idealism Reassessed*. Oxford: Clarendon Press, 1995.

Lorimer, James. *The Institute of the Law of Nations: A Treatise of the Jural Relations of Separate Political Communities*. Two Volumes. Edinburgh and London: William Blackwood & Sons, 1884.

Lynch, Cecilia. "Kant, the Republican Peace, and Moral Guidance in International Law." *Ethics and International Affairs* 8 (1994): 39–58.

Mangone, Gerard J. *A Short History of International Organization*. New York: McGraw-Hill Book Company, 1954.

Mannheim, Karl. *Ideology and Utopia: An Introduction to the Sociology of Knowledge*. Translated by Louis Wirth and Edward Shils. London: Routledge & Kegan Paul, 1954; first published in England, 1936.

Mayer, Peter, ed. *The Pacifist Conscience*. Hammondsworth: Penguin, 1966.

Mead, Edwin D. "Immanuel Kant's Internationalism." *Contemporary Review* CVII (February 1915): 226–32.

Mead, Edwin D. "Organize the World!" in *Tracts on Peace and War, 1875–1902*. British Library, 8245, BBB 68: 1–11. Reprinted from New *England Magazine* (December 1898): p. 11.

Mertens, Thomas. "Cosmopolitanism and Citizenship: Kant Against Habermas." *European Journal of Philosophy* 4 (December 1996): 328–47.

Meyer, Cord. *Facing Reality: From World Federalism to the CIA*. New York: Harper & Row Publishers, 1980.

Mitrany, David. *The Progress of International Government*. London: George Allen & Unwin, 1933.

Mitrany, David. *A Working Peace System*. Chicago: Quadrangle Books, 1966; first published 1943.

Morrow, Dwight Whitney. *The Society of Free States*. New York and London: Harper & Bros., 1919.

Mowat, R.B. *The European States System: A Study of International Relations*. Second Edition. London: Oxford University Press, 1929; first published in 1923.

Mulholland, Leslie A. "Kant on War and International Justice." *Kant-Studien* 78 (1987): 25–41.

Mulholland, Leslie A. *Kant's System of Rights*. New York: Columbia University Press, 1990.

Murray, P. and Rich, P., eds. *Visions of European Unity*. Boulder, CO: Westview Press, 1996.

Negretto, Gabriel L. "Kant and the Illusion of Collective Security." *Journal of International Affairs* 46 (Winter 1993): 501–24.

Northedge, F.S. *The League of Nations: Its Life and Times, 1920–1946.* Leicester: Leicester University Press, 1986.

Pangle, Thomas L. and Ahrensdorf, Peter J. *Justice Among Nations: On the Moral Basis of Power and Peace.* Lawrence, Kansas: University Press of Kansas, 1999.

Parkinson, F. *The Philosophy of International Relations.* Volume 52, Sage Library of Social Research. London, Beverly Hills: Sage Publication, 1977.

Paulsen, Friedrich. *Immanuel Kant: His Life and Doctrine.* Translated from the revised German edition by J.E. Creighton and Albert Lefevre. New York: Charles Scribner & Sons, 1902.

Pinder, John. "The Federal Idea and the British Liberal Tradition" in Bosco, Andrea, ed., *The Federal Idea: The History of Federalism from Enlightenment to 1945.* Volume I. London: Lothian Foundation Press, 1991: 99–118.

Puchala, Donald J. *Theory and History in International Relations.* New York: Routledge, 2003.

Raulet, G. "Citizenship, Otherness, and Cosmopolitanism in Kant." *Social Science Research* 35 (September 1996): 437–46.

Rawls, John. *The Law of Peoples.* Cambridge, MA: Harvard University Press, 1999.

Ray, James Lee. *Democracy and International Conflict: An Evaluation of the Democratic Peace Proposition.* Columbia, S.C.: University of South Carolina Press, 1995.

Riley, Patrick. *Kant's Political Philosophy.* Totowa, NJ: Rowman & Littlefield, 1983.

Ritchie, David George. *Studies in Political and Social Ethics.* London: Swan Sonnenschein & Co., 1902.

Robbins, Lionel. *Economic Planning and International Order.* London: MacMillan, 1937.

Roberts, Adam and Kingsbury, Benedict. "Introduction: The UN's Roles in International Society since 1945" in Roberts, Adam and Kingsbury, Benedict, eds., *United Nations, Divided World: The UN's Roles in International Relations.* Second Edition. Oxford: Clarendon Press, 1993: 1–62.

Roberts, Adam and Kingsbury, Benedict, eds. *United Nations, Divided World: The UN's Roles in International Relations.* Second Edition. Oxford: Clarendon Press, 1993.

Robinson, Hoke, ed. *Proceedings of the Eighth International Kant Congress.* Two Volumes. Milwaukee: Marquette University Press, 1995.

Rosenau, James N. *The United Nations in a Turbulent World.* International Peace Academy, Occasional Paper Series. Boulder and London: Lynne Rienner Publishers, 1992.

Rummell, R.J. *Understanding Conflict and War.* Volumes 1–5. Los Angeles: Sage, 1975–1981.

Russett, Bruce. *Controlling the Sword: The Democratic Governance of National Security.* Cambridge, MA: Harvard University Press, 1990.

Russett, Bruce. *Grasping the Democratic Peace: Principles for a Post-Cold War Order.* Princeton: Princeton University Press, 1993.

Russett, Bruce and Starr, Harvey. *World Politics: The Menu for Choice*. New York: W.H. Freeman, 1981.

Sacksteder, William. "Kant's Analysis of International Relations." *The Journal of Philosophy* 51 (December 1954): 848–55.

Schuman, F.L. *The Commonwealth of Man. An Inquiry into Power Politics and World Government*. London: Robert Hale, 1954.

Schwarz, Wolfgang. "Kant's Philosophy of Law and International Peace." *Philosophy and Phenomenological Research* 23 (1962): 71–80.

Shell, Susan Meld. *The Rights of Reason: A Study of Kant's Philosophy and Politics*. Toronto, London, and Buffalo: University of Toronto Press, 1980.

Siep, Ludwig. "Kant and Hegel on Peace and International Law" in Robinson, Hoke, ed., *Proceedings of the Eighth International Kant Congress*. Two Volumes. Milwaukee: Marquette University Press, 1995: 259–72.

Singer, J.D. and Associates. *Explaining War: Selected Papers from the Correlates of War Project*. London: Sage Publications, 1979.

Skinner, Quentin. *Meaning and Context: Quentin Skinner and His Critics*. Edited by James Tully. Cambridge: Polity Press, 1988.

Small, Melvin and Singer, J. David. *Resort to Arms*. Beverly Hills, CA: Sage Publications, 1982.

Smith, Anthony. "Kant's Political Philosophy: Rechtsstaat or Council Democracy?" *Review of Politics* 47 (April 1985): 253–80.

Smith, Steve. "The Forty Years' Detour: The Resurgence of Normative Theory in International Relations." *Millennium* 12 (3) (Winter 1992): 489–506.

Smith, Thomas W. *History and International Relations*. Routledge Advances in International Relations and Politics. London and New York: Routledge, 1999.

Spiro, D. "The Insignificance of the Liberal Peace." *International Security* 19 (1994): 50–86.

Stapfer. *Life of Immanuel Kant*. Translated by Hodge. Library of Useful Tracts. Volume Three. Edinburgh: Thomas Clark, 1836.

Starr, H. "Why Don't Democracies Fight One Another?: Evaluating the Theory-Findings Feedback Loop." *Jerusalem Journal of International Relations* 14 (1992): 41–59.

Stawall, Mehan F. *The Growth of International Thought*. London: Thornton Butterworth, 1929.

Stuckenberg, J.H.W. *The Life of Immanuel Kant*. London: The MacMillan Co., 1882.

Suganami, Hidemi. *Domestic Analogy in Proposals for World Order, 1814–1945: The Transfer of Legal and Political Principles from the Domestic to the International Sphere in Thought on International Law and Relations*. University of London, Ph.D. Thesis, 1985.

Sullivan, Roger J. *Immanuel Kant's Moral Theory*. Cambridge: Cambridge University Press, 1989.

Sumner, Charles. "The War System of the Commonwealth of Nations: An Address before the American Peace Society at its Anniversary in Boston, May 28, 1849" in

Tracts on War, 1825–1869. Boston: Ticknor, Reed & Fields, British Library, Rare Books, 8425, G15, Number 3: 1–71.

Tesòn, Fernando R. "The Kantian Theory of International Law." *Columbia Law Review* 92 (January 1992): 53–102.

Trueblood, Benjamin F. *The Federation of the World*. Cambridge: The Riverside Press, 1899.

Trueblood, Benjamin F. "The Historical Development of the Peace Idea." Paper presented at the Summer School of Religious History, Haverford, Pennsylvania, June 1900.

Thompson, Kenneth W. *Fathers of International Thought: The Legacy of Political Theory*. Baton Rouge and London: Louisiana State University Press, 1994.

Urquhart, Brian. "The UN and International Security after the Cold War" in Roberts, Adam and Kingsbury, Benedict, eds., *United Nations, Divided World: The UN's Role in International Relations*. Second Edition. Oxford: Clarendon Press, 1993: 81–103.

Van der Linden, Harry. *Kantian Ethics and Socialism*. Indianapolis: Hackett Publishing Co., 1988.

Van der Linden, Harry. "Kant: the Duty to Promote International Peace and Political Intervention" in Robinson, Hoke, ed., *Proceedings of the Eighth International Kant Congress*. Two Volumes. Milwaukee: Marquette University Press, 1995: 71–79.

Vaughn, C.E. *Studies in the History of Political Philosophy Before and After Rousseau*. Edited by A.G. Little. Manchester: Manchester University Press, 1925.

Walker, R.B.J. *Inside/Outside: International Relations as Political Theory*. Cambridge: Cambridge University Press, 1993.

Wallenstein, Peter. *Structure and War: On International Relations 1820–1968*. Stockholm: Raben and Sjogren, 1973.

Waltz, Kenneth N. *Man, the State, and War*. New York: Columbia University Press, 1959.

Waltz, Kenneth N. "Kant, Liberalism, and War." *American Political Science Review* 56 (1962): 331–40.

Waltz, Kenneth N. *Theory of International Politics*. London: Sage Publications, 1979.

Walzer, Michael. *Just and Unjust Wars: A Moral Argument with Historical Illustrations*. New York: Basic Books, 1977.

Wheaton, Henry. *History of the Law of Nations in Europe and America*. New York: Gould, Banks and Co., 1845.

Wight, Martin. *International Theory: The Three Traditions*. Edited by Gabriele Wright and Brian Porter. Introduction Essay by Hedley Bull. Leicester: Leicester University Press for the Royal Institute of International Affairs, 1991.

Wilenski, Peter. "The Structure of the UN in the Post-Cold War Period" in Roberts, Adam and Kingsbury, Benedict, eds., *United Nations, Divided World: The UN's Roles in International Relations*. Second Edition. Oxford: Clarendon Press, 1993: 437–67.

Williams, Howard. *Kant's Political Philosophy*. New York: St. Martin's Press, 1983.

Williams, Howard. *International Relations in Political Theory*. Milton Keynes: Open University Press, 1992.

Williams, Howard, ed. *Essays on Kant's Political Philosophy*. Chicago: Chicago University Press, 1992.

Williams, Howard. *International Relations and the Limits of Political Theory*. Basingstoke: MacMillan, 1996.

Williams, Howard. *Kant's Critique of Hobbes: Sovereignty & Cosmopolitanism*. Political Philosophy Now. Cardiff: University of Wales Press, 2003.

Williams, Howard and Booth, Ken. "Kant: Theorist beyond Limits" in Clark, Ian and Neumann, Iver B., eds., *Classical Theories of International Relations*. Houndmills, Basingstoke, Hampshire, and London: MacMillan Press, 1996: 71–98.

Williams, H., Sullivan, D., and Matthews, E. Gwynn. *Francis Fukayama and the End of History*. Political Philosophy Now. Cardiff: University of Wales Press, 1997.

Williams, H., Wright, M., and Evans, A., eds. *A Reader in International Relations and Political Theory*. Milton Keynes: Open University Press, 1993.

Williams, Michael C. "Reason and Realpolitik: Kant's Critique of International Politics." *Canadian Journal of Political Science* 25 (March 1992): 99–119.

Wilson, Peter. "The New Europe Debate in Wartime Britain" in Murray, P. and Rich, P., eds., *Visions of European Unity*. Boulder, CO: Westview Press, 1996: 39–62.

Wilson, Peter. *The International Theory of Leonard Woolf: An Exposition, Analysis, and Assessment in the Light of His Reputation as a Utopian*. University of London, Ph.D. Thesis, 1997.

Wood, Allen. "Kant's Project for Perpetual Peace" in Robinson, Hoke, ed., *Proceedings of the Eighth International Kant Congress*. Two Volumes. Milwaukee: Marquette University Press, 1995: 3–18.

Woolf, Leonard. "Review of Kant's 'Perpetual Peace.'" *New Statesman* (July 31, 1915): 398–99.

Woolf, Leonard. *International Government*. London: George Allen & Unwin, July 1916.

Woolf, Leonard. *The Future of International Government*. The Labour Party: Transport House, 1940.

Woolf, Leonard. *The War for Peace*. London: George Routledge, 1940.

Woolf, Leonard. *The International Postwar Settlement*. London: Fabian Publications, 1944.

Zakaria, Fareed. "The Rise of Illiberal Democracy." *Foreign Affairs* 76 (6) (November/December 1997): 22–43.

Zimmern, Alfred. *The League of Nations and the Rule of Law, 1918–1935*. London: MacMillan & Co., 1939.

Index